# Equality in America

# EQUALITY IN AMERICA

## The View from the Top

Sidney Verba and Gary R. Orren

Harvard University Press

Cambridge, Massachusetts, and London, England   1985

This book is printed on acid-free paper, and its binding materials
have been chosen for strength and durability.

Library of Congress Cataloging in Publication Data

Verba, Sidney.
  Equality in America.

  Bibliography: p.
  Includes index.
  1. Equality—United States.   I. Orren, Gary R.
II. Title.
JC575.V47   1985        323.4'2'0973        84-19756
ISBN 0-674-25960-2 (alk. paper)
ISBN 0-674-25961-0 (pbk. : alk. paper)

*To*
*Cynthia and Merle,*
*who often remind us that*
*equality begins at home.*

# Preface

A group of English socialists reportedly invited the author of a newly published book, *Inequalities*, to speak to them. As the blackboard grew dense with algebraic equations, the listeners realized their mistake: the speaker, G. H. Hardy, was not a political economist at all, but a mathematician. Indeed, there are many kinds of inequality, and our book does not address them all.

The complexities of equality—the puzzles, ironies, and seemingly insoluble issues—drew us to the subject and command attention in this book. Can it be that the United States is at once the epitome of equality, as some claim, and the paragon of inequality, as others argue? How can we reconcile economic inequality, which is the inevitable result of a capitalist economy, with political equality, which is the crux of democracy?

The contradictions surrounding equality are more than philosophical conundrums. They are also important in everyday political life. Equality lies at the heart of policymaking and political struggle. The public agenda in 1984, for example, brimmed with equality issues—debates over the role of blacks and women, disagreements over who should shoulder what share of the tax burden, charges of unfairness hurled at one political party, countercharges that special interests wielded too much influence leveled at the other.

The purpose of this book is therefore both practical and theoretical. The bulk of the book describes and analyzes American values about equality, particularly the values of American leaders, in order to give a better understanding of American politics. This material serves as the foundation for the last four chapters, which examine the more theoretical properties of equality, particularly the similarities and differences between political and economic equality and the linkage between the two equalities. This latter section in turn illuminates the role of values about equality in American politics.

The first two chapters place the issue of equality in comparative, theoretical, and historical context. Chapter 1 analyzes what makes the American political and economic system so special compared with other democratic nations. It introduces crucial distinctions between economics and politics, between the real and the ideal, between individual and group equality, and between equality of opportunity and equality of result. Chapter 2, which traces the equality debate in America from its pre-Revolutionary roots to the present day, shows that these four distinctions have been embodied in battles over equality for more than two hundred years.

The remainder of the book concerns the views of central characters in this endless debate on equality—leaders from significant sectors of American society, including business, labor, the media, the political parties, and the feminist and civil rights movements. Chapter 3 describes these leaders and tells how they were selected for study. Although the leaders come from similar social and economic backgrounds, Chapter 4 reveals that they hold widely divergent views on equality. They disagree sharply on such matters as the fairness of the American socioeconomic system and the proper role of government in dealing with inequality. At the same time, they are almost unanimous in upholding equal opportunity, and they decry the use of quotas in hiring.

Chapter 5 investigates the structure of these attitudes toward equality—not *what* the leaders think but *how* they think. Whether the leaders of different groups agree or disagree, they share an understanding of what the issues are; individual views are remarkably consistent from one issue to another; and the leaders in general speak the same "language" of equality. Chapter 6 shows that groups too, such as business and labor, have attitudes that are predictable and distinct. Indeed, what shapes the leaders' attitudes is not so much their life circumstances as their group affiliation. This is especially true of political party leaders, as spotlighted in Chapter 7. On the surface, Democratic and Republican leaders face the same kinds of influence. They are at once pushed away from the ideological center by special interest groups and pulled back toward it by the rank-

and-file. Furthermore, both parties have confronted three cardinal equality issues in the same chronological order: first economics, then race, and finally gender. Yet each party is impelled by different interest groups, and each has broached the equality issues at different times; hence, the views of the two parties scarcely overlap.

Chapters 8, 9, and 10, the theoretical heart of the book, examine economic equality, political equality, and the relationship between the two. They also show how the contrast between economic and political equality is connected with the contrast between real and ideal equality. In the case of income, the real matches the ideal fairly closely. But in the case of political influence, almost no group of leaders is content with the status quo.

Chapter 11 again places the equality issue in comparative, historical, and theoretical contexts. The views of American leaders are compared with those of Swedish leaders to show that American values encourage a remarkable degree of economic inequality. The history of contemporary American politics, where matters of equality figure prominently in the policies of the Reagan administration and in the strategies of the 1984 election, demonstrates that equality is not a remote, abstract idea but a relevant, concrete issue. Finally, the theory that values—contrary to both the free market and the Marxist models—are not merely rationalizations for people's self-interest but also separate and potent entities explains the profound impact of beliefs about equality on social conditions and public policy.

ONE of the greatest rewards of a lengthy project is the many debts incurred along the way. The basic data came from a survey of American leaders conducted jointly by the Washington *Post* and the Center for International Affairs at Harvard University. Barry Sussman, director of polls for the *Post*, worked intimately with us in both the development of the survey and the early analysis of the data. His commitment to our joint enterprise was crucial.

G. Donald Ferree, currently an associate director of the Institute for Social Inquiry at the University of Connecticut, was a close collaborator throughout the research, making major contributions to the design, administration, and analysis of the surveys. His virtuosity in manipulating and illuminating massive quantities of data was indispensable.

A group of talented, hard-working Harvard students served invaluably as research assistants: Michael Dawson, James Duane, Philip

Guentert, Helen Milner, Stephen Shuff, Stuart Smith, and Lars-Gunnar Wigemark. We benefited enormously from the thoughtful criticism of Morton Keller, Steven Kelman, Robert Klitgaard, J. R. Pole, Thomas Schelling, and Richard Zeckhauser, who sharpened our thinking about equality. Jennifer Hochshild, William Kristol, Jane Mansbridge, and Kay Lehman Schlozman provided thorough critiques of the entire manuscript that saved us from factual errors and ambiguities. David Brittan, John Donahue, and Virginia LaPlante made heroic attempts to trim our prose and protect our reputations against obscure expression, poor punctuation, and outrageous syntax.

The Ford Foundation provided generous funding for the data analysis. The Center for International Affairs and the John F. Kennedy School of Government of Harvard University supplied research support and intellectually stimulating environments.

Jennifer Olson typed and retyped chapters with good cheer and rare competence. Evelyn Brew typed the manuscript, drew and redrew the figures, watched over the research assistants, and held the entire effort together, all with a special grace.

None contributed more than Cynthia Verba and Merle Orren. They were there at the beginning and there at the end—which is going a long way. Throughout, they were a source of emotional support and encouragement.

Even with all this help, we have only come a little way to a full understanding of the role of equality in America. Our study remains exploratory and not definitive. We take comfort, however, in the Talmudic injunction: "We are not called upon to complete the task, but neither are we free to evade it."

# Contents

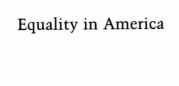

Equality in America

Observing some beggars in the street as we walked along, I said to him I supposed that there was no civilized country in the world where the misery of want in the lowest classes of the people was prevented. Johnson [replied]: "I believe Sir, there is not; but it is better that some should be unhappy, than that none should be happy, which would be the case in a general state of equality."

Boswell, *Life of Johnson*

We may naturally believe that it is not the prosperity of the few, but the greater well-being of all that is most pleasing in the sight of the Creator and Preserver of men . . . A state of equality is perhaps less elevated, but it is more just: and its justice constitutes its greatness and its beauty.

Tocqueville, *Democracy in America*

# 1

## Egalitarian Dilemmas

Few issues have sparked more controversy or held more sway over the course of history than has equality. Ships have been launched, lives given, governments toppled—all in the name of this one ideal.

The fight goes on. Equality, one of the earliest of political ideals, is also among the most elusive. Some vision of equality underpins political views ranging from branches of classical political philosophy to modern revolutionary doctrine. Yet the essential ambiguity of the concept endures. Indeed, the blunt term *equality* cannot convey all that is at stake. Equality has many meanings, often contradictory; it is not one issue but a complex of issues. In the United States this complex is particularly intriguing. Many observers, especially foreigners, have noted the unique egalitarianism of social relations in America. But America is also a land of inequality, a place where riches and poverty exist side by side.

Much has been said and written about equality in America. But most of the discourse has dealt with either the musings of scholars or the sentiments of the general public. The views of American leaders have so far gained little attention. There is a second, quite different gap: writers on equality too rarely acknowledge the importance of values. Instead they hug the coastline of less perilous territory, such as demographics or politics. Yet American leaders' views on equality—and the values that shape those views—can illuminate the mysteries surrounding the condition of equality in America, and the public policies which affect it.

**Importance of Values**

Many approaches to equality, especially economic equality, leave little place for underlying beliefs or values. According to the dominant economic model, equality and inequality result from the decisions made in market encounters among rational, utility-maximizing individuals. Peoples' basic beliefs are regarded as givens, embodied in "utility functions," and are revealed by individual market behavior. But utility functions can explain everything and therefore nothing. To take personal values as given and assume that people maximize them is, as Lester Thurow has observed, "just a fancy way of saying that individuals do whatever individuals do. By definition, there is no such thing as an individual who does not maximize his utility."[1] Ironically, the major analytical alternative to the standard market economic view, Marxist analysis, also permits little room for values. Marxism denies that ideas exert an independent force in history. Cultural values and ideology are mere camouflage, rationalizations of objective class interests.

But the influence of values on the distribution of resources is at once stronger and more complex than either the market economist or the Marxist analyst would allow. Americans have a distinctive set of beliefs about equality. In particular, they have a stronger taste for political than for economic equality. These beliefs have deep cultural roots. Values shape individuals' economic and political behavior. More important, shared values set the rules of play for both the market and the political arena. Finally, values are instrumental in shaping the public policies that give practical effect to political belief.

In defending the importance of values in matters of equality, Michael Walzer has argued that the principle of fairness which should govern distribution within different spheres, such as money, power, health, or love, must be determined by the dominant values citizens hold toward each type of goods. Discourse on justice and equality must take seriously the "collective values" and "shared understandings" of a society, the "deeper opinions" reflecting the "social meanings that constitute our common life."[2] An appreciation for "deeper opinions" must underlie any attempt to delve into the issue of equality. This holds true as much for the social scientist as for the policy maker who must gauge the obstacles that face egalitarian initiatives.

It is impossible without such appreciation to understand fully how a government develops policies relevant to equality. The government must decide whether its welfare programs will provide a broad array of social services to all, or only a safety net for the neediest. It must decide whether and how much to intervene in the matter of income redistribution. And it must decide on programs of affirmative action.

The policies which result are usually explained either as products of objective economic and demographic factors, such as level of affluence or age distribution, or as reflections of social choices made by particular groups and individuals—in other words, politics.[3] Yet both explanations overlook the degree to which political decisions on equality hinge on values. The decisions are bound up in the responsibilities of the state to individual welfare, and in the definition of a just society. They depend on how American leaders conceptualize equality, and how they balance its different aspects. These views, in turn, support the particular mixture of policies in America by setting the boundaries of potential consensus around varying definitions of equality.

Values or attitudes are not rigidly determined. They do not simply reflect interests inherent in one's social position, nor do they always reflect one's personal interests. Leaders of the two political parties, for example, have similar demographic profiles, but their attitudes toward equality are strikingly different.

Furthermore, values affect the nature of political conflict within a nation. For one thing, they set the bounds of dispute. Republican and Democratic leaders may disagree on matters of equality, but they agree on the parameters of the debate. This agreement places certain issues, such as radical income redistribution, outside the range of discourse over policy options. At the same time, the issues on which there is a value difference among leaders fill the political agenda and fuel the battles over equality.

## Importance of Leaders

The issue of equality has been addressed at various levels. Among scholars, such as social scientists and philosophers, no other area of social policy has been discussed so extensively. The issue is also of interest to the mass public, which concerns itself less with broad philosophical matters than with concrete social policies. Opinion surveys have charted the contour of the public's views. These surveys can also be used to study views that may be even more illuminating, those of American leaders.

Leaders provide a middle level of discourse between the abstract analyses of scholars and the day-to-day concerns of citizens. They hold the fairly well-reasoned positions of those directly engaged in the political process. Their views define the substance of policy disputes over these issues. American leaders' opinions may lack the sophistication of scholarly discourse, but they are likely to be based on some reflection, to be relatively coherent, and to confront real policy issues. Perhaps most important, leaders are pivotal decision-makers. In large measure their beliefs mold the reality of equality in America.

To FIND OUT what that reality is, and whether American society is truly egalitarian, one can travel the country and talk to its citizens, or survey the public for more systematic knowledge. One can read American history, study laws and customs, peruse the accounts of foreign travelers, and scrutinize the vast body of statistics on the subject. But the harder one looks, the more ambiguous the answer seems. In some respects, America is an egalitarian society: political equality based on broad suffrage with no property qualifications developed in the United States before it appeared anywhere else and was furthered by political parties organized to bring out the vote; feudal hierarchies never dominated soical life; and for the most part, Americans have been free to follow the careers for which their talents best suit them. Similarly, the American people seem to be egalitarian: their democratic customs have delighted, amused, and shocked foreign visitors, as has their opposition to hierarchy and domination in private and public life.[4] Yet from another perspective, America is not egalitarian at all: a market economy promotes wide disparities in income, and the government's commitment to welfare measures, especially to redistribution, is feeble compared with that of other nations. Nor is the American public uniformly egalitarian: it generally tolerates these income disparities, and its devotion to careers open to talent promotes drastic differences in the life circumstances of people. The history of racial inequality represents a particularly serious departure from the fabled American egalitarianism.

Many of the characteristics that make America exceptional derive from the ambivalent nature of equality in the United States. The country is at once more and less egalitarian than other societies. This ambivalence is possible in part because there are many different forms of equality, and they are not always consistent one with another.[5] Almost all Americans claim the label of egalitarianism; they differ, though, on what equality means.[6] To be egalitarian in one way may require being inegalitarian in another.

## Equality of Opportunity or Result

One reason for the ambivalence about equality in America is that people often confuse equal opportunity with equal results. At issue here is how much equality people really want. Equal opportunity to make of oneself what one can has been the dominant norm in America.[7] People should have equal rights and opportunities to develop their talents; ability and effort should be rewarded. The notion that everyone should have an equal chance to get ahead glorifies personal achievement. In David Riesman's words, "equality of opportunity was a ladder for the bourgeoisie to climb on."[8]

This ideology has recently met fierce opposition. Many observers, including philosophers, social scientists, and even a President, have pointed out that equality of opportunity undermines equality of result.[9] The goal of social policy, say the new egalitarians, should be not simply free competition but equality of condition. They propose a wide range of social policies to accomplish this objective, including tax reform, more transfer payments, and public service jobs. The most controversial proposals call for compensatory programs, affirmative action, and quotas for the disadvantaged. No other social policies in recent memory have caused different groups to collide so violently. The explosive outbursts are hardly surprising, for as Daniel Bell has observed: "What is at stake today is the redefinition of equality. A principle which was the weapon for changing a vast social system, the principle of equality of opportunity, is now seen as leading to a new hierarchy, and the current demand is that the 'just precedence' of society, in Locke's phrase, requires the reduction of all inequality, or the creation of equality of result—in income, status, and power—for all men in society. *This issue is the central value problem of the postindustrial society.*"[10]

Few critics of the current state of equality in America hope for full equality of condition. Rather, the issue is over the acceptable size of the gap. How much disparity ought there to be among individuals and groups? Policy clashes arise when egalitarian goals go beyond opening up opportunities for advancement to specifying particular outcomes. The conflicts have to do with the upper limits, lower limits, and distribution in between.

Equality of result can be achieved only by containing the effects of equality of opportunity. This can be done by creating a lower limit, or "floor," beneath which individuals cannot fall; an upper limit, or "ceiling," above which they cannot rise; or both. A floor is a minimum guaranteed bundle of political, economic, or social rights that is available to all, requiring little or no skill or effort to attain. A ceiling is a level above which one cannot rise in economic, social, or political position, no matter how much skill, money, or motivation one applies. In practice, floors include minimum income guarantees or the right to vote, while ceilings include upper bounds on income or the traditional restriction of one vote to each elector. If the floor is high enough and the ceiling low enough, one comes close to full equality of result, since the rewards for talent and effort are blocked at the top and all have equal shares available at the bottom.

Floors and ceilings, by definition, violate the sanctity of individual achievement associated with equality of opportunity. Each tampers with the hierarchy that individual effort would produce. A ceiling, however, is likely to be seen as the greater affront to the value of individual achievement. All a floor does is to take something away from those closer to the top and give it to those closer to the bottom, such as income redistributed to the poor or, more subtly, political influence shared with the politically impotent; the effect on those at the top is indirect and has the laudable purpose of relieving those at the bottom. A ceiling, in contrast, directly limits the ability of those high on the ladder to keep climbing.

## Individual or Group Equality

Because of this emphasis on personal achievement, Americans, perhaps more than other people, tend to think of equality in terms of individuals rather than of groups. But equality in America refers just as much to the relative positions of groups. It means equality for ethnic minorities, for women, for the handicapped, and for other groups who believe they are getting a raw deal.

The main issues relating to disadvantaged groups are discrimination and its inverse, affirmative action. With the establishment of a floor under political and economic conditions, a set of basic political rights for all, and a set of minimum economic benefits, individuals are in principle free to compete in the "area of opportunity" above the floor. But members of certain groups find that discrimination places a special ceiling on what they can attain. These groups enter the economic or political struggggle with such handicaps that their members wind up disproportionately clustered at the bottom of the scale. Such groups argue for the removal of discriminatory barriers to fair competition. At times they also argue for compensatory programs to help overcome the disadvantages inherited from previous discrimination. The removal of barriers arouses little debate, falling as it does under the rubric of more equal opportunity, but the notion of compensation creates serious division.

In the eyes of its supporters, affirmative action falls outside the issue of group versus individual equality. Its intent, supporters claim, is simply to spread among all groups the privilege unfairly monopolized by one group, white males. Because the proponents of affirmative action believe that it would ultimately give all members of society an equal chance to achieve happiness, they also believe that they are upholding the ideal of individualism. They regard opposition to affirmative action as group inegalitarianism disguised as individualism.

Despite Americans' individualism, equality has typically become a political issue only when it concerns disparities between groups. If there are wide differences among individuals in income or occupational level or political influence, but the distributions are random in relation to categories of individuals, the inequality is less likely to provoke an outcry. Inequalities have greater political significance when the disadvantaged share traits that help them identify their common plight. Such traits help the disadvantaged to "find each other" and to form a coalition. Alliances built in this way tend to be more durable than those lacking the cement of a common social background.

## Economic or Political Equality

Another source of confusion among Americans is that their sentiments are far more egalitarian in some areas than in others. They assign different goods to different spheres of justice.[11] There are spheres for money, political power, welfare, leisure time, and love. People do not balance all goods by the same distributional criteria. For example, Americans generally believe that the distribution of money should be governed by free exchange; that the assignment of professions should be determined by merit; and that provision for welfare should be based on need. The aim of egalitarianism is not the elimination of all differences, which would be impossible, nor even the elimination of differences within any one of these spheres, which might also be impossible unless the state continually intervened. Rather, the goal is to keep the spheres autonomous and their boundaries intact.[12] Success in one sphere should not be convertible into success in another sphere. Political power, which is the most dangerous social good because it is the easiest to convert, must be constrained against transmutation into economic power, and vice versa.

Equality is central to any conception of democracy. Democracy implies a certain degree of political equality—if not full equality of political influence among citizens, at least some limit to inequality. If control over political decisions is monopolized by a small segment of the population, democracy is vitiated in its essence. The issue of *how much* political equality is necessary for practical democracy, however, is not settled.

Americans have always been more egalitarian in the political than in the economic realm. In politics the ideal is democracy and one person, one vote. This ideal condemns gross disparities of political power among individuals and groups, and hence approaches equality of result. The ideal implies both a floor and a ceiling: No preferences ought to be totally ignored in the political system, nor should the preferences of any one individual or group predominate. The floor under political influence is established by institutions such as universal suffrage and First Amendment rights that guarantee to all the freedom to express political preferences at minimum cost. The ceiling is manifested in the one-vote limit, periodic attempts to curb the "big interests," and the recent campaign finance laws.

In economics, by contrast, the dominant norm is capitalism, a system in which income and other rewards accrue to talent and effort. Here the ideal is equal opportunity. Since the New Deal, Americans have accepted a floor under economic conditions. Yet they would be much less likely to tolerate an economic ceiling. Above the floor, the ideal is unbridled competition. Since the inevitable result is inequality of condition, the American system is one in which economic disparities exist side by side with the ideal of equal degrees of political influence. As Charles Beard put it, "Modern equalitarian democracy, which reckons all heads as equal and alike, cuts sharply athwart the philosophy and practice of the past century. Nevertheless, the democratic device of universal suffrage does not destroy economic classes or economic inequalities. It ignores them. Herein lies the paradox, the most astounding political contradiction that the world has ever witnessed."[13] Economic inequality and political equality coexist in many democracies. In America, however, the commitment to each is particularly strong, and so is the tension between them.

Americans' ambivalent stance toward equality, particularly in terms of the political-economic distinction, shows up clearly in comparison with other industrialized democracies at a roughly similar level of development and affluence. International comparisons of the extent of equality are difficult, for the measures are uncertain and the data are not always the best. No single measure will do, but comparisons across a range of indicators reveal that the United States ranks among the most open and participatory of modern democracies when it comes to politics and among the least egalitarian when it comes to economic matters. The nation embodies democratic polity and capitalist economy at their fullest! In both the economic and political realms, this pattern shows up in the timing of the adoption of equality-producing policies, the current policy commitment to equality, and the resulting level of equality in society (Table 1.1).

On the score of economic equality, Congress passed legislation creating Medicare and Medicaid in 1965, committing the U.S. government for the first time to a broad-based, though not comprehensive, system of medical care. Germany (Prussia) had undertaken such a policy in 1883, and in the meantime most other industrialized democracies had followed suit. The American version, limited to care for the elderly or the indigent, is much less extensive than that of other nations. With medical care, as with other social welfare measures, such as old-age pensions, unemployment insurance, family allowances, and comprehensive health insurance, the United States has been much more of a latecomer than its material development would have suggested. In fact, two of these measures were adopted well after they had been embraced by the other countries, and two have yet to be adopted. This nation also followed others in adopting other social programs of a welfare sort.

The extent of government commitment to policies fostering economic equality presents a similar but more striking pattern. The measures here include the level of expenditures for social security, income maintenance, and income transfer programs, in addition to the progressivity of income tax. On all of these measures the United States ranks quite low among the nations, well below the median and usually close to the bottom of the distribution.

**Table 1.1**

Economic Equality Worldwide

| Indicators of economic equality | U.S. rank[a] | Number of nations ranked |
|---|---|---|
| Date social and economic measures adopted | | |
| Old-age pensions[b] | 7 (1935) | 7 |
| Unemployment insurance[b] | 6 (1935) | 7 |
| Family allowance[b] | 6 (none yet) | 6 |
| Comprehensive health insurance[b] | 6 (none yet) | 6 |
| Policies supporting economic equality | | |
| Index of social insurance coverage, (1970)[b] | 14 | 14 |
| Public income maintenance expenditure as a percent of GDP (1972)[b] | 12 | 17 |
| Percent of GNP spent on social security (1971)[c] | 14 | 18 |
| Total public expenditures as percent of GNP (1975)[b] | 13 | 14 |
| Social transfers as percent of GNP (1975)[b] | 10 | 14 |
| Progressivity of tax[d] | 12 | 17 |
| Resulting economic equality | | |
| Gini Index of post-tax income equality[e] | 9 | 12 |
| Quintile income equality (Difference in after-tax income of top and bottom quintiles)[c] | 8 | 12 |
| Change in income distribution due to taxes[f] | 9 | 13 |

a. The lower the number, the more egalitarian the nation.

b. Peter Flora and Arnold J. Heidenheimer, ed., *The Development of the Welfare State in Europe and America* (New Brunswick, N.J.: Transaction Books, 1981), pp. 55, 83, 85, 87, 310, 317.

c. David Cameron, "Politics, Public Policy, and Economic Inequality: A Comparative Analysis," 1981 (based on OECD data).

d. OECD, *National Accounts of OECD Countries, 1975,* vol. 2 (Paris: OECD, 1978).

e. Malcolm Sawyer, "Income Distribution in OECD Countries," OECD Economic Outlook, *Occasional Papers* (Paris: OECD, 1976), p. 19. When standardized for household size, the United States ranks 9 out of 11.

f. Alexander Hicks and Duane H. Swank, "Governmental Redistribution in Rich Capitalist Democracies," paper presented at Annual Meeting of American Political Science Association, Chicago, Sept. 1983.

Finally, the equality of the income distribution in a number of nations, based on the Gini index and a quintile income equality measure, gives the United States a somewhat different rank, but still well on the unequal side of the median.[14] Furthermore, the distribution of income has been remarkably stable over time in the United States, despite massive social and economic changes as well as the introduction of new government programs. Time series comparisons of income shares are a matter of controversy, and so is the degree of stability.[15] The only consistent statistics, income before taxes and in-kind government transfers, nevertheless suggest that the distribution of income became more equal during the Depression and

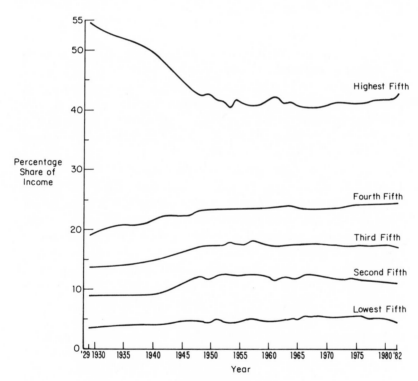

**Figure 1.1**
Distribution of Family Income in the United States by Quintile,
1929–1982[a]
Source: 1929–1944, compiled from E. C. Budd, *Inequality and Poverty* (New York: W. W. Norton, 1967), p. xiii, table 1. 1947–1982, compiled from *Current Population Reports, Series P-60, No. 142* (Feb. 1984), Bureau of the Census, U.S. Department of Commerce, pp. 47–49, table 17.
a. Before taxes and in-kind government transfers.

World War II and has hardly changed in the postwar period (Figure 1.1). If taxes and transfers are taken into account, there was a slight tendency toward reduction in inequality up to 1979, after which recession and the policies of the Reagan administration reversed the trend. The income inequality trends for blacks and whites are different. Throughout the postwar period the distribution of income among blacks has been more unequal than among whites. Through 1967 income inequality declined for both racial groups. However, since then, inequality has increased for both blacks and whites, although more slowly for whites. The result is that income inequality for whites in 1982 was virtually identical to what it had been in 1947. For blacks, there was a dramatic increase in income inequality over those years.

The change in income distribution owing to taxes bears more directly on the question of whether government intervention reduces income inequality. It refers to the percentage reduction in the Gini index of inequality between pretax and post-tax income. On this measure of the extent to which taxes reduce inequality, U.S. policy produces little redistribution, and the United States ranks near the bottom of the industrial nations. These data are consistent with an appraisal of the United States as a nation which tolerates, even celebrates, economic hierarchy.

One area in which governmental spending in the United States has exceeded that in other nations is education. The United States ranks first in per capita spending on schooling and first in the percentage of the population that has received higher education. But educational expenditure differs from other outlays in that it promotes equal opportunity rather than equal results. Support for public education harmonizes perfectly with American ideology. The educational system has been the main channel for upward mobility. In that sense, it is a source of economic inequality rather than equality.[16]

Whereas the United States may lag in legislation fostering economic equality, it has been the leading innovator in policies and institutions that further citizens' participation in political life (Table 1.2). Not the least of these innovations was the founding of a republic in which the legislature and the executive were elected by and responsible to the public. At the start of the nineteenth century, moreover, the United States spawned relatively stable political parties with a mass electoral base. These, the first such parties in the world, were another crucial contribution to popular democracy.

Where the United States ranks in the timing of universal suffrage

**Table 1.2**
Political Equality Worldwide

| Indicators of political equality | U.S. rank | Number of countries ranked |
|---|---|---|
| Date political measures adopted | | |
| Executive popularly elected or | | |
| responsible to elected assembly[a] | 1 | 14+ |
| Universal male suffrage[b] | 3 | 14 |
| Policies to support political equality | | |
| Press freedom[c] | 5 | 14+ |
| Resulting political equality | | |
| % saying they can do something | | |
| about an unjust law | | |
| 1959[d] Local | 1 | 5 |
| National | 1 | 5 |
| 1974[e] Local | 1 | 5 |
| National | 1 | 5 |
| Voter turnout[c] | 14 | 14+ |
| Proportion regular voters[f] | 3 | 6 |
| Proportion active beyond vote[g] | 2 | 6 |
| Organizationally active[h] | 1 or 2 | 6 |
| Diffusion of participation[i] | 1 | 6 |

a. Christopher Hewitt, "The Effect of Political Democracy and Social Democracy on Equality in Industrial Societies: A Cross-national Comparison," *American Sociological Review* 42 (June 1977): 450–464.

b. Hewitt, "The Effect of Political Democracy and Social Democracy on Equality." Prussia had universal male suffrage in 1867, which would rank it ahead of the United States, but the voters were not weighed equally. If one took white male suffrage, the United States would rank first.

c. Charles L. Taylor and Michael C. Hudson, ed., *World Handbook of Political and Social Indicators*, 2nd ed. (New Haven: Yale University Press, 1972), pp. 51–56.

d. Gabriel Almond and Sidney Verba, *The Civic Culture* (Princeton: Princeton University Press, 1963), p. 219.

e. Samuel Barnes and Max Kaase, ed., *Political Action* (Beverly Hills: Sage Publications, 1980), p. 144.

f. Jae-on Kim, Norman Nie, and Sidney Verba, "The Amount and Concentration of Political Participation," *Political Methodology*, Spring 1974, pp. 105–132; Sidney Verba, Norman Nie, and Jae-on Kim, *Participation and Political Equality* (New York: Cambridge University Press, 1979).

g. Verba, Nie, and Kim, *Participation and Political Equality.* The first ranking nation in this measure is Yugoslavia, which may make for an inappropriate comparison, given its different participatory structure. Its high rank derives from widespread participation in workers' organizations, local councils, and community actions—

depends on whether one looks at white male suffrage (where it ranks first), or male suffrage (where it ranks high), or universal suffrage (where it ranks nearer the middle). Full suffrage for men and women is the fullest test of equal political access. But given the norms of the nineteenth century, the United States can be credited with the first great strides toward such access, even though the result of the Jacksonian revolution was only white male suffrage and the result of the Fifteenth Amendment was only male suffrage regardless of race.

In many other ways the United States pioneered in mass participatory institutions open to all citizens. The early New England town meetings came closer to true direct democracy than any other modern attempt. And along with Switzerland, a number of American states were innovators in the direct democracy devices of the referendum, initiative, and recall. The United States also set a precedent in establishing a constitution under which the upper house of the legislature was popularly chosen. America's "House of Lords" was the elected Senate.[17] Finally, with the development of the direct primary early in the twentieth century, the United States became the first nation to give the public a major voice in nominating public officials.

Current legislation to foster mass political participation presents a mixed picture, but one that generally confirms the United States' leadership on such policies. The low marks are for voting laws. Other nations pursue administrative policies that are much more egalitarian in their effects on voting, such as permanent and automatic registration of all citizens, elections on Sunday, and little or no residency requirements. Starting in the late nineteenth century, the United States imposed laws to make registration more difficult. The purpose in most cases was to correct electoral abuses. One could even say that the purpose was to equalize voting access by eliminating double voting or "gravestone" voting. The result, however, was clearly to limit voter turnout, particularly among lower-status citizens.

In other ways, though, the United States has encouraged participation. The impressive degree of press freedom indicates the system's

a set of activities somewhat different from those used to categorize the other nations.

h. Verba, Nie, and Kim, *Participation and Political Equality*, p. 58. Two somewhat different measures yield different results. The first ranking is as active member in an organization that deals with community affairs; the second is on working through a group to deal with community affairs.

i. Adjusted index of participatory equality, without voting. Verba, Nie, and Kim, *Participation and Political Equality*.

openness to varied political views. Even more to the point are laws that allow widespread participation in the political process. The data do not exist to rank nations on these matters but the United States would surely stand near the top on any such scale. One reason is direct primaries, which have grown in scope and importance in recent years. It is likely that many more citizens take part in nominating political candidates in America than in any other nation. Another factor is the wide opportunities Americans enjoy to run for public office. In the United States many more offices, from coroner to congressman, are elective than in other countries.

So much for the means of political life; what of the results? How much political equality is there? Political equality cannot be gauged in the same way as economic equality. There is no metric such as money, no statistic such as the Gini index, and no body of data comparing countries. There are, however, relevant data on political participation. Most of the measures do not directly trace participatory equality. Instead, they measure the level of political activity, or of attitudes promoting such activity, in various nations. Political equality is presumably greater when more citizens are politically active or efficacious. On all scales but the voting rate, the United States ranks high.

Another aspect of political equality is the diffusion of participation, how equally political activity is dispersed among citizens. At one extreme, most activity rests in the hands of a small stratum of activists who engage in many different political acts with great frequency. At the opposite extreme, most people are moderately active, with no one group predominating. The United States leads in the diffusion of political activity.

Relative to other industrialized democracies, then, the United States is inegalitarian in economic matters and egalitarian in political matters. Even so, the economic hierarchy spills over into the political sphere, often undercutting the equality of participation that American values would otherwise permit. Although the potentially corrosive effect of money in politics is a traditional American concern, the United States poses fewer obstacles than do other industrialized democracies to the exploitation of economic resources for political purposes.

In part, this freedom to turn economic resources to political advantage derives from the acceptance—even by much of the American left—of economic stratification. American leaders from all parts of the political spectrum concede the legitimacy of fairly wide disparities between rich and poor. And the absence of a class-based, redistributionist ideology in America lowers the awareness of economic and class differences and makes it easier to spin gold into influence. Hence the implicit political privilege enjoyed by business interests is by no means coincidental.[18]

To be sure, Americans are not blind to this power of privilege, and there have been many attempts at reform. Nevertheless, at least in recent years, such attempts have focused more often on increasing the representation of minority groups or of women than on increasing that of the poor or uneducated. This may result in a definite class bias in political representation. Thus, reforms undertaken after 1968 to make the delegates to Democratic Party conventions more representative in terms of age, sex, and race were quite successful, but they yielded an assembly still heavily skewed toward those with higher social status.[19]

The United States lags behind other nations in regulating private expenditures for partisan political purposes. Most other democracies have long had limits on the use of private funds in elections. The role of private campaign contributions can be curbed through ceilings on spending, and through public funding of elections. The United States compares poorly in both areas (Figure 1.2). Before 1974 the United States and Switzerland were the only nations that neither provided public funds nor limited private donations. Even after the campaign funding reforms of 1974, the limits on private contributions in the United States remained feeble. Indeed, the growth of political action committees and the continued legality of private direct support of candidates has increased the role of private funds in U.S. elections. The Supreme Court's ruling on campaign contributions neatly juxtaposes the egalitarian value of a limitation on the use of money in politics with the libertarian value of freedom to support the candidate of one's choice. The United States is even more distinct among democracies in permitting political candidates to purchase advertising time on television, another way in which private money can be converted into a political resource. Most democracies—including Britain, France, Germany, and Italy—deny candidates this opportunity. Again egalitarians, who would restrict the use of money in politics, clash with libertarians, who want to encourage free speech.[20]

Although the United States ranks first in the diffusion of political participation, having a much higher proportion of moderately active citizens than in comparable nations, it also ranks first or second in

Private Finance

|  | No limits | Limits |
|---|---|---|
| **None** | U.S. (pre-1974)[a]<br>Switzerland[b] | France[a] |
| Quite limited (usually matching funds or indirect subsidies) |  | U.S. (post-1974)[a]<br>Canada[c]<br>Ireland[b]<br>Australia[b] |
| Most or all funding public | Finland[a]<br>Norway[a]<br>Denmark[b]<br>Netherlands[b] | United Kingdom[a]<br>Sweden[a]<br>Italy[a]<br>West Germany[a]<br>Austria[c]<br>Japan[b] |

(left axis label: Public Finance)

**Figure 1.2**

Campaign Financing in Democracies

a. "Dollar Politics," *Congressional Quarterly* 2 (Oct. 1974): 55–60.

b. David Butler, Howard R. Penniman, and Austin Ranney, ed., *Democracy at the Polls* (Washington, D.C.: American Enterprise Institute, 1981).

c. *Government Financing of National Elections* (Washington, D.C.: Library of Congress, 1979), vol. 1.

the correlation between participation and socioeconomic status (Table 1.3). In other words, there are proportionately fewer activists in other nations, but they represent a wider variety of income and educational levels. In the United States, activists come disproportionately from the better educated and more affluent.

This correlation, together with the one anomaly in social policy, the fact that the United States exceeds other nations in spending on education, produces a vicious cycle of inequality. Education fosters increasing disparities in income and occupational status. In turn, people who are better educated, more affluent, and higher in occupational status are more likely to participate in politics. The politically active are more concerned about education, as both a personal and a community need, than are the less active or the inactive citizens, whose highest priority is immediate economic problems. Consequently, public officials, attuned to the concerns of politically active Americans, perceive far more public support for educational

**Table 1.3**
Relationship of Economic and Political Equality Worldwide

| Correlation of socioeconomic status and participation | U.S. rank | Number of countries ranked |
|---|---|---|
| 1959[a] | 1 | 5 |
| 1967–1970[b] | 2 | 7 |

a. Sidney Verba and Norman Nie, *Participation in America* (New York: Harper and Row, 1972), based on data from Gabriel A. Almond and Sidney Verba, *The Civic Culture* (Princeton: Princeton University Press, 1963).

b. Sidney Verba, Norman Nie, and Jae-on Kim, *Participation and Political Equality* (New York: Cambridge University Press, 1979).

programs than for other social policies. As the government responds to this support by strengthening education, the cycle of inequality begins anew.[21]

### Reality or Ideal of Equality

As Herbert McClosky has noted, "If Americans concur most strongly about liberty in the abstract, they disagree most strongly about equality . . . Both the political stratum and the public divide sharply on . . . political as well as social and economic equality. Both are torn not only on the empirical question of whether men are *in fact* equal but also on the normative issue of whether they should be *regarded* as equal. Neither comes close to achieving consensus on such questions." For the public at large, then, and for political leaders in particular, a gap is likely to exist between the reality and the ideal of equality in the domains of both economics and politics.[22] The ambivalence about equality is thus heightened. Not only are there separate standards of equality for economics and politics, but each domain evokes, in turn, both divergent ideals and varying views of reality. The narrowing of the ideal-real gap may entail bringing economic reality into line with the economic ideal of equal opportunity, or bringing political reality into line with the political ideal of equality of result. It may also involve a challenge to economic reality from the political ideal, and vice versa.

The challenge to economic reality from the political ideal embodies the notion of social and economic citizenship, the right to equal treatment in social and economic matters as an extension of one's basic political equality as a citizen. When political rights were broadened in the nineteenth century to encompass universal white male suffrage, many observers—including both proponents and opponents—believed that the tension between the new political equality and the fact of economic inequality would lead to government intervention aimed at leveling economic conditions. Full political democracy, it was felt, would wipe out free market capitalism and its inherent inequalities.

Of course, this has not happened. At times, primarily in the New Deal and the Great Society eras, political forces have led to major modifications of and limitations on the market system. But the economy has remained, in reality and ideal, a model of inequality. One reason the ideal of political democracy has had less impact on the reality of economic inequality than had been hoped, or feared, is that the existence of economic hierarchy, in both reality and ideal, erodes equality of result in the political sphere. Thus, the other challenge is to political equality from the fact of economic inequality. The latter provides some citizens and groups with a disproportionate share of the resources necessary for effective political action. This disparity impedes the realization of the ideal embodied in formal political equality. Furthermore, the ideal of economic inequality legitimizes the political use of economic resources.

The result is a constant tension between the two spheres. Inequality in the economic sphere, as both ideal and reality, shapes politics as those with more economic resources use them for political gain. Political equality, also as ideal and reality, poses a constant challenge to economic inequality as disadvantaged groups petition the state for redress. Egalitarian demands lead to equalizing legislation, such as the progressive income tax. But the continuing disparities in the economic sphere work to limit the effectiveness of such laws, as the economically advantaged groups unleash their greater resources in the political sphere. These groups lobby for tax loopholes, hire lawyers and accountants to maximize their benefit from tax laws, and then deduct the costs.

The gulf between reality and ideal produces ambivalence about equality not only in the confrontation between economic and political life but also within each domain. For example, despite the American commitment to the ideal of equal opportunity, tolerance of economic inequality is by no means universal in this country. But opposition to economic inequality usually manifests itself only in the advocacy of a floor under incomes to eliminate extreme poverty. It rarely takes the form of a belief in a ceiling on income to limit extreme wealth. On the tough questions, such as how much inequality and how much poverty people are actually willing to accept, all consensus vanishes. There is debate on the necessity of a floor and, more important, on how many people need how much protection.

In the field of politics, equality of result may be the dominant norm, but disparities in political influence, even if deplored, are widely tolerated. Americans are unwilling to place too solid a floor below political activity or too rigid a ceiling above it. Citizens are urged to exercise their political rights, but there is little interest in stamping out "political poverty" by requiring all citizens to vote. In the absence of a solid floor, some groups, the disproportionately poor ones, exercise little or no political influence. Ceilings are more widely tolerated. One person, one vote is an established principle. But a ceiling on other kinds of political activity is harder to establish, and support for it is more diffuse. Campaign finance and lobbying laws, for example, are typically weak and ineffectual.[23]

The tension between real and ideal within and across the two domains of equality is heightened by the lack of agreement on the nature of the real. This is particularly true in the political sphere. The issue of political equality in particular turns more on how much equality there is than of how much there should be. The debate centers more on who does govern than on who should govern. Even if Americans concur on the egalitarian ideal for political rights, they still argue about how far the nation is from that ideal.

MUCH OF THE STORY of equality told in this book hinges on these four distinctions: the tension between economics and politics, the contrast between current reality and normative ideals, the clash between individual-based and group-based formulas, and the conflict between opportunity and result. These polarities, in various combinations, set the tone and color the content of American beliefs about equality. The distinctions are never far from view as the story unfolds.

# The Two Hundred Years' War

The issue of equality is one that recurs throughout American history. The demand for equality has lain at the epicenter of the major upheavals that have erupted on the American political scene: the Revolution, the Jacksonian era, the Civil War and Reconstruction, the Populist-Progressive period, the New Deal, and the tumultuous 1960s and 1970s. Often these outbursts were fueled with fiery egalitarian rhetoric; at other times the egalitarian discourse was more muted. But through all these crises, the equality issue remained central. As J. R. Pole observes, the "tenacity" of the egalitarian principle is a characteristic feature of political debate in the United States, where equality has "entered into the language of justice in a more explicit and more public manner than in most contemporaneous political systems."[1]

Moreover, the four key distinctions within the concept of equality—opportunity or result, group or individual, economics or politics, and reality or ideal—are not merely an academic construct. The relations and tensions among the domains of equality have been articulated by contending factions in each period of egalitarian fervor, and the nature of that debate has implications for the contemporary struggle over the issue.

In each period, the challenging groups sought both political and economic equality, for themselves and on behalf of others. Inevitably, after each battle, some progress was made toward egalitarianism on both fronts. In the end, however, each upheaval did relatively little to disturb inequalities in the distribution of income and wealth. The enduring and significant result of these historical battles was rather the achievement of greater political equality through the expansion of political rights or the dispersion of political influence. In other words, the principal legacy of the drives for equality in the United States has been a steadily increasing democratization.

The progression of political equality in America may seem obvious, since democracies are characterized by a singular concern for the individual and for equal rights. The United States in particular has a well-defined and widely appreciated tradition of political egalitarianism. But the salience of equality issues should not be confused with the unambiguous and universal advocacy of equality itself. Throughout the history of the United States, segments of the population have ignored or even promoted political inequality. The framers of the Constitution deliberately fashioned a republican form of government; not only were the citizens separated by a system of indirect representation from the actual levers of government, but only a few were given the right to vote in that system. The political tyranny of a popular majority was one of their primary concerns, and an elaborate mechanism of checks on popular power was built into the political apparatus. Similarly, at a later period the Progressives, for all their democratic reform, were most interested in a government run not by the citizen but by the expert. And political scientists, both past and present, have expressed reservations about the extent to which the ordinary citizen can or should rule. The emphasis has been on "realistic" conceptions of democracy which acknowledge the limited competence, idealism, and rationality of the common citizen. Even practitioners of politics are wary of extensive political involvement by the masses.

Thus, movements for political equality can hardly be taken for granted in American society, whatever its unequivocal and self-proclaimed ideals. Simply put, the reason for the historical disparity among spheres of equality is that economic equality has had fewer proponents than has political equality, and economic reformers have faced greater obstacles and achieved less success. But equality in the United States, whatever its form, has never been a foregone conclusion.

The counterplay of political and economic equality is not the only current issue that has been a main theme of American history. The dominant commitment to equality of opportunity also runs as an ideological leitmotif through history. The gaps between the rich and the poor, the landed and the unlanded, the workers and the industrial barons are all noted continuously, and the inequalities lamented. But the argument that something ought to be done about them is easily refuted, for such inequalities are believed to derive from the workings of a fair system in which effort and talent are rewarded, or at least such inequalities are thought ultimately to benefit most people through their contribution to economic growth. It is not the role of the state to interfere with that process.

The dominant view of equality is individualistic. Some categories of individuals may be deprived, but the remedy is usually individual advancement. However, the group-based idea of equality, under which one identifies particular groups of individuals who are disadvantaged and who have to overcome that disadvantage as a group, appears again and again. And it arises most often in relation to the two groups that have dominated much of the contemporary debate over equality: women and blacks. The theme of slavery and, later, rights for the ex-slaves is a constant counterpoint to the general debate on equality, usually stirring up more passion than the more general considerations of the issue. And the theme of rights for women, though more muted, appears early in American history. In both of these domains, the main issues are political, and the main progress, when progress is made, is in the realm of political rights and political equality.

The group-based perspective on equality is two-sided: some groups suffer disadvantages, other groups are blamed for them. Each historical period has its groups to blame, its perceived cabal of oppressors. These groups are resented for their special privilege and power, their favored status representing an unacceptable violation of the egalitarian ideal. Extremes of privilege have always been considered unfair, from the monopolists in Jackson's time to the trusts at the turn of the century. Such groups have served as a focus for egalitarian agitation. They are perceived to obstruct the equality that, as Tocqueville argued, Americans see as the natural order. The "special interests" that form the target of American popular suspicion have usually but not always been the moneyed interests that combine privileged power with privileged wealth. Special interests can also be big government, big labor, or others whose special position of influence is seen to unbalance the political process. In this way, any intervention into the natural order of equality is suspect, even interventions that might foster more equal allocations. This paradoxical opposition to unequal power when, as has happened at certain periods of economic reform in America, that power might be used to foster equality is reconciled by the commitment to equality of opportunity. Equal opportunity, where each individual is an equal competitor and the role of the government is the negative one of sweeping aside the obstacles that stand in the way of an equal chance to get ahead, provides a hidden hand of just allocation free of the intervention by any more powerful special interest.

Central to the history of the debate over equality are certain assumptions about the role and nature of the state. Americans might lament economic inequality, but it was not thought to be the role of the state to do anything about it. Equality, with the exception of political equality, was not an issue for public policy during most of American history. The movement from equality as a matter of philosophical debate or moral exhortation to equality as an issue of legislation and public policy was impeded by the conflict of equality with another American value, an antipathy toward power, particularly power of the state. In the earliest days of the nation direct intervention by the government on behalf of a social objective like equality would have been considered an intolerable breach of personal liberty. By the twentieth century this negative conception of liberty had in part given way to a positive one, wherein individuals' freedom to explore their potential is safeguarded and promoted by the state. The antipathy toward power has come to be directed at undue influence in private hands as much as in public; the government's power is seen to countervail private power in the name of balance and equity. Through history, the focus of suspicion has shifted from political power to economic power.

The history of equality illustrates yet another major theme that has persisted to this day, the autonomous importance of ideas about equality. To be sure, the issue revolves around substantive matters of advantage and disadvantage. The rich invoke arguments that would protect their position; the poor provide counterarguments. Those without political rights are more likely to call for the extension of such rights than are those whose position in the political hierarchy is established. Self-interest is rarely far from center stage. But self-interested groups are usually not neatly polarized around those interests. People of similar social and economic position take quite different philosophical positions. Likewise, people of different backgrounds share similar views. The ideology of individualistic opportunity is not mere superstructure or false consciousness; it has a life of its own. Indeed, one of the most important features of the history of equality is its religious base. The positions taken by Americans derive from, or at minimum are consistent with, their fundamental religious beliefs.

Equality can be analyzed into its many components, but these components are closely interconnected. Historically, the many aspects of equality have been linked in political discourse. The issue of economic equality has consistently appeared in the debates on political equality. The moral principle demanding the equal treatment of one oppressed group inevitably spread to others, in what Pole refers to as the "indivisibility" of the equality concept. Ironically, the opponents were often more conscious of this infectiousness than were the reformers. That equality for one group would imply equality for others was often used as a justification for denying it to the first.

### The Revolutionary War

The egalitarian fervor of the American Revolution had no equal before it, but it did have a foundation in the increasing scrutiny the new liberals were giving to the ancient notion of a Divine Order. No longer was it assumed that inequality was the natural condition, that everything and everyone had a preordained place in the "great chain" beneath the Creator. To regard man not as an element of the hierarchy but as an individual, one with the power to choose, led logically to considering society as a contract into which that individual chose to enter. At least as signatories to an agreement, men were equals.[2]

Early American conceptions of equality were not always deep or dearly held; rather they expressed the rhetoric of revolution. But rhetoric should not be dismissed, for rhetoric can become attitude, and attitude policy. The Revolutionary rhetoric became an American ideal because it was so explicitly codified in the founding documents of the nation. This particular egalitarian rhetoric was adopted in part as a reaction to British rule. At first the Americans wanted nothing more than to be treated as true British subjects themselves, with the same rights. Soon it appeared that the only way to assert their political equality was to renounce that subject status through revolution. By this time, the deprivation of common law protections had made inequality an American issue. As Virginia lawyer Richard Bland pronounced, "I am speaking of the *rights* of a people, *rights* imply equality."[3] A high-minded and moral pronouncement on the "self-evident truth" of man's equality served well as a call to arms, it was a principled cause worthy of sacrifice. Of course, few principles are more difficult to contain. To its credit, the new nation continued to let equality guide it, in many aspects of public life, when the crisis had passed.

Bernard Bailyn relates the liberal spirit of the Revolution to the seventeenth- and eighteenth-century British protest literature "devoured by the colonists." Social conditions were right for these liberal sentiments to flourish: the lack of a feudal tradition in America allowed for an unorthodox rejection of rigid hierarchy in society. Allan Nevins and Henry Steele Commager remark, "America was a fertile soil for doctrines of a republican or quasi-republican character. The population for a century and a half had been living in an atmosphere of democracy or 'leveling.' "[4]

America's egalitarian tradition is part and parcel of its religious tradition. The German theologian Philip Schaff wrote that in America "everything had a Protestant beginning." The nation's political values are those of seventeenth century Protestantism. Political behavior has assumed the trappings of a religion itself, as Samuel Huntington observes, with the Declaration of Independence as its holy scripture.[5] It is no coincidence that most of the political explosions throughout American history have been accompanied by a religious revival. Conventional moral precepts preceding each upheaval were inadequate guides to social reform. The hopes of the Jacksonians for the common man and a new society were founded in tenets of the religious revival of the early 1800s. The social issues of industrialization were addressed by both the political Progressives and the next wave of evangelicals one century later.[6]

The first Great Awakening of 1730–1760 prepared the way for the break with Britain. Protestant values of moralism and individualism "took up the ground left vacant by the absence of political experience" before the Revolution, values reflected in tracts from the street-corner pamphlet to the Declaration of Independence. Edmund Burke believed that religious dissent when transplanted in America bloomed into a healthy aversion to "submission of mind and opinion," certainly a critical element in the creation of a society where all opinions are accorded equal protection.[7]

The use of the term *revolution* to describe the war over these values is misleading. Unlike later revolts along the French or Marxist lines, the American Revolution was not rooted in class: merchants, farmers, employers, and the employed could be found on both the

Revolutionary and the Tory sides of the conflict. The taking up of arms against England effected not economic, not social, but dramatic political change, backed by new political ideas. Among the many changes were the abolition of legal vestiges of feudalism like entail and quitrents, reform of the penal codes, the enactment of bills of rights, the abolition of slavery in Northern states, the separation of church and state, and the break with the Crown. The ideas embodied in these changes were simple but radical: the notion that government derived its legitimate powers from the consent of the governed, a rejection of the institutionalization and legal protection of privilege, and a dedication to the norm of political equality. These ideas constituted the heart of the Revolution and are the essence of national identity even today:

> In what was a truly novel event in world history, Americans did not assert their independence because their ethnicity, language, culture, or religion differentiated them from their British brethren. The United States came into existence at a particular moment in time—July 4, 1776—and it was the product of a conscious political act based on explicit political principles. "We hold these truths to be self-evident," says the Declaration. Who holds these truths? Americans hold these truths. Who are Americans? People who adhere to these truths. National identity and political principle were inseparable. From the beginning, as Croly noted, the American past was "informed by an idea."[8]

Yet for all they promised in political equality to the young nation, these values had few social or economic implications. In the words of Pole, "the American Revolution introduced an egalitarian rhetoric to an unequal society." Economic and social inequalities remained essentially intact. Though slavery was attacked, white servitude was not. Though America had rejected hereditary rulership, its own gentry retained the power and esteem it had enjoyed for generations, not because of practical strictures on social mobility but because of the limited allegiance to true egalitarian values. As Martin Diamond points out, "the Declaration does not mean by equal anything at all like the general human equality which so many now make their political standard."[9] Thomas Jefferson and the other framers held no illusions that men had been born equal in their endowments of intellect or virtue; for that reason, it seemed prudent to them that participation in governance be limited to those who had proved themselves equal to the task, say by accumulating wealth and property in a competitive society. But they were determined to grant individuals the right to life, liberty, and the pursuit of happiness to the extent that their personal assets allowed. And they would allow government to take action to facilitate those choices—an act of courage on the part of those so recently exposed to the despotism of state authority. These ideas were in every sense of the word revolutionary.

The new equality was a political ideal. It was, in addition, a general commitment to the equal worth of individuals as individuals, as creatures with "inalienable rights." It was not a commitment to substantive equality of wealth or social standing. Differences between rich and poor were deemed legitimate. These attitudes about the legitimacy of wealth have both religious and practical roots. The "Rule of Equity" prohibited the Calvinist from coveting the fortune of another, a moral injunction which contributed to the continued absence of redistribution from the social agenda. As a rationale for the economic order, Protestant religious values were of great practical consequence. Because equal opportunity justified unequal results, Americans could reconcile the ambition, acquisitiveness, and entrepreneurial character of their society with formal stipulations of equality in law and politics. Pole notes, "The emotions released by the Revolution left many Americans deeply dedicated to the aim of keeping in being a society whose members, whatever their differences in wealth, education, fortune, or social style, would respect one another as equals," in political and legal terms.[10]

Some, it is true, came to believe that the "respect of equals" was unlikely among citizens who were unequal in so many ways, particularly in wealth. Thomas Skidmore, a New York reformer during the Jacksonian era, believed that Jefferson evaded the most important issue of equity with the vague "pursuit of happiness." Without property, the guarantee of this pursuit was hollow. The poor cannot be happy, nor can their rights be preserved. Equality of property is in itself a right. Skidmore's conception of equality was radical, but he argued that he wanted only to complete the logic of the ideals that the Founding Fathers had themselves defined.[11] He was one of a few who advocated the granting of land to slaves, recognizing that they would be free only if they were economically independent.

One of the Founding Fathers seems to have shared this concern over unequal wealth. James Madison felt that laws should have a general, mild, almost silent tendency to lessen differences in wealth. He discussed "the unequal and various distribution of property" in the Federalist papers. This inequality was the "most common and durable source" of the factionalism he so feared. Yet he proposed no remedy for that source, no role for government in economic equality. Indeed, his was the only mention of equality in the Federalist papers.

Nor did Madison's fellow patriots seek a remedy for unequal wealth. Their revolution began with a society unequal in wealth, and so did it end. Before the war, exploitative practices by absentee landowners perpetuated the gap between the rich and the poor in colonial America. Poverty persisted despite the plenitude of a flourishing economy, particularly in the cities. On the eve of the Revolution, 29 percent of Boston residents were too poor to be taxed—a city where 10 percent of the residents owned more than half of the wealth. Boston's population had doubled between 1687 and 1771, while its percentage of property-poor increased fourfold.[12]

The immense political changes wrought by independence from Britain did nothing to alter that gap. Egalitarian rhetoric and indentured servitude both reached new heights. Nearly a third of the North's white population owned little more than their immediate personal belongings. Even owning land was no guarantee of happiness or the freedom to pursue it: 60 percent of Maryland planters made only enough to cover the barest necessities of existence.[13] Despite the pervasiveness of economic inequality, most landed Americans chose to bask in their newly won political rights.

### The Jacksonian Era

The periods of egalitarian fervor that punctuate American history were each an age of the common man: a renewal of faith in his abilities and a reaffirmation of his right to participate freely in the political and economic systems. In 1828 with the election of Andrew Jackson the common man assumed the highest office in the land. Jackson had been born into poverty himself and had the Westerner's distrust of the powerful Eastern establishment, particularly its financiers. He hoped to restore the rightful rule of public opinion.[14] Once again, the impulse toward equality took a political direction.

Jackson's liberal sentiments were mirrored in the new politician of the time, whom Richard Hofstadter terms the "technician of mass leadership":

These leaders encouraged the common feeling that popular will should control the choice of public officers and the formation of public policy. They directed popular resentment of closed political corporations against the caucus system, which they branded as a flagrant usurpation of the rights of the people, and spread the conviction that politics and administration must be taken from the hands of a social elite or a body of bureaucratic specialists and opened to mass participation. Success through politics, it was implied, must become a legitimate aspiration of the many.[15]

The advent of direct primaries and the civil service brought a new measure of political equality and enfranchisement to American society, reforms among the many swept forward by "the great new democratic wave."[16] Suffrage was extended through the elimination of property restrictions in many states. Even social manners became more democratic. In toppling the gentry and the experts, the Jacksonians hoped to achieve, in their words, the "great principle of amalgamating all orders of society."[17]

Special classes of Americans who fell outside the principles of equality that were applied to landed white males began to press for better treatment. The abolition movement advanced the cause of the slaves by claiming their share of the equality rhetoric. The pre-Revolutionary claims that Britain had reduced the colonies to "slavery" had caused some discomfort to Southerners when the logical implications of such a metaphor were considered, for moral principles of equality are hard to apply selectively.[18] Women found their political voice by joining in the abolitionist movement. Inevitably their new consciousness of the blacks' plight extended to their own predicament, and they used their new political experience to link the equality issues of race and gender. When women were excluded from the World Antislavery Convention in 1840, as they were excluded from so many abolitionist organizations, Lucretia Mott and Elizabeth Cady Stanton agreed that women must organize politically to throw over their own subjugation. Their 1845 Women's Rights Convention approved a Declaration of Sentiments which held it "self-evident that all men and women are created equal."[19]

Political activity flourished. The American proclivity for voluntary association was given free rein during the Jacksonian period. There was a substantial increase in voting participation, and new interest groups and political parties contributed much to the new democratization of power. Interest in and access to the political system reached new heights.

Labor was included in the expanding sphere of political consciousness. The first signs appeared of an economic class division and discontent that would come to dominate the later politics of the New Deal. As Pole observes of the Eastern cities, "the growing concentration of industrial plants, together with the separation of capital and management from the work force, was bringing about the beginnings of [a] resentfully self-conscious urban skilled working class." Leaders of the working-class interests saw that privileges in education and social rank undermined formal guarantees of equality; the very concept of equality became the "central intellectual commitment" of the labor movement in Jackson's time. The worker's faith in American egalitarianism demonstrated that abstract notions of rights had turned into legitimate social expectations.[20]

But Jackson was content with equal protection under the law. Like the Founding Fathers, he was convinced that unequal economic conditions were the immutable result of unequal abilities. In Jackson's words, "Distinctions in society will always exist under every just government. Equality of talents, or education, or of wealth cannot be produced by human institutions."[21] If political equality could produce equal opportunity, that would suffice. Equal opportunity included the opportunity to fail while others moved ahead; such failure was held to be almost a moral issue and certainly a matter of personal responsibility.[22] There was a certain pragmatism in this attitude as well. Unequal achievement and economic progress were thought to go hand in hand. Economic progress was all-important; unequal achievement would have to be tolerated, and equality sought in some other domain.

The people shared his belief that equal economic opportunity had finally been achieved. Their touchstone was Jackson's destruction of the Bank of the United States, a symbol of economic favor and state-sanctioned monopoly. Laissez-faire was the order of the day. The market was regarded as the ultimate democracy because it discriminated against no man's money. In this generation's view, equality of opportunity was to be protected by government. They believed that the government should act to protect the natural economic order, a charge which encompassed both a rejection of economic "privilege" and a tolerance of great disparities in wealth. The Jacksonians were understandably more aware of explicit charters of monopoly than of the surreptitious forces that continued to thwart the economic opportunities they so cherished. This conception of what government should do about equality was still defined by the American hostility toward centralized power, particularly that of the state. The elimination of the Bank is thus the quintessential equality policy of the time, a symbol for Jacksonians and historians alike.

There was no pretense at all about extending these same opportunities to blacks. Jackson cared little about racial equality. As he had sought equality across class, it was left to others in other times to extend it across race.[23] Nevertheless, these limitations should not obscure the truly great transformations wrought in this, the second revolution of equality.

### The Civil War and Reconstruction

The Civil War fostered equality by ending slavery. This was a momentous step in the American effort toward full equality for its citizens. Yet the step was a limited one. With Reconstruction came the political rights of citizenship and the vote. Yet these rights were to become largely empty formalities. And there was no movement at all toward substantive social or economic rights.

The call for emancipation had served the same purpose as the claim for rights before the Revolution: a rhetoric of equality justifying the sacrifice of war. This is not to say that few were sincere in their espousal of the egalitarian ideal; once the war had been won, attitudes again translated into substantial social change. The victory over the South had taken on a moral significance, like the moralism of other American political upheavals. Intellectuals of the time were optimistic and eager to play a part in the reforms to come.

There were reforms, but the spirit of change in the name of American ideals died more quickly than it had in the other upheavals. The Republican radicals were fought by Southerners long after the last shot had been fired, and the radicals' strength was sapped by dissension within the ranks of their own party. Perhaps American society had undergone a convulsion too dramatic to sustain another upheaval. Once the crisis had passed, the nation needed to reserve its energy for practical rebuilding, not idealistic reform. The contagion of egalitarianism had frightened the conservatives into a serious defense of the status quo. There was no knowing what other rights might be claimed next by what other groups, and what sacrifices this would entail of the wealthy, the powerful. Conservatives watched as Republican Joseph Fowler "fearlessly proceeded from the principle of equality as applied to individuals regardless of property or race to equality regardless of sex."[24] Abolitionist Wendell Phillips, like a nineteenth century Ralph Nader, had come to stand for a multitude of causes: equal rights for women, temperance, justice for the American Indian, self-determination for Ireland, elimination of capital punishment, concern for the mentally ill.[25] In building coalitions for the support of their political agenda, Republican radicals played upon the natural affinity among the oppressed. "The man who is the enemy of the black laboring man is the enemy of the white laboring man the world over," declared Massachusetts senator Henry Wilson. "The same influences that go to keep down and crush down the rights of the poor black bear down and oppress the poor white laboring man."[26] The barriers between types of equality were fragile, and they were being broached in only one, ever-expanding egalitarian direction.

Traditional qualms about state activism, still considered a matter of liberty, also came between equality as an ideal and equality as a reality, much as they had in the Jacksonian and Revolutionary periods. The size and power of a wartime government had alarmed many Americans. This certainly did not aid the cause of radical Republicans, whose plans for the reconstruction of the South would have required an unprecedented intervention by government in local affairs, all in the name of a fragile ideal.

The most important obstacle to the Radical platform was the President himself. Andrew Johnson, a conservative Southerner, found himself the duly elected head of a government dominated by Republicans committed to an egalitarian reconstruction. He availed himself of the antigovernment sentiment and latent racism in vetoing their legislative proposals to remake the South in the classic Republican image: small farms, free schools, and political freedom.[27]

The President was not without support among the populace at large. Democratic successes in the off-year elections of 1867 revealed significant discontent with the plans to make freedmen the white man's equal. Much of the "anthropology" of the late nineteenth century was devoted to establishing the biological inferiority of the Negro race. It was commonly accepted that, whatever the rights given to them, blacks did not in fact have the intellectual capacity to become the white man's equal. As Pole points out, this conception may actually have eased fears about according blacks those new rights. Nevertheless, whites still felt threatened by a society in which blacks lived free, no matter how superior whites may have believed their race to be.

The Republicans were in many cases overly sanguine about the immediate prospects for racial equality and complacent about the measures necessary to achieve it. In this respect they were their own worst enemies, as shown by the contrast between Senator Charles Sumner and Representative Thaddeus Stevens. Both were zealous advocates of equality in their respective houses, but Stevens was much more willing to use the powers of the state to enforce economic justice as well as political. Sumner's beliefs, and those of his contemporary Radical colleagues, were reminiscent of those of the Jacksonians: government was not responsible for the economic aims of society.[28] As Pole observes:

> The failure of the Radical plan to distribute land to the freedmen . . . placed a heavy burden on the efficacy of the political weapon that did remain in Negro hands after the Fifteenth Amendment. The right of suffrage satisfied the demands of other Republicans who stood on the principle of political individualism without looking too closely into the social context in which it had to be exercised. Most of the freedmen's political allies, in fact, were quite satisfied that the suffrage alone would bring their other needs within reach. Even such a determined antislavery campaigner as Wendell Phillips could take a remarkable degree of satisfaction in the efficacy of suffrage. "A man with a ballot in his hand," he said in supporting the Fifteenth Amendment, "is the master of the situation. He defines all his other rights. What is not already given to him, he takes . . . The Ballot is opportunity, education, fair play, right to office, and elbow room."[29]

Upon passage of the Fifteenth Amendment, a number of abolition groups disbanded, believing the black was finally a free citizen like any other.[30]

Some Republicans did not even pay lip service to the party's stance on equality, for racism pervaded the North as well as the South. Other Republicans found it not in their hearts but in their self-interest to support equality. Some of these advocated Reconstruction as a means of keeping the freedmen in the South; others saw in black suffrage the advent of an important constituency that would keep the Republican party in power. Without those votes, there were fears that the Southerners and their Northern sympathizers would combine in the legislature to repudiate the war debt and ruin the credit of the nation. As a liberal of the day described it, "The highest requirements of abstract justice coincide with the lowest requirements of political prudence."[31]

Despite political opposition, popular misgivings, and an unrealistic optimism, the Radicals pressed on, and many of their ideas about justice found their way into postbellum public policy. Their achievements were significant. A civil rights bill that rejected *Dred Scott*'s racially exclusive definition of citizenship and legislation strengthening the Freedmen's Bureau passed in 1866 over the President's veto. The Fourteenth and Fifteenth Amendments to the Constitution proposed a race-blind citizenship which could be preserved from the states' interference through the interposition of the federal government. The Fifteenth Amendment forbade states from abridging the right to vote on the basis of "race, color, or previous condition of servitude," a guarantee of black suffrage not included in the Fourteenth. With this legislation, Jackson's notion of equal protection of the laws became an explicit and codified policy of the government.

Blacks did begin to make modest advances in their social condition. Their expectations rose, if slowly, and they cautiously organized to press for their legally allotted place in the political system. Though not without instances of corruption and inefficiency, the Freedmen's Bureau did what it could with its modest powers and budget to ease blacks' transition to free citizenship. Its expenditures represented the sole federal contribution to the education of blacks in the postbellum years; between 1870 and 1880 the enrollment of black children had increased sixfold.[32]

But as the political passion of the 1860s cooled, the momentum for realizing blacks' rights was gradually lost. Congress eliminated the Freedmen's Bureau, the only real agency for racial change, in 1869. Republicans emasculated their own Civil Rights Bill of 1875, passed as little more than a tribute to the late Charles Sumner. The Supreme Court steadily eroded the scope of Reconstruction legislation; the Fourteenth Amendment was invoked more often to protect corporations from government regulation than to preserve black suffrage from state prejudice. The limited language of the Fifteenth Amendment failed to prevent devices like literacy tests and poll taxes from disenfranchising blacks. The political gains for blacks of this period were more durable than the economic, but even the former rested on shaky ground.

The translation of ideals into realities was laborious during the Reconstruction years, and not only for reasons of pragmatic politics, vested interests, and ingrained prejudice. The egalitarians were faced with vexing questions about the relationship between different spheres of equality. No longer could they espouse a general egalitarian ideal; the paradoxes had become too obvious. They had failed to heed the warnings of two of the most important thinkers the South produced before the war. John C. Calhoun "faced with more candor than many of his contemporaries the conflicts arising from concomitant commitments to equality of opportunity and equality of condition."[33] He agreed that equality under the law is essential to the free society. Yet that equality also gives free rein to the unequal abilities of its citizens; a gross inequality of condition inevitably arises which is itself essential to progress. His argument resembled in its conclusion that of George Fitzhugh, who believed that "liberty and equality throw the whole weight of society on its weakest members."[34] To Fitzhugh, egalitarianism was fundamentally inconsistent with the realities of human nature.

The egalitarians were not swayed by Calhoun's and Fitzhugh's vision of a normatively unequal and paternalistic society. Yet they had begun to realize that they held beliefs about not only the distribution of power and wealth but the means of achieving it as well. It would be necessary to extend the authority of the state to realize fully their standards for equality, both political and economic. Social critics and visionaries like Henry George and Edward Bellamy would later espouse this belief, sowing the intellectual seeds of Progressivism and the New Deal.

## The Populist and Progressive Eras

In the late nineteenth century, industrialization transformed the United States. The quintessential American was no longer the yeoman farmer; he had become the business entrepreneur whose "rugged individualism" the government would preserve with a laissez-faire attitude toward the regulation of commercial activity. In truth, the American individual as economic actor had been replaced by the American corporation. The railroads spread across the miles of land granted by the government; in turn, those tracks allowed mining and lumbering to take place on an unprecedented scale. As trusts and pyramids multiplied, the wealth from this new productivity flowed to a relative few. These men felt that the money and power they had accumulated was deserved in the name of a greater good for society: progress. They "wanted an industrial America under [their] custodianship. [They] wanted the entire social system bent to the needs of industrialization . . . governmental power committed to policies and programs on behalf of the ascendant industrial order."[35] Government for its part seemed willing to oblige, as did the Supreme

Court. Laissez-faire was useful as an ideal only where it suited the interests of business.

A tendency toward economic concentration continued through the century. The mobility between classes that so impressed Tocqueville proved deceptive; not only did the rich get richer, but for the most part the poor stayed poor. The economic order became more hierarchical by occupational level as well as income. Capital and management separated from labor. By the second half of the nineteenth century, two-thirds of all participants in the economic system were employees.[36] The homeowner was being replaced by the tenant, the landowner by the farm laborer. At the end of the century 25 percent of all farmland was owned by only 0.006 percent of the population.[37]

The fortunes of the new "captains of industry" were so unseemly that for the first time studies were conducted on the distribution of income. In 1893 the Census Bureau estimated that 9 percent of the nation's families held 71 percent of the wealth.[38] Farmers saw this as a threat to the American way of life. Yet they also had tangible economic grievances. As debtors, they wanted "soft" money and inflationary policies; business wanted "hard" or scarce money. Increased productivity and overseas competition had undermined crop prices. The freight charges by the railroad monopolies were regarded as onerous. The Farmers' Alliances of the South and Plains States evolved and combined to form the cadre of the Populist party in the 1880s.

Populism was more than a party. It gave voice to rural frustrations with the new industrial age. These passions stoked the beginnings of a political upheaval in the midst of a social and economic one. Like the other upheavals, it was figuratively and sometimes literally religious in its fervor. A Kansas Populist leader urged the 1894 state party convention "to make a platform that talks less about free silver and more about salvation; less about finance and more about religion."[39]

The Populists restored nonracial themes of equality to American political discourse. And their claim was economic as well as political. As the social heirs of the "plain people" who carried the day in the American Revolution, they felt that they deserved a better fate than victimization at the hands of the new industrialists. They also believed that their colonial predecessors had had a bigger piece of the economic pie; the Populists advocated a graduated income tax to restore the parity of wealth that had been lost. They declared that "the forces of reform this day organized will never cease to move forward until every wrong is remedied, with equal rights and equal privileges securely established for all the men and women in this country."[40] The mention of women was notable. Remarked novelist Hamlin Garland, "No other movement in history—not even the anti-slavery cause—appealed to the women like this [Populist] movement here in Kansas." Women orators, until then a rarity in American politics, assumed prominence in Populist politics.[41]

For all the Populist rhetoric about equality, their egalitarianism did not extend much further than to their female compatriots. This was a time when the homogeneity of the country's Northern European stock was being challenged by immigration both from other parts of Europe and from Asia. The Populists, as well as most Americans, distrusted the foreign labor crowding the cities and swelling the ranks of industry. Small-town, Protestant America was under attack but hotly defended. Racial restrictionism made its first appearance in public policy with the Chinese Exclusion Act of 1882. "Scientific" theories of racism relegated peoples outside the Anglo-Saxon strain to a genetically inferior status.

The domestic labor movement shared the Populist sentiment toward immigrants, but the Populists' support in turn for the organized working class was at best halfhearted. Farmers were accustomed to long hours and thought little of attempts to legislate a shorter day for city workers. The wage demands of urban labor seemed excessive, and the farmers resented the fact that those demands contributed to the spiraling cost of the material used in agriculture. In turn, their demands for higher crop prices meant higher food prices for laborers. The tactics of industrial unions were just another symbol of urban corruption.[42]

Though the American farmer may also have resented the political strength of the unions, unions were in fact none too strong relative to the clout of capital during this period. The government was no friend of organized labor: wages had to be kept low to permit the continued high rate of capital investment by management, to say nothing of the high rate of profit. There was little improvement in real wages between 1896 and 1914, a period during which productivity increased tremendously.[43]

Reflecting the weakness of its position, the labor movement stood for a "business unionism" that rejected socialist and syndicalist solutions. Labor's weakness was compounded by its ideological reservations over what little power it had. Equal economic opportunity was still interpreted as free capitalist competition; the success of the industrial order legitimized its power. In effect, management had coopted the egalitarian values that would have rightly worked in labor's favor. The unions were trapped into mouthing sentiments about the mutual interests of capital and labor.[44]

Unions were weak, but their political zenith lay ahead of them; the preeminence of the farmer was a thing of the past. By the end of the nineteenth century non-farm employment was growing three times faster than the agricultural labor force. In the sixty years after the Civil War the rural population fell from 80 percent of the total to less than half.[45]

As urban politics began to overshadow rural politics, Populism gave way to the Progressive movement. Progressive reform had a more patrician aura than the Populist platform. The torch of political change in this period of ferment passed from the lower class to the middle class. The Bull Moose movement of 1912 was, to quote William Allen White, "in the main and in its heart of hearts *petit bourgeois*, a movement of little businessmen, professional men, the well-to-do farmer, the skilled artisans from the upper brackets of organized labor."[46]

The Progressives were better educated and less provincial than the Populists, and their ideas more complex. They had a Yankee Protestant sense of responsibility for social ills and their solution. Progressive thought took various forms. One was best exemplified by the muckrakers, journalists like Lincoln Steffens who sought to expose the corruption that inevitably accompanied the grand size of contemporary institutions. Their egalitarian sensibilities and laissez-faire philosophy motivated a vision of society where the common man could run things if only he were allowed. The Jeffersonian strain of Progressivism embraced by political figures like Brandeis and Wilson shared this egalitarian sensibility and also advocated trust-busting as a means of restoring a more competitive economy.

The Hamiltonian school of Progressivism reacted less reflexively to the characteristics of industrial America. The organization of political and economic life may be accompanied by many evils, but it would take organization itself to control those evils. Herbert Croly, a spokesman for this philosophy, argued that it was not enough to tinker with the democratic machinery and hope that the better men would take the opportunity to lead. Big business and organized politics were here to stay. The public good must be represented by an equally vigorous countervailing power, the federal government. And for the goal of popular rule to have any positive content, that government must have in hand an explicit social program.[47]

Croly argued that egalitarian reform failed to achieve its potential again and again because "equality was not a concrete aim but a mode of protest." No one was against equality. The platforms of both parties, then as now, reaffirmed their commitment to equality every four years. As rhetoric, the ideal of equality, Croly claimed, was a trap. He returned to the theme developed earlier by Calhoun, the contradiction between equal opportunity and equal condition. What was at fault was the principle of equality, not Americans' imperfect adherence to it; the American commitment to "equal rights" obscured the contradiction. According to Croly, "The principle of equal rights encourages mutual suspicion and disloyalty. It tends to attribute individual and social ills, for which general moral, economic, and social causes are usually in large measure responsible, to individual wrong-doing; and in this way it arouses and intensifies that personal and class hatred, which never in any society lies far below the surface."[48]

Disparities of wealth, inequalities of power, and divisions among races at the beginning of the twentieth century posed a great challenge to the cause of egalitarianism. The Progressives had a formidable task in their plans for reform, which in the American tradition were plans for more political democracy rather than more economic equality. A number of their reforms genuinely improved and broadened popular control over public affairs. For example, the direct election of Senators and the recall made the electoral system more responsive to its constituents. The constituency itself was enlarged by the granting of suffrage to women.

Some of the Progressives' reforms, however, undercut the increasing democratization of politics. Intentionally or not, certain of their proposals may have sharpened the economic bias against the political participation of lower-class citizens. Most directly, voting registration procedures introduced during this period did much to keep lower-class voters from the polls. Other reforms for popular rule also gave a bigger voice to the upper strata. By taking power away from political parties, the new devices of the referendum and the direct primary may have taken power away from the lower classes as well, for it was the political party that mobilized the lower-class vote. Furthermore, an alert minority could exert its will through the complex ballot initiatives that alienated the average voter. Ultimately the party bosses were replaced by a wealthier, better-educated elite and by a new politics that relied on the expert rather than the common man. Under Progressivism, concentrations of power were moved about rather than dispersed.

This effect of Progressive reform highlights one of the ambiguities of equality. In the United States an inequality of wealth is more legitimate than an inequality of political rights or political power. The legitimacy of economic inequality, however, leads to the easy acceptance of the translation of wealth into political power, which in turn leads to de facto inequality in the political realm. The Progressives focused on making the political process more formally equal. In so doing, they increased the informal influence of wealth and status on political participation.

In any event, as Croly predicted, the political kingpins found their way back to political control. The tendency toward economic oligopoly had not been reversed. "In their search for mechanical guarantees of continued popular control," notes Hofstadter, "the reformers were trying to do something altogether impossible—to institutionalize a mood. When the mood passed, some of the more concrete reforms remained; but the formal gains for popular government, while still on the books, lost meaning because the ability of the public to use them effectively lapsed with the political revival that brought them in, and the bosses and the special interests promptly filtered back."[49] Another upheaval had passed, leaving to the next upheaval the job of institutionalizing its ideals. The adoption of the Progressives' national income tax is the most notable exception to the limits of the ideal of economic equality. Theodore Roosevelt shocked his party in 1906 by advocating "the adoption of some such scheme as that of the progressive income tax on all fortunes." But even many conservative Republicans had been won over to an income tax as a means of reducing the tariff rates, for by the 1890s the nation had become a net exporter and its high tariffs were no longer politically or economically desirable. The income tax seemed to be the obvious source of alternative revenue. Reform-minded Democrats held the Populist view that the income tax was a valuable tool in the redistribution of wealth. By 1912, the Sixteenth Amendment had been ratified, giving Congress the power "to lay and collect taxes on incomes, from whatever source derived."[50]

## The New Deal

The objective of the New Deal, unlike that of the earlier movements, was not political reform but economic recovery. Political reform, however, was undeniably the New Deal's result. According to William Leuchtenburg, "the New Deal achieved a more just society by recognizing groups which had been largely unrepresented."[51] Thus, Franklin D. Roosevelt's economic programs had significant consequences for the politics of equality.

This period was not marked by the moral fervor of the others; its vision was more pragmatic than utopian. But dramatic social change became possible with an equally dramatic change in society's expectations. The election of Roosevelt portended the light at the end of the Depression's tunnel, and people were gripped with the euphoria of new possibilities. Roosevelt's assumption of the Presidency, wrote Walter Lippman, was a boost to public morale equal to the "second battle of the Marne in the summer of 1916."[52] A certain egalitarianism motivated the New Deal, as it had the reform movements of the past, but in this instance it took the form of a more overt concern for economic equality. Samuel Beer states that "the egalitarianism of the New Deal was a response to what was seen as a twofold problem: a maldistribution of income and a concentration of economic power." New Deal policies provided some measure of security against severe economic deprivation, but little redistribution of wealth was either sought or achieved. Indeed, the most significant consequences of the concern for economic equality were political.[53]

Making labor the equal of management was the boldest political stroke of the New Deal. The Wagner Act addressed "the inequality of bargaining power between employees who do not possess full freedom of association or actual liberty of contract and employers who are organized in the corporate or other forms of ownership association." It created the National Labor Relations Board, charged with the protection of the workers' right to bargain collectively and the oversight of the process by which the workers' representatives were chosen. This unprecedented grant of power to an economic group fostered a boom in labor organizing; union membership rose from 4 million in 1935 to 9 million in 1947. The government was now in the equality business without reservation, but the equalization was political. It provided "countervailing power" to groups too weak to make their own case for social justice.[54]

While the New Deal promoted equality within the political sphere and, to some extent, in the economic sphere, it also heightened the tension between them by making economics a more political issue. Egalitarian politics coexists at best with difficulty next to an inegalitarian economy. The more that political decisions affect economic distributions, the more that the relationship between the two systems becomes strained. If the state does very little in relation to the economy, there will be less tension when the market performs under its principle of equal opportunity and unequal reward while the polity operates under its principle of equal political access.

The social service state of the New Deal undermined such a separation. Economic allocations increasingly came to depend on government decisions as the arena of economic conflict shifted from the market to the polity. Critics of such a change see it as a destructive intrusion of the state into the economy, arguing that when economic benefits are allocated by governmental fiat in response to the political demands of groups, the result is gross inefficiency. Conservatives deplore the loss of incentive when economic reward can be had through politics rather than productivity. They also object to the loss of liberty and growing dependency on government. Supporters of social welfare policies see them as a healthy involvement of the government in the economy to compensate for the inequities of the market and the inability of an unregulated economy to satisfy basic human needs. Under either interpretation, the state has become more active in the economy, and the domains of politics and economics have become intertwined. One of the final barriers between the two spheres of equality is thus breached, but with increasing dissension over the practical limits of that American ideal.

The politicization of economic distribution brings a new twist to the politics of equality, the conflict over group equality rather than individual equality. As Beer points out, individual equality sought "to give each the same right without regard to group or class identity ... The Wagner Act departed from this principle by creating rights for a special group." In the unregulated market, the dominant norm of equality is equality of opportunity for individuals. Political conflict, in contrast, is among groups. The New Deal's wedding of the two domains went only so far as to carry the principle of reward based on effort and talent, a principle usually applied to individuals, over to the new group-based political conflict. This limited approach might have been expected in a society so ambivalent about equality. As Beer notes, the Wagner Act "retained the essence of the old rationale since, once these rights were guaranteed by law, it was up to the group to utilize them."[55] The government did not meet the demands of labor; labor was given the countervailing power to seek its goals itself.

The New Deal thus held high the promise of political equality at least as much as economic equality, but the political struggle was defined in economic terms. The contenders in the dual struggle over economic policies and political power were the major economic actors, business and labor. In this sense, the New Deal represents a high point in class conflict in a nation where conflict has usually had few class overtones. The partisan alignment of the New Deal was by no means based entirely on class, for the strength of the Democratic party in the solid South cut across class lines, but it had a significant class flavor, with labor as the mainstay of the Democratic coalition and business closely allied with the Republican party.

The New Deal gave no significant impetus to two major aspects of equality: race and gender equality. Roosevelt never made a commitment to racial equality per se; that issue was kept off the agenda as the electoral price of maintaining the support of the South and the momentum for economic reform. Appalled at his failure to propose civil rights legislation, the NAACP broke with him in 1935. Many interpreted his plan to pack the Supreme Court as a possible retrenchment in the area of racial equality. Wrote one liberal, "If I were a Negro I would be raging and tearing my hair over this proposal."[56]

Nevertheless, the New Deal accomplished much for blacks in tackling the Depression. The social service package of the New Deal, the aid to unionization, and the economic recovery program helped significant portions of the black population, as it did white Americans who were disadvantaged. Roosevelt appointed blacks to the most important posts they had yet held. As early as 1932 Robert Vann, publisher of the Pittsburgh *Courier*, told black voters: "My friends, go turn Lincoln's picture to the wall. That debt has been paid in full."[57] The Democratic party was not yet the champion of racial equality, but the groundwork was laid.

The New Deal evinced some indirect commitment to gender equality. Its modest successes included the example of Eleanor Roosevelt and a new network of female administrators, such as Secretary of Labor Frances Perkins, the first female cabinet member.[58] But gender equality, like racial equality, was not on the New Deal agenda.

**The 1960s and 1970s**

The 1960s and 1970s saw the rebirth of egalitarianism in yet another fit of political passion. The concern for and rhetoric of equality were so intense that an entire movement, neoconservatism, sprang up in reaction to what its exponents felt were dangerous excesses. Irving Kristol warned against those people who "prize equality more than liberty." His colleague Robert Nisbet felt the call for equality to be "the single greatest threat to liberty and social initiative."[59] The federal government, having entered into the allocation of wealth and power, could not easily retreat; it was called upon to reaffirm its commitment to equality. A "superjudiciary" asserted itself where the bureaucracy was unresponsive, eliminating racial segregation by fiat.

The Great Society was founded on a belief in government's capacity to do good. Like the New Deal, it had programs that aimed at economic equity but were not fundamentally redistributive. Also like the New Deal, these programs singled out economic groups for special attention—but this time for explicit economic not political assistance. Where, before, social programs like Social Security did not discriminate by class or race, new measures with economic means tests, like Aid to Families with Dependent Children (AFDC), singled out the poor and thus blacks as a particular beneficiary. This hardly amounted to an equalization of wealth, but considerations of economic equity had finally entered the mainstream of American political discourse and public policy.

Political reform with an egalitarian bent bloomed in the '60s as it had in the other periods of political flux. There were fewer restrictions on voting, more presidential primaries, delegate quotas by race and gender at Democratic conventions, new campaign finance laws, and freedom-of-information legislation—all aimed to reallocate power from vested political interests. As Huntington points out, some legislation backfired. "Sunshine laws" often forced political dealing further under cover. Party reforms may have wrested the primaries from one elite and handed them to another. Without a doubt, the restrictions on campaign funding redounded to the benefit of incumbent politicians.[60]

Both youth and blacks renewed their activism on behalf of egalitarian goals. The right to vote was given to the eighteen-year-old; blacks in ever-increasing numbers exercised their right to vote. Their demonstrations against "the Establishment" called into question the legitimacy of hierarchies of authority and posed an egalitarian, if nihilistic, alternative to inequality in the American social structure. Practical measures for equality emerged from the turmoil in the streets, thanks to the diligence of the cadre of reformers. Their most notable success, and Lyndon Johnson's great pride, was the Voting Rights Act of 1965. The dramatic march by Martin Luther King and his followers at Selma, Alabama, had focused the public's attention on the need for action and on Congress' inactivity. Within a year of the Voting Rights Act, civil rights legislation had been amended to prohibit discrimination in the selection of juries, protect the physical safety of blacks, and prevent racial bias in the provision of housing.[61]

When Congress did act, it affirmed, and the Supreme Court upheld, its right to intervene where the states failed to offer equal protection to the rights of its citizens. The liability of Reconstruction, its failure to compel the states so to behave, was erased, and the promise of Reconstruction, its grant of suffrage to blacks, was finally realized. Constitutional lawyers were coming to the realization that "equality itself had emerged as the guiding principle in the dominant areas of public interest."[62]

The blacks' bid for equality was largely successful, socially and politically, but not economically. The seven years after the Voting Rights Act saw one million blacks added to the voting rolls. During that same period the percentage of Southern black children attending all-black schools fell from 98 percent to 9 percent. And there were economic gains in real terms for black wage-earners. Yet relative to their white colleagues they had made little headway, and the growing "feminization of poverty" found more and more female-headed black families sinking into destitution. The proportion of black families headed by women rose dramatically in the 1970s. Although the average black adult earned 68 percent of what the white adult earned, black children typically lived in families making only 55 percent of the income of white children's families, because 43 percent of those black children received no financial support from their fathers.[63]

Women, like blacks, demanded their equal rights, but achieved them differently: they did not avail themselves to the same extent of the politics of protest. They may not have needed that particular public forum when their private channel, access to white males, was more effective than that of the blacks. In some respects, victories for blacks smoothed the way for victories by women: black suffrage was the precedent for extending the vote to women in 1920. Yet the same paternalism used to keep blacks from advancing after the theoretical argument for equality had been won was used against women. The industrial work environment at the turn of the century had provided the justification for protective laws, such as limitations on exertion and work hours, which ultimately stigmatized women as inferiors. Those same industrial conditions allowed women to demonstrate their worth as they replaced the men sent abroad during World War I.[64]

Yet even by the 1960s few women were integrated into the mainstream of American professional life. Only 3.8 percent of the nation's lawyers and less than one percent of its engineers were female.[65] Their legislative victories were primarily political. Through political maneuvering, sexual discrimination was added to the other types of discrimination prohibited by the Civil Rights Act of 1964, whereby sexual equality became an official policy of the U.S. government.[66] Although the Equal Rights Amendment, the more explicit statement of that principle, failed to become law, women, like blacks, had won a great social victory. Sexual discrimination was no longer acceptable in public policy, though it might remain in private attitudes and behavior.

To the extent that the 1960s are not yet "history," it is impossible to judge which of its measures for equality will survive. As in other periods of upheaval, however, the political will probably overshadow the economic. The young were given a political tool, the vote. The use of that tool was guaranteed to blacks, but this has not translated into direct or dramatic economic gain. The gap in earnings between blacks and women on the one hand and white males on the other persists into the 1980s. These disadvantaged groups have made relative advances in political power; their relative economic improvement is much less obvious.

President Johnson articulated the ideal that guided the reforms of his Great Society: "We seek not just freedom but opportunity—not just legal equity but human ability—not just equality as a right and a theory but equality as a fact and a result."[67] The ambiguity of this formulation reflects the modern drive to tie the domains of equality ever tighter together without resolving the paradoxes that their juxtaposition represents. The civil rights movement and the feminist movement complicate the equality issue by intensifying these ambiguities and possibly creating new ones. For example, the conflict between equality as similar opportunity versus equality as similar condition has been heightened. Women and racial minorities believe that the history of inequality in opportunity makes the opening of opportunity today an inadequate means of closing the gap between themselves and the more advantaged segments of society. Thus they call for mandated equality of result through quotas or affirmative action and other compensatory programs. Much of the tension of the current debate revolves around this set of demands.

The new equality issues also increase the old tension between individual and group equality. Pole characterizes the traditional perspective on equality in terms of a "principle of interchangeability."[68] Any American, if given the training and opportunities denied his or her group because of prejudice, could assume the place of any other American in society, make the same contribution, and command the same respect. Yet ingrained biases and sensitivity to status frustrated the realization of this principle. In fact, those whose group identities subjected them to discrimination were increasingly reluctant to forsake them. Ethnic groups clung to their culture and resisted complete assimilation. Religious groups did not offer up their unique beliefs for the sake of a homogeneity that could buy them a new station in life. Soon the government was asked to heed group differences rather than ignore them. The New Deal moved away from the traditional individualistic definition of equality to a group-based definition in its recognition of organized labor as a legitimate contender in the economic and political arenas. "Equality of result" is a norm most clearly applicable to individuals, whereas "proportional pluralism," to use Pole's term, is the norm for the new politics of group equality.[69] In *Fullilove v. Klutznick* (1980) the Supreme Court decided that setting aside government contracts for minority-owned businesses is compatible with the constitutional guarantee of equal protection. The Court upheld the limited use of quotas as a remedy for past discrimination. The group identities of race and gender have figured prominently in the equality debates of the past two decades.

The tension among the various equality issues has increased over the past twenty years. Racial equality versus gender equality is a tension faced by many civil rights and feminist groups; the conflict between programs for blacks and programs for other ethnic groups has also created problems. These tensions are not merely conflicts over the amount of attention that should be paid to one form of inequality or another. The difficulty is often that to attempt to achieve one type of equality, such as equal pay for women, may undermine the attainment of other types of equality, such as equal pay between blacks and whites.

The result is a political agenda with equality issues at the fore. Those issues are presented in such a way that the many ambivalences and ambiguities of the American public with regard to equality are at center stage.

AMERICA has experienced periods of political leveling that produced little economic change. The Revolution established new political rights for the new American citizen but left the relative wealth or poverty of each American intact. This pattern persisted in the next century. The policies of the Jacksonians, for example, enhanced political democracy but did little to stem the increasing inequalities in the distribution of wealth. Although Jackson attacked economic institutions like the Bank of the United States, he did so only where they wielded or symbolized inordinate political power. The upheaval of the Civil War held out the promise of economic redistribution, but here again the aftermath—Reconstruction—established equal access only to power, not to property. Progressives too perpetuated the legacy of strictly political reform, couching their agenda in moral rather than economic terms. And the New Deal, which provided gains in social and economic security, brought little redistribution. Public policies of the 1930s, which narrowed the power gap between business and labor, and changes in the 1960s and 1970s, that increased the political influence of blacks, women, and youth, typified American social change since the Revolution—a change that produced durable political reform but little economic leveling.

Though many of the reforms wrought during these periods are still with us, the distribution of wealth in this nation has from its beginning remained essentially the same. Concentrations of wealth were unequal but stable during the colonial era. In the cities the concentration grew greater with the influx of the young and the propertyless. In the South, concentration increased as property did. But these effects were balanced by the shift to the frontier, where wealth was distributed more equally and grew faster per capita. During the next century, however, wealth became more unequally distributed over the nation as a whole. This was most pronounced in the antebellum period, coincident with an increasing wage premium for skilled labor.[70]

The nineteenth century surge in economic inequality was balanced by three periods of equalization. The first and most dramatic was the emancipation of the slaves. The second was the sharp reduction in the gap between rich and poor during World War I, possibly the result of a shortage of unskilled labor, increased product demand, inflation, and greater mobility between classes. The last and most important period of equalization was the income revolution that leveled wealth distribution between the 1920s and the mid-century; inflation and a more balanced growth across sectors favored unskilled labor once again. Since World War II, a slight increase in pretax inequality has been balanced by government transfers producing a fairly stable distribution. Overall, as Jeffrey Williamson and Peter Lindert have found, "inequality of wealth today resembles what it was on the eve of the Declaration of Independence."[71]

One explanation for this continuing inequality lies in Americans' perceptions of the issue. Efforts at economic redistribution have been limited by the perception that a great deal of equality already exists, in wealth and otherwise. Many have assumed, wrongly, that the American egalitarian ideal necessarily reflects a significant degree of actual equality among the citizens who so strongly support it. Another reason for the limited redistribution is a practical one. The logistics of transferring resources from the rich to the poor are certainly more complex than amending voting laws, which, though not always easily enforced, are effected with the stroke of a pen. The periods of political upheaval have been too short to sustain the extended institutional efforts necessary for the redistribution of wealth. Finally, the most important reason for the persistent inequality of wealth is that the American ideal of equality does not embrace redistribution. Americans have developed a philosophy that justifies disparities of riches but not of power. In Huntington's words, Americans have an "ambivalence about wealth." Wealth on any scale is tolerated as long as it cannot be translated into political advantage. The American celebration of philanthropy stems from the belief that great fortunes can and should exist. When Jackson attacked the U.S. Bank and the financial elite, for example, he did not covet their money; he feared their power. The American tradition of antitrust is a long-standing effort to determine at what point money actually becomes power.[72]

This distinction between the relative legitimacy of wealth and of power helps explain why periods of reform are marked by a concern for political rather than economic justice. The intense moralism of the upheavals in American history appears to be incompatible with people's materialistic concerns and better suited to social than to economic reform. Hence, concern over intangible rights, like the vote, supplant disputes over the distribution of goods. In the decades following the Depression, for instance, the Old Left represented class politics and economic issues. Yet the passion of the 1960s spawned the New Left, which took a moral stance on social issues like the Vietnam War and the Equal Rights Amendment.

The limits to redistribution are the limits of American beliefs about equality. Those limits are in large measure defined by the more affluent classes. Members of the higher socioeconomic strata are the most ideological in their perspective on public life, and historically they have assumed the greatest responsibility for articulating and carrying out the ideal of equality. As Henry George said of the Grange, reform was proposed by a class that "is the one least likely to accept radical ideas. It is warmly supported by men who hold five, twenty, fifty thousand acres of land."[73] Nevertheless, their ideology is conditioned by their personal interests, and their attempts at reform are not likely to be founded on values that would prove self-destructive. As Huntington observes, the poorer classes "have an interest in substantial economic change, but they lack the ideological motivation to make that change a reality, and indeed, they are mobilized for political action by appeals to values which guarantee that major economic change will not become a reality."[74] Throughout American history these values have not been limited to those in the top brackets; resistance to economic equality has been and continues to be, much more pervasive.

# 3

## The Leaders

The issue of equality has many levels. At an abstract philosophical level, it poses such questions as the justification of egalitarian values, the relationship of the individual to society, and the meaning of equality itself. At a more pragmatic though still general level, the subject of equality is concerned with broad policies and fundamental social objectives, such as the proper degree of income differentiation, the relationship between income distribution and incentives, and the extent to which the government should intervene to remedy historical patterns of discrimination. And at the most finite level, the equality issue directs attention toward particular laws or regulations, such as a specific tax structure or an affirmative action plan.

The leadership study focused on the middle level of the equality issue, the broad shape of policy, rather than on philosophical matters or specific laws. Policy is of course related to the other levels. It forms a bridge between the philosophy of equality addressed by scholars and the reality of equality expressed in the formulation and implementation of particular statutes.

### Picking the Leaders

This concern with policy guided the choice of participants in the leadership study. The primary interest was not with the views of

This chapter was written with G. Donald Ferree, Jr.

scholars on matters of equality but rather with the views of those actively engaged in the political process. Thus the leaders were selected from those sectors of American society for which the issue of equality is most important and which are most active in the political struggle over it. Their views have the most immediate and lasting effects on the course of that struggle. Furthermore, the views of such a group of leaders are presumably more consistent, more stable, and more carefully considered than are the views of ordinary citizens. Involvement in the issue of equality does not necessarily require that an individual's job deal explicitly with equality. Thus, no effort was made to seek out affirmative action officers or representatives of tax lobbies.

Admittedly, the views of the general public are important to the issue of equality. This issue is one of the central themes of American political culture and inevitably involves the social and economic position of each citizen. Nevertheless, the evolution of the issue as a subject of political controversy depends more upon the attitudes and actions of leaders. Their views influence both the political establishment and the public at large.

The leaders in the study represent many different sectors of American society and a broad range of views on equality. The conflict over equality involves both the attempt of one segment of society to protect a distribution of resources favorable to itself and the attempt of another segment to improve its share of the distribution. The position of a group can therefore be defensive or offensive: group A challenges the current distribution, group B defends it. Sometimes, however, a challenge to the current distribution is not perceived as a threat by any established group, or a group may become more protective of its status even in the absence of challenge.

Because both defense and challenge are central to the issue of equality, the study included established groups and challenging groups alike: groups whose position in the American distributional scheme is reasonably secure and groups that are raising questions about that distribution. The distinction is by no means hard and fast. A group can be both established and challenging: it may defend its position against those who attack it and at the same time challenge other groups for new advantage. Organized labor has this dual nature. It enjoys a well-established position in the American economic and political system and at the same time challenges the business community in an attempt to gain ground.

Established groups were represented in the study by the three traditional economic sectors: business, organized labor, and farming. The farm sector, though weaker than the other two sectors, is nevertheless an important voice. The challenging sectors were represented by the civil rights movement and the feminist movement. The study dealt not with all blacks and all women but with the organized movements for blacks' and women's causes, because neither all blacks nor all women lay a challenge to the current distribution of positions in America. There are many other challenging groups, including ethnic and linguistic minority groups, gays, poor people, and the handicapped, all claiming that the distribution of privileges and positions in American society is skewed against them, and all calling for redress. The study certainly did not exhaust the field of challenging groups. However, the civil rights and feminist movements represent two of the most effective and important challenges to the current state of American equality.

Three other sectors of society that play an intermediary role in policies on equality were also represented in the study: political parties, intellectuals, and the media. The media play a significant role in setting the agenda on matters of equality, through the expression of editorial opinion as well as in subtler ways, such as selecting the materials to be covered or slanting stories one way or another. Parties also play an important role in the policy debate. Despite the growing weakness of the two major American parties, there are persistent differences between them on issues associated with equality, which are manifested in many ways, as in the attitudes of rank-and-file members and of party leaders, the party platforms, the votes of members of Congress, and administration policies. Differing policies on equality often arise from differing party positions. Intellectuals are a much less defined or structured category than the other two intermediary groups. Whereas leaders in the media and the parties wear their institutional affiliations on their sleeves, intellectuals have no such precise identifications. Nevertheless, academics, essayists, scientists, and creative artists, to mention a few, play an important role in public debates over equality.

Finally, the survey included future leaders in the form of youths, half of them female and half of them male. The policy debate will continue for a long time, and the debaters of today will in the future be replaced by these youths. There is evidence that young people, particularly the more affluent and better educated, hold views on issues of equality that are radical in comparison with those of older people. Although this radicalism may simply represent the leftism of youth, soon to be replaced by a more conservative maturity, it is important to know where tomorrow's leaders stand today.

The nine sectors of society tapped in the study—business, farm, organized labor, the civil rights and feminist movements, the media, political parties, intellectuals, and youth—are by no means exhaustive. One obvious omission is leaders within the government, such as members of Congress or administrative agencies. The task of getting samples of a range of government officials was beyond the study's resources. Another sector that might have been included is the new technocratic elites associated with the postindustrial society. These leaders could not be defined precisely enough to identify the organizations that speak for them.

Choosing individual leaders from within each of the nine sectors was difficult. The problem of how to identify the leadership of a community, an organization, or a nation is an old one in political science. One can rely upon reputation and thus ask knowledgeable observers. One can go by institutional position. One can observe particular disputes or decisions and trace who exercises the most influence on the process. Or one can observe whose preferences are favored by the outcome. There is no single appropriate technique. The technique chosen depends upon a study's purpose and resources.

The main purpose of the leadership study was to find articulate spokespersons from the various sectors engaged in the equality debate. It was not to search for the power elite or the most influential individuals in each sector, though in fact the study probably included a high proportion of individuals who are influential in their sectors. The emphasis on articulate spokespersons led to a definition of leadership in terms of institutional position, because organized opinion is likely to carry more weight in the policy debate, and leaders with an organizational base are typically more active and visible. Furthermore, those who occupy formal positions of leadership are more likely to have views representative of others associated with the organization. Those in prominent institutional positions may not be the primary decision-makers, who often operate more informally behind the scenes. However, the major power-holders *per se* were not essential to the study. And the use of designated role-holders has a practical advantage. It is easier to make selections from a list of institutions or organizations than it is to rely upon reputation or other intangible signs of leadership to find the real powers. The use of organizational position was feasible for all of the study's social sectors except intellectuals and youth. For these two groups the study selected samples of individuals.

The choice of institutional leaders presented other problems as well. For one thing, some sectors have both an organized and an unorganized component that differ in orientation. The feminist movement, for example, is actually several related movements. One segment stresses political goals, structured organizational hierarchy, and leadership. Another segment focuses on self-improvement and individual advancement and deliberately avoids organization and hierarchy.[1] It would have been difficult to conduct a leadership survey in a group that claims to have no leadership, so the study concentrated on the formally organized branch of the movement, which wields considerable political influence.

In addition, the leaders chosen from most sectors were either national or local in orientation. National leaders came from institutions with a national scope. Local leaders, all chosen from the same set of localities, came from comparable positions within major market areas.

The leadership groups included the following individuals (see also Appendix A):

*Business*

National: Chairman of the board or president of a sample of the largest nonbanking corporations in the *Fortune* 500 and chairman of the board or president of a sample of the 200 largest banks in the country.

Local: President of the largest local bank and chief executive officer of the local Chamber of Commerce.

These leaders are heads of the largest business enterprises both nationally and locally. The heads of local Chambers of Commerce are prominent local businessmen, not organizational bureaucrats of the Chamber of Commerce.

*Labor*

National: Top three or four officers of the largest international labor unions.

Local: President of two of the locals from those unions, drawn in rotation.

*Farm*

National: National officers of the three largest farm membership organizations and presidents of the major commodity associations.

Local: Local presidents of the farm membership organizations.
These leaders are not major farm operators but heads of organizations representing farm interests.

*Intellectuals*

Random sample drawn from *Who's Who*-type directories for the natural sciences, humanities, social sciences, and arts.

Unlike most of the other groups, these leaders were chosen not as representatives of organizations but as individuals.

*Media*

National: Members of the press, radio, and television galleries of Congress.

Local: Managing editors of the largest-circulation local newspaper and news directors of the highest-rated local television station.

These leaders are working journalists and those who make news decisions, not the corporate heads of media organizations.

*Parties*

National: Members of the Republican and Democratic National Committees.

Local: Local and/or county chairmen of the two parties.

These leaders are party professionals, not elected officials.

*Blacks*

Highest local elected black official, local president of the NAACP and/or Urban League, and random sample of other black elected officials, including members of the Congressional Black Caucus.

These leaders, the only government officials in the study, represent a significant and fairly well-organized segment of black leadership.

*Feminists*

Local officers of the National Organization for Women, the National Women's Political Caucus, the Coalition of Labor Union Women, the Women's Equity Action League, Federally Employed Women, and the State Commissions on the Status of Women.

These leaders represent organizations that are feminist in orientation. Although these organizations are neither conservative nor neutral on women's issues, they do not represent the most radical, antiorganizational segment of the feminist movement.

*College Youth*
Random sample of seniors from ten elite colleges in the major geographical areas of the country.

The survey of leaders was conducted by mail questionnaire in 1976 and 1977. The overall response rate was 56 percent, with over 50 percent of the sample for each group responding, which was quite reasonable for a mailed questionnaire. The study yielded a grand total of 2,762 respondents (Table 3.1; see also Appendix A). Comparison of early and late responses revealed no systematic differences, suggesting the absence of significant bias between respondents and nonrespondents.

In addition to the mailed survey of leaders, a telephone survey was conducted of a national sample of the public (see Appendix B).

**Table 3.1**
Leadership Response Rates to Mail Questionnaire

| Group | Questionnaires returned | | |
|---|---|---|---|
| | Number | | % |
| National business | 145 | 312 | 52 |
| Local business | 167 | | 57 |
| National labor | 141 | 266 | 52 |
| Local labor | 125 | | 52 |
| National farm | 114 | 266 | 52 |
| Local farm | 152 | | 54 |
| Intellectuals | | 296 | 57 |
| National media | 163 | 318 | 57 |
| Local media | 155 | | 52 |
| National parties | 149 | 307 | 52 |
| Local parties | 158 | | 55 |
| Blacks | | 266 | 52 |
| Feminists | | 367 | 67 |
| College youth | | 374 | 63 |
| Total | | 2762 | 56 |

This survey was relatively brief and did not contain all the questions asked of the leaders. But a number of questions paralleled those in the leadership survey, allowing for a comparison between the mass public and the leaders.

All of the groups in the study are in some sense in the mainstream. There are other segments of American society whose views on issues of equality fall to the left or the right of these groups, including radical redistributionists and radical opponents of any interference with the inequalities that emerge from a market system. Their views are certainly not irrelevant. Such groups sometimes are important participants in the policy process. Also, though now outside the mainstream, they may someday enter it, or it may come to them; the mainstream of American politics at times shifts its bed. But the study stayed with the current mainstream because it roughly defines the range of views on equality that will dominate political debate in coming years. Nor is the mainstream narrow; the views held by the various groups display great diversity. There is both a remarkable consensus across these groups on certain fundamentals relating to equality and a sharp disagreement over other aspects of the issue. The consensus defines the limits of the policy debate; the differences fuel the debate over policy alternatives.

## Social Background

A profile of American leaders emerged from the study which shows that they are distinctive in social, economic, and political terms. These leaders, especially in the established groups, are likely to come disproportionately from the more advantaged social categories: white males of upper social and economic status. In most societies, in fact, there is a systematic bias in the recruitment of leaders that leads to a preponderance of individuals from relatively privileged backgrounds—more affluent, better-educated, and higher-status. The implication of such unrepresentativeness is uncertain. Many studies have demonstrated the weak connection between social background and political views.[2] A leadership group that differs in social background from the population at large does not necessarily differ in its political views. Nor does a group of leaders constitute a closed power elite simply because of a shared social background. The political views of institutional leaders are more likely to stem from the process of their selection and their institutional affiliation than from their social background.

This is certainly the case for the American leadership groups. The difference in political outlook between business and labor leaders corresponds far more closely to their group affiliation than to their social background. The same holds true for black, feminist, or party leaders. It is possible that leaders are socialized into certain views while in office, but more likely that they move into certain positions because of their views. In either case, social background merely defines a recruitment pool; it is not the breeding ground for political attitudes.

Yet the social background of leaders is not irrelevant. Knowing whether leaders hail from a variety of social strata or from the same middle-class, well-educated origins contributes to an understanding of equality itself. These social characteristics reveal whether the leadership positions in the various groups are differentially open to members from all backgrounds, which in itself is evidence for the state of equality in America.

The leadership groups in the study are relatively unrepresentative of the general population in terms of their educational and occupational backgrounds (Table 3.2). In half the cases, one-quarter or more of the leadership group come from a family in which the father has a college degree, and about a fifth come from homes where the mother has a college degree. Furthermore, over half in most groups, and close to two-thirds in some groups, have fathers in professional, technical, or managerial occupations. These proportions are well beyond those of the general population.

There are interesting variations, however. College youths are even more likely than the other groups to come from families with college-educated parents and high-status occupations. This is due mostly to their age. Their parents are, on average, a generation younger than those of the adult leadership groups. By contrast, among labor, farm, and black groups only about ten percent of the leaders' fathers have a college education, and only about one-quarter of the fathers are in high-status occupations. Between leaders of black and feminist groups, which constitute the leading edge of criticism of the state of equality in America, there is a sharp social division. The feminist leaders have middle-class backgrounds, like those of such established groups as business or party leaders. This is substantially less true of black leaders.

The leaders are also unrepresentative of the population as a whole in terms of their own educational attainment (Table 3.3). A high proportion of them have achieved a college education or better, as compared to the 17 percent of the general population with a college

**Table 3.2**
Education and Occupation of Parents of Leaders (%)

| Group | Fathers with college degree | Mothers with college degree | Fathers in professional, technical, or management position |
|---|---|---|---|
| Business | 21 | 18 | 67 |
| Farm | 11 | 11 | 21 |
| Labor | 11 | 5 | 28 |
| Intellectuals | 30 | 18 | 66 |
| Media | 32 | 20 | 63 |
| Republicans | 28 | 20 | 62 |
| Democrats | 25 | 15 | 55 |
| Blacks | 13 | 9 | 24 |
| Feminists | 28 | 19 | 56 |
| Youth | 68 | 46 | 81 |
| Population over 35[a] | — | — | 22 |

a. University of Michigan, Center for Political Studies, 1976 American National Election Study.

education. Intellectuals, not surprisingly, have the highest educational level. Compared with the other groups, farm leaders and labor leaders are much less likely to have a college education or to have done graduate work. Labor leaders stand out in this respect; fewer than one in three graduated from college. Like farmers, they are distinguished from the other leaders by their working-class origins. A *Fortune* study of business leaders conducted in the same year similarly found that 86 percent were college graduates and 56 percent had done graduate work.[3]

The black leaders are among the least advantaged groups in terms of parental education, but are quite like other groups with respect to their own education. This difference clearly reflects the rapid improvement in the overall educational opportunities of the black community during the past generation. It also reflects the weight placed on advanced education as a criterion for organizational leadership. As a result, black leaders, like the leaders of most groups, are unrepresentative of the general population in their educational attainment. In a group defined by race, religion, or gender, leadership naturally depends in almost all cases on membership in that category. Beyond that, educational and occupational criteria are likely

**Table 3.3**
Educational Background of Leaders (%)

| Group | College graduates | Graduate work | Elite college or graduate school |
|---|---|---|---|
| Business | 81 | 52 | 36 |
| Farm | 44 | 22 | 11 |
| Labor | 31 | 18 | 11 |
| Intellectuals | 94 | 91 | 48 |
| Media | 74 | 36 | 26 |
| Republicans | 74 | 48 | 26 |
| Democrats | 73 | 60 | 22 |
| Blacks | 70 | 55 | 16 |
| Feminists | 73 | 56 | 20 |
| Population over 35[a] | 17 | — | — |

a. University of Michigan, Center for Political Studies, 1976 American National Election Study.

to be paramount.[4] Thus feminist and black leaders, though they represent groups challenging the distributional system in the United States, are as well educated as leaders of the other groups.[5] Labor and farm leaders, in contrast, have generally lower levels of formal education as a result of the greater significance that must necessarily be attached to other factors in the selection of leaders within those groups. When a group is defined in terms of a social class characteristic such as occupation, leadership cannot be so easily skewed toward the upper reaches of the educational or occupational scales—unless, as in the case of business leadership, the occupation is itself of high social status.

Finally, most of the leaders are white males (Table 3.4). There are more women among the party leaders than among most of the other groups, as a result in part of the tradition of tandem male and female party leadership positions. The only two exceptions to the race and sex uniformity of the leadership groups are, predictably, the black and feminist leaders.[6] In light of the sex and race distribution of the other groups, leadership within organizations dedicated to the interests of a disadvantaged group like blacks or women may be an important channel of mobility for certain members of the group.

The organization of a social group is often regarded as a key to effective political activity on behalf of those individuals. Organizations of blacks and women, the study suggests, perform an additional function: they provide a unique opportunity for members of the group to obtain leadership positions, along with the training in managerial skills, access to other leaders, institutional resources, and prestige that such positions provide. Since leadership of a significant institution in the private sector is often a stepping-stone to political or governmental leadership, the availability of such positions for a disadvantaged group may make it easier for members of that group to rise to top public positions than would otherwise be the case.

In sum, American leaders are not typical of the groups they lead. This is especially the case for leaders of groups having an actual or potential mass following, such as the leaders of farm, labor, black, and feminist organizations and of the two political parties. In each instance, the leaders are more likely to be middle-class and well educated. The disparity is especially striking among black and feminist leaders. In addition, there are sharp disparities between leaders and followers when it comes to race or sex. The significance of these deviations depends upon how closely the leaders' unrepresentative traits are related to their policy positions. The leaders are not demographic replicas of the masses for whom they purport to speak. If they represent the views of those masses, such similarity of views has nothing to do with a full similarity of background.

**Table 3.4**
Race and Sex of Leaders (%)

| Group | White | Male |
|---|---|---|
| Business | 99 | 98 |
| Farm | 98 | 94 |
| Labor | 96 | 95 |
| Intellectuals | 95 | 85 |
| Media | 96 | 90 |
| Republicans | 97 | 75 |
| Democrats | 95 | 67 |
| Blacks | 3 | 86 |
| Feminists | 92 | 1 |
| Youth | 93 | 54 |

## Political Orientation and Activity

The groups of leaders vary in their partisan affiliation (Table 3.5). Business leans in the Republican direction, as does farming, albeit less decisively. All of the other groups lean toward the Democratic party. But within these general tendencies partisanship varies from group to group. Only in two groups do a majority of the leaders express allegiance to a single party: more than half of the black and labor leaders are self-identified Democrats. Leaders of the other Democratic-leaning groups—intellectuals, media people, feminists, and youths—are most likely to see themselves as "Independent, but leaning closer to Democrats." In this, they are similar to business-people who call themselves "Independent Republicans." Indeed, the category of Independents who lean toward one party or the other subsumes most of the leaders in every group except blacks and labor. American leaders have partisan inclinations but maintain some psychological distance from the major parties.

In terms of political ideology, very few leaders describe themselves as being on either the far left or the far right (Table 3.6). The most conservative groups are business, farm, and Republican leaders. The feminists are much more liberal than any other group. All the other leaders lean in a liberal direction. This leftward tilt reflects which groups were included and which ones excluded from the study; that is, blacks and feminists were studied, not leaders of white ethnic groups or of Moral Majority-type organizations.

The partisan profile of the public at large presents no distinctive differences from the leaders' profile. Some leadership groups contain more Democrats than the public; others contain less. The same applies to the Independent and Republican categories. On the question of ideological self-identification, the public is similar to the leaders in the sense that few in either group put themselves in the extreme categories. But more of the public place themselves in the center of the ideological spectrum. Leaders are more likely to be committed in one political direction or another.

The study did not measure how much weight America's various leaders actually carry in political life. It did supply data, however, on the extent to which leaders within specific sectors also play some leadership or activist role in the general political system. The data reveal differences across the various groups in the level and type of political activity. This information not only illuminates the back-

**Table 3.5**

Political Partisanship of Leaders (%)

| Group | Strong Democrat | Democrat | Independent, closer to Democrat | Independent | Independent, closer to Republican | Republican | Strong Republican |
|---|---|---|---|---|---|---|---|
| Business | <1 | 6 | 10 | 4 | 39 | 32 | 10 |
| Farm | 14 | 13 | 13 | 7 | 25 | 22 | 6 |
| Labor | 36 | 29 | 25 | 7 | 3 | 1 | 0 |
| Intellectuals | 8 | 15 | 36 | 13 | 15 | 11 | 2 |
| Media | 4 | 14 | 40 | 20 | 14 | 5 | 2 |
| Blacks | 18 | 37 | 30 | 9 | 2 | 4 | 1 |
| Feminists | 21 | 23 | 36 | 9 | 4 | 4 | 2 |
| Youth | 5 | 14 | 36 | 22 | 16 | 6 | 1 |
| Population over 35[a] | 11 | 24 | 14 | 18 | 11 | 14 | 6 |

a. University of Michigan, Center for Political Studies, 1976 American National Election Study.

**Table 3.6**
Political Ideology of Leaders (%)

| Group | Far left | Very liberal | Somewhat liberal | Moderate | Somewhat conservative | Very conservative | Far right |
|---|---|---|---|---|---|---|---|
| Business | 0 | <1 | 13 | 24 | 53 | 10 | <1 |
| Farm | 0 | 5 | 16 | 22 | 44 | 13 | 0 |
| Labor | 2 | 20 | 42 | 26 | 9 | 1 | 0 |
| Intellectuals | 3 | 12 | 41 | 21 | 21 | 2 | 1 |
| Media | 2 | 10 | 38 | 33 | 14 | 3 | 1 |
| Republicans | 1 | 2 | 4 | 35 | 41 | 18 | 1 |
| Democrats | 2 | 21 | 49 | 23 | 5 | 1 | 0 |
| Blacks | 4 | 29 | 38 | 23 | 5 | <1 | 0 |
| Feminists | 6 | 42 | 33 | 15 | 4 | 0 | 0 |
| Youth | 2 | 20 | 42 | 26 | 9 | 1 | 0 |
| Population over 35[a] | 2 | 12 | 15 | 39 | 18 | 12 | 2 |

a. University of Michigan, Center for Political Studies, 1976 American National Election Study.

ground of the leaders but contributes to an understanding of equality of influence among different sectors of society.

A powerful resource in American politics is knowing people in high places. Indeed, this camaraderie is what binds an elite group together, according to most theories of American politics. C. Wright Mills saw the power elite as being bound together by personal ties, dating back to school and college days and reinforced by friendship, social contact, and common membership in clubs and organizations.[7] Each American is free to write to his or her member of Congress or to a newspaper, or to complain to an administrative official. But the effectiveness with which such channels are used depends in part upon how well one knows the person whose assistance one seeks. Each citizen has a member of Congress to whom letters can be written, but few know a member of Congress personally. Few know someone in the media or the administration.

Acquaintanceship, however, does not always guarantee influence. A government official or media person may respond in the same way to the familiar caller as to the unfamiliar. Indeed, callers who become too familiar may suddenly find their influence much diminished. Nevertheless, acquaintance implies access, and the widely connected leader has a better chance of being influential than the leader with few personal contacts. As one indicator of the potential political influence of American leaders, the study asked them whether they had acquaintances among four types of public figure: senator, congressman, cabinet member, and top government official (bureau chief or higher) (Table 3.7). American leaders turn out to be widely acquainted with public figures, as shown by the high proportion of leaders in the various categories who personally know their senator or congressional representative. Almost all the party leaders are acquainted with members of Congress, as one would expect, but so are most members of the media as well as business leaders. Farm, labor, and black leaders are somewhat less well-connected, though over half of them know a senator and three-quarters of them know a member of the House. Feminist leaders and intellectuals are better acquainted with government officials than are average citizens, but a good deal less so than are the other leaders. That this should be the case among intellectual leaders, who were not selected for their organizational positions, is hardly surprising. Many intellectuals have no need or desire to know political and governmental figures. What is unexpected is that feminist leaders, who head organizations with a political platform, are not better acquainted with those in political power. Feminist leaders are apparently less well-integrated into the informal communication networks that characterize much political interaction.

**Table 3.7**
Political Acquaintances of Leaders (%)

| Group | Acquaintance | | | |
| | Senator | Member of house | Cabinet member | Top bureaucrat |
|---|---|---|---|---|
| Business | 78 | 86 | 27 | 42 |
| Farm | 61 | 74 | 23 | 29 |
| Labor | 65 | 76 | 21 | 35 |
| Intellectuals | 28 | 36 | 4 | 17 |
| Media | 72 | 83 | 19 | 40 |
| Republicans | 80 | 87 | 41 | 51 |
| Democrats | 88 | 95 | 7 | 28 |
| Blacks | 67 | 78 | 13 | 26 |
| Feminists | 48 | 56 | 7 | 28 |

The question about acquaintance with high administration figures, namely members of the cabinet and top bureaucrats, was intended to distinguish those uncommon leaders with exceptionally good connections. It was expected that few leaders would know a cabinet member. Yet a surprisingly large number of leaders, more than one out of five, in the established groups of business, labor, and farming are acquainted with a cabinet member, as are one out of five of the media leaders. Black and feminist leaders rank much lower, though once again well ahead of the intellectuals. A similar pattern is seen in relation to acquaintance with a top bureaucrat.

The access that some groups have to central governmental decision-makers is even stronger among national as distinct from local leaders. The proportion of national leaders who know a cabinet official is 37 percent for business leaders, 40 percent for farm leaders, and 33 percent for labor leaders. And at least half of each of these national groups report knowing a top bureaucrat. In a sense, the figures are most striking for the business leaders. National farm and labor leaders head organizations that are located mostly in Washington. A large part of their job is to secure political representation of their organizations' interests, a task that would create close contact with the Agriculture or Labor Department. National business leaders, however, head corporations that are rarely headquartered in Washington. One would expect political representation to be a smaller part of their activities. But their acquaintance with top officials is quite extensive.

To determine how active American leaders are in the political process on behalf of the interests they represent, the leaders were asked about the frequency with which they wrote to or spoke with a member of Congress (Table 3.8). In comparison with the general population, the leaders are clearly activists. A very small percentage of the public at large has direct contact with members of Congress, as shown by a 1978 study in which only 15 percent reported that they or a family member had contacted their representative.[8] In contrast, a substantial proportion of most groups in the leadership study report writing or speaking to a member of Congress. The least active group by far is intellectuals. Although they are an elite group in terms of education and recognition, they lack the representative organizational roles of the other leaders. As a result, the proportion of intellectuals who have talked to a member of Congress is less than one-third that of any of the other leadership groups.

**Table 3.8**
Contact with Government by Leaders (%)

| Group | Have written to a member of Congress a few times a year or more | Have talked to a member of Congress a few times a year or more |
|---|---|---|
| Business | 84 | 86 |
| Farm | 72 | 62 |
| Labor | 82 | 68 |
| Intellectuals | 28 | 18 |
| Media | 30 | 90 |
| Republicans | 89 | 91 |
| Democrats | 83 | 95 |
| Blacks | 69 | 75 |
| Feminists | 82 | 57 |
| Public in general[a] | 15 | 15 |

a. Someone in household has contacted a member of Congress. University of Michigan, Center for Political Studies, 1978 American National Election Study.

The distinction between writing and talking to an official is crucial. Anyone can write to a member of Congress, whereas face-to-face conversation requires significant personal and economic resources. For media and party leaders this direct contact is part and parcel of their professional activity. For business leaders, the high frequency of personal contacts with members of Congress is a further indication of the active role of business in the political process. Most business leaders in the study are managers of businesses, not official representatives of business. Yet they engage in more direct political contact than do leaders whose job it is to speak officially for their constituents.

This distinction between direct contact and more distant communication is significant in the feminist pattern of response as well. Feminist leaders are about as likely to write to a member of Congress as are business, labor, and party leaders, and they are more likely to do so than are farm or black leaders. But in frequency of face-to-face contact they fall far below all these other groups. This disparity parallels the data on personal acquaintance, which reveals that feminists are much less likely to know top government officials. Since members of Congress tend to pay more attention to a face-to-face statement than to a mailed communication, feminists are at a disadvantage.

AMERICAN leaders typically are well educated, middle-class white males, active in political life. All in all, the leaders are unrepresentative of the population as a whole. They are by no means homogeneous in social background, and yet are not widely diverse either. Most important, it is these leaders, with their divergent views on equality, who set the terms of the political debate.

# 4

## Accord and Discord

American leaders' views on equality are no less complex than the issue itself. Simply to label them egalitarian or inegalitarian would be to overlook crucial philosophical nuances. Where leaders stand on matters of equality depends upon whether the issue is equality of result or of opportunity, of politics or of economics, among individuals or among groups, and the perceived reality of equality or the desired ideal. In addition, there are matters on which most leaders agree and matters on which there is sharp disagreement across the leadership groups.

### The Ideal of Economic Equality

The contrast between equality of opportunity and equality of result, albeit an oversimplified distinction, is commonly used to divide American attitudes toward equality. The vision of economic equality in the United States is an ideal of opportunity. Americans have never striven to ensure that all people live alike. Rather, they have always followed the ideal of an equal start in the race so that those with greater ability and drive are allowed, and encouraged, to come out ahead.[1] This belief in an equal race, not an equal position at the finish line, is what might be expected from those already established in American society; equality of opportunity is a decidedly middle-class ideal. What is supposedly unique about the American attitude is that all groups—middle-class and working-class, advantaged and disadvantaged—subscribe to an ideal of equal opportunity, not equal result.

The study tested whether this supposition is borne out in the attitudes of American leaders. In particular, it focused on whether the challenging groups—black and feminist leaders as well as college youth—are committed to equality of opportunity rather than equality of result. They were asked whether they preferred "equality of opportunity: giving each person an equal chance for a good education and to develop his or her ability" or "equality of results: giving each person a relatively equal income regardless of his or her education and ability." They were also asked whether a fairer economic system would be one in which "people with more ability would earn higher salaries" or one in which "all people would earn about the same."

Equality of opportunity, not of result, is clearly the dominant ideal for American leaders (Table 4.1). It is not surprising to find business leaders, farm leaders, or leaders of the Republican party almost unanimously disposed to this view. Yet this consensus extends to all leadership groups. More than four out of five members of each group favor equality of opportunity, and fewer than one out of ten in any group endorses equality of result. This near unanimity runs across labor, blacks, feminists, and college youth.

**Table 4.1**
Attitudes on Equality of Opportunity and Result (%)[a]

| Group | How best to deal with inequality | | What is a fair economic system | |
|---|---|---|---|---|
| | Equality of opportunity | Equality of result | Earnings based on ability | All earnings about the same |
| Business | 98 | 1 | 98 | 1 |
| Labor | 86 | 4 | 80 | 11 |
| Farm | 93 | 2 | 90 | 4 |
| Intellectuals | 89 | 3 | 89 | 7 |
| Media | 96 | 1 | 93 | 3 |
| Republicans | 98 | 0 | 99 | 0 |
| Democrats | 84 | 8 | 79 | 12 |
| Blacks | 86 | 7 | 67 | 17 |
| Feminists | 84 | 7 | 71 | 15 |
| Youth | 87 | 7 | 74 | 14 |

a. Percentages do not add to 100 because some individuals had no opinion or took a middle position.

The question on equality of earnings produces a more mixed result across the groups. The ideal of fairly equal pay finds some support among black leaders, feminist leaders, college youth, labor leaders, and Democratic leaders. But in no case does the proportion of those in favor reach 20 percent of any group. And in every case, the dominant opinion leans clearly in the direction of earnings based on ability. In short, equality of opportunity is the American ideal even among leaders who might be expected to advance more radical goals. This suggests, at least in the abstract, that the groups most vocal in their demands for greater equality want to earn that equality rather than have it handed to them and, perhaps, that these groups assume they could do so if unfair barriers were removed.[2]

## The Reality of Economic Equality

Although American leaders agree on the ideal of economic equality, there is much less consensus on the extent to which the American social and economic system lives up to that ideal. To assess the extent to which the various groups believe that opportunities are indeed equally available to all, four questions were designed to probe their views on the causes of inequality. First, they were asked whether the main cause of poverty in America is that "the American system doesn't give all people an equal chance" or that "those who are poor almost always have themselves to blame." A similar question focused on whether the cause of poverty among American blacks is that the system does not give them an equal chance or that they do not try hard enough. Another question dealt with whether discrimination prevents women from getting jobs equal to their ability or whether it is their own fault. Finally, the leaders were asked whether they believed that the free enterprise system generally provides a fair share to workers.

The resounding agreement on the ideal disappears in the leaders' perceptions of the real (Table 4.2). On the cause of poverty in America, labor and business leaders, who are in accord about the ideal of equality, differ sharply. Business leaders generally consider poverty to be the fault of the poor themselves. Fewer than one in ten see it as the fault of the economic system. This position is shared by farm leaders and by leaders of the Republican party. Yet labor takes the opposite view.

More is at stake here than the simple fact that "businessmen are generally conservative." For at least two reasons, one would expect

**Table 4.2**

Perceptions of Equality (%)[a]

| Group | Poverty in America | | Black poverty | | Unequal jobs for women | | Free enterprise | |
|---|---|---|---|---|---|---|---|---|
| | Fault of poor | Fault of system | Fault of blacks | Fault of system | Fault of women | Fault of system | Fair to workers | Unfair to workers |
| Business | 57 | 9 | 28 | 40 | 25 | 32 | 93 | 3 |
| Labor | 15 | 56 | 23 | 52 | 21 | 54 | 44 | 38 |
| Farm | 52 | 19 | 50 | 26 | 34 | 31 | 73 | 14 |
| Intellectuals | 23 | 44 | 18 | 65 | 17 | 60 | 50 | 30 |
| Media | 21 | 50 | 12 | 64 | 17 | 61 | 59 | 26 |
| Republicans | 55 | 13 | 32 | 37 | 25 | 40 | 88 | 6 |
| Democrats | 5 | 68 | 10 | 73 | 11 | 72 | 47 | 31 |
| Blacks | 5 | 86 | 9 | 82 | 17 | 67 | 31 | 44 |
| Feminists | 9 | 76 | 6 | 83 | 3 | 92 | 23 | 50 |
| Youth | 16 | 61 | 17 | 69 | 12 | 74 | 41 | 40 |

a. Percentages do not add to 100 because some individuals had no opinion or chose a middle position.

business leaders to be less likely than most groups, especially labor, to blame the system for poverty. First, they are the real economic elites, the ones who have been most successful in the economic world. Self-esteem and self-respect doubtless require that they see their economic accomplishment as the result of individual talent and hard work, not as the result of an arbitrary, unfair, and impersonal system where the lucky end up ahead and others end up at the bottom through no fault of their own. Therefore, seeing those at the bottom as responsible for their lot is a necessary corollary of the belief that the winners have mostly themselves to thank.

Second, business leaders are less apt to blame the economic system because they are now in a real sense the owners and managers of that system. Consequently, they are not only the ones who receive the benefits of economic stratification but also the ones who distribute those economic rewards. It is therefore doubly important for them to see the system as fair rather than as subject to blind chance or, worse yet, to groundless discrimination, in order to justify both their past achievement and their present occupation. Business leaders are not the only ones who engage in self-justification. Leaders of less well-off groups may also justify lower achievement by blaming the system.

The view of labor that the system is the main cause of poverty is held even more strongly by leaders of the Democratic party, black leaders, feminist leaders, and college youth. Intellectuals and leaders of the media are more likely to blame the system, but a substantial number blame the poor.

The disagreement over the cause of poverty in America takes different forms. Consider, for example, the sharp polarization between leaders of the business community and leaders of the challenging groups. Only 9 percent of the business leaders believe that poverty is the fault of the economic system, whereas 86 percent of the black leaders and 76 percent of the feminist leaders see it that way. The leaders of the two political parties are in substantial agreement on the ideal of equal opportunity. In their perceptions of reality, however, leaders of each party side with those groups from whom they receive their major support. Republican leaders line up with business; Democratic leaders line up with labor, blacks, and feminists.

There is also a polarity of opinion on the causes of black poverty and of inequality in job achievement for women, but with interesting variations from the causes of poverty in general. Every group except farm leaders assigns greater blame for black poverty to the system than to the blacks themselves. In fact, the leaders are more likely to take this attitude toward black poverty than toward poverty in general. Business and Republican leaders largely blame poverty on the poor, but they are more likely to see black poverty as the product of discrimination within the system than as blacks' own doing. That conservative groups sympathize more with poor blacks than with the poor in general illustrates the impact of the racial issue on American political consciousness. Traditionally, social class explanations of economic inequality have been unpopular in the United States.[3] Moreover, during the past three decades, Americans have been more inclined to see racial discrimination as the cause of economic disadvantage among blacks than to see class discrimination as the cause of poverty in general. Intellectuals and media leaders share this perception.

Those groups that tend to see poverty in general as the result of the system make less distinction between the cause of poverty among the population as a whole and among blacks. The only two groups who are not more likely to blame the system for poverty among blacks than for poverty in general are organized labor and, surprisingly, black leaders themselves. Labor's attitude is only one sign of the conservative strain within the union leadership over racial issues. As for blacks, the difference between their views on the causes of poverty in general and of black poverty in particular is small, and they probably perceived the referent of the general question on poverty to be the American black population.

American leadership groups are closer together on the cause of unequal job achievement between men and women. Only among farm leaders does a larger proportion, but still less than half, believe that lower job achievement on the part of women arises from their lack of effort rather than from discrimination within the system. Among all other groups, leaders tend to fault discrimination rather than women themselves, but in widely varying degrees. Only one out of three business leaders and only two out of five Republican leaders see systematic discrimination at work, in contrast to nine out of ten feminist leaders and seven out of ten Democratic leaders. Black leaders lean toward blaming discrimination, but less strongly than feminists or Democrats. That only two-thirds of them are aligned with this view is one indication that black leaders give less support to feminist causes than one might expect, or than the feminists give to black causes.

Although the leaders of both political parties are more likely to attribute inequality to the system than to the lack of individual effort on the part of blacks or women, the differences between the two party groups remain sharp. The Republicans are somewhat divided in their assessment. The Democrats overwhelmingly place the blame on the social and economic system.

Blacks and feminists differ on the causes of poverty:

| *Feminists* | | *Blacks* | |
|---|---|---|---|
| Unequal jobs for women are fault of system | 92% | Black poverty is fault of system | 82% |
| Poverty in general is fault of system | 76% | Poverty in general is fault of system | 86% |
| Difference | 16% | | −4% |

Nearly all feminist leaders ascribe women's inequality to an unfair system, while fewer fault the system for poverty in general. In contrast, the vast majority of blacks blame both overall poverty and the poverty of blacks on the system. Feminist leaders probably are less likely than their black counterparts to see themselves as the referent of the question on poverty, that is, as "the poor." Since 1976 when the leadership study was conducted, the nation has witnessed a growing "feminization of poverty," as the numbers of female-headed households and women on government welfare benefits have swollen. Partly as a response to this trend, the feminist movement has identified the economic improvement of women as a higher priority in their efforts. Consequently, the differences in perception between blacks and feminists on the causes of poverty have probably dwindled in the years since the survey.

On the question of whether the free enterprise system in America is fair to workers, there is again substantial divergence across the groups. Business and Republican leaders overwhelmingly endorse the fairness of the free enterprise system; farm leaders generally share this view. Other groups are more divided, though only among leaders of black and feminist organizations (not among labor or Democratic party leaders) does a plurality consider the system unfair.

Leaders across a wide spectrum of American life concur in their vision of equal opportunity as the ideal form of equality. This agreement runs across the established parts of the American economy, such as the business and farm sectors, and across both political parties, and it encompasses the leaders of challenging groups as well. However, there is a good deal of diversity in the leaders' perceptions of how well the American system actually provides equal opportunities. Certain groups, of which business and Republican leaders form the core, usually joined by farm leaders, find the system generally fair and attribute inequality to individual failure rather than to the failure of the system, though they are more likely to cite the system in explaining poverty among blacks and women. At the other extreme, leaders of the challenging groups tend to see the system as unfair in the opportunities it offers, a belief in which they are joined by many leaders of the Democratic party, organized labor, and college youth.

College youth tend to line up with the black and feminist leaders on equality issues. The similarity between these college seniors and the black and feminist leaders is all the more striking in that the students represent the class of 1976. These are not the young idealists of the late 1960s and early 1970s but the supposedly more staid, career-minded undergraduates of the post-Vietnam generation.

## The Role of Government

Those who want a more equal distribution of income do not necessarily want more government intervention to achieve it. This may be because they think that the current government effort will eventually lead to more equality, or that government is not an effective means to that end, or that the risks of harmful side effects are too great.

If one endorses government action, a number of public policies might be pursued in order to reduce inequality. The rich could be taxed to help the poor, for example, or the government could actively attempt to reduce the income gap between rich and poor through its social programs. Each of these policies represents a governmental commitment to redistribution, but one that would allow income differentials to persist. Furthermore, each is consistent with the government's current use of an income tax system and transfer payments to effect moderate redistribution. A third policy calls for a stronger redistributive role for the government, requiring a change from current policy and posing a challenge to the ideology of opportunities open to those with ability and drive. It calls for government to establish a ceiling on individual income. American leaders were asked what they thought about these three policies to reduce inequality. The public at large was also asked about two of the government policies: the more moderate policy of reducing the income gap between rich and poor and the more extreme policy of setting an upper limit on income.

The leadership groups hold widely disparate views on the two more moderate policies (Table 4.3). Business and Republican leaders oppose active government redistribution of income. These groups presumably feel that they are already taxed at a higher rate than is fair and that the economy in general suffers from the reduction of incentives brought about by high tax rates. Not surprisingly, feminist and black leaders take the opposite position, as do Democratic leaders. Labor leaders also support a redistributive role for the government, but to a lesser extent.

The difference between the attitudes of leaders of the two political parties are striking. More than three-quarters of the Democratic leaders consider these policies to be a proper role for the government, while fewer than one out of five Republican leaders concur. Democratic and Republican partisans in the public at large also diverge in their attitudes toward the wisdom of such government policies, but not as substantially. This is especially true for the Republican party. Seventy-five percent of Democratic leaders support the idea of government intervention to reduce the income gap, compared to 65 percent of their followers. The Republican leaders deviate in a conservative direction from their fellow partisans, with only 14 per-

**Table 4.3**
Attitudes on Government Intervention to Equalize Income (%)

| Group | Fair to tax rich to help poor | Government should reduce income gap between rich and poor | Government should put top limit on income |
|---|---|---|---|
| Business | 22 | 14 | 2 |
| Labor | 63 | 68 | 13 |
| Farm | 24 | 33 | 10 |
| Intellectuals | 60 | 62 | 20 |
| Media | 55 | 50 | 7 |
| Republicans | 19 | 14 | 2 |
| Democrats | 78 | 75 | 17 |
| Blacks | 72 | 82 | 16 |
| Feminists | 71 | 76 | 23 |
| Youth | 64 | 64 | 19 |
| Public-at-large | — | 58 | 9 |

cent of the leaders favoring such a policy, compared to 42 percent of Republicans in the electorate.

Reactions to the more radical proposal of placing a ceiling on individual earnings contrast sharply with reactions to the more moderate redistributive policies. Imposing a ceiling would not necessarily give the government a more radical redistributive role than would taxing the rich to help the poor or narrowing the gap between the two economic extremes. Such a limit might be more intrusive and controversial, yet the degree of radicalism would depend on how low the income limit was and on what kind of income equalizing taxes or transfer payments were imposed. However, American leaders interpret the cap on earnings as a stronger government action. The proportion of each leadership group endorsing this proposal is small. Only among feminists does more than 20 percent of a group favor a ceiling, and even among that group the proportion is less than one in four. Democratic and black leaders, despite their strong approval of more moderate redistributive policies, also oppose an income ceiling. Indeed, the proportion of each group favoring a policy to tax the rich to help the poor is between three and ten times larger than the proportion of each group favoring an income limit. And the public apparently agrees with its leaders. A majority favors some government effort to reduce the income gap, but the bulk of Americans oppose the establishment of an upper limit on income.

American leaders' staunch opposition to a ceiling on income reflects more than a simple aversion to government intrusiveness. While ceilings interfere with the "natural" movements of individuals up and down the economic hierarchy by dint of their own talent and effort, so do floors, which are widely endorsed. Yet ceilings are considered more coercive than floors. To give the poor a boost through resources taxed from the more affluent involves taking something from the rich—justly or unjustly, depending upon one's view as to the causes of poverty and the responsibility of the government. But the limitation that such taxes impose on the affluent individual's freedom to achieve is indirect. In comparison, a ceiling on income is a direct limit on one's ability to achieve.

Surveys of the public at large clarify the attitudes of Americans toward ceilings and floors on income. Both a ceiling on income and a floor beneath it are deviations from the dominant commitment to equality of opportunity, although a ceiling is a more drastic and coercive deviation. The public, like the leaders, rejects a ceiling but is more amenable toward a floor (Figure 4.1). Only 9 percent of the public favors an income ceiling, whereas 32 percent favors a floor in the form of a government guarantee of a minimum income. The consensual support for a floor depends on whether that floor is compatible with the public's dedication to equality of opportunity. When asked whether they favor a government guarantee of sufficient work so that a family breadwinner can earn a minimum income, 81 percent of the public says yes. Significantly, the less skilled respondents are somewhat more favorably disposed toward this kind of floor than are the professionals. Thus, on the issue of a ceiling there is consistent opposition across all levels; on the issue of a floor compatible with equality of opportunity, namely a guaranteed job to earn a minimum income, there is support across all levels. In contrast, the public as a whole is widely divided among occupation levels on a floor compatible with equality of result, namely a minimum income not linked to a job, and more widely divided among occupation levels as well. There is no consensus on such an income guarantee. The public clearly approves of government intervention in support of income equality if that support can somehow be made consistent with the dominant view that an earnings difference based on skill and effort is legitimate and ought not to be interfered with by redistributive policies.

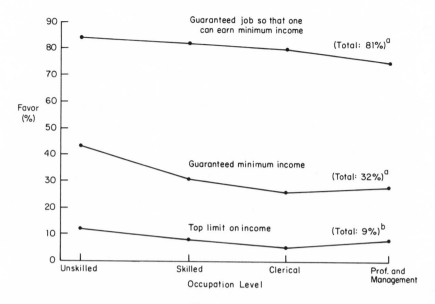

**Figure 4.1**
Public Attitudes on Income Floors and Ceilings
a. Gallup Poll, Dec. 1968 (n = 3155).
b. Metropolitan Workforce Survey, April 1976 (n = 1370). The composite occupational levels in the Metropolitan Survey approximate the Gallup Poll categories listed here. See Kay Lehman Schlozman and Sidney Verba, *Injury to Insult: Unemployment, Class, and Political Response* (Cambridge: Harvard University Press, 1979), pp. 55, 359.

These attitudes toward government action to redistribute income reflect the way in which the issue appears on the political agenda. Relatively moderate redistribution policies divide American leaders. On one side is a fairly conservative opposition to such redistributive efforts, centered in the business community and leaders of the Republican party. This opposition is to some extent shared by other groups, in particular by farm leaders and rank-and-file Republican voters. Arrayed against them is the leadership of the Democratic party, as well as the leadership of the new challenging groups such as blacks and feminists. These groups have the support of intellectuals, youth, and labor. The conflict suggests continuing pressure for governmental redistributive policies, resisted by business and the Republican party. However, the commitment to redistribution has its boundaries. Even among those groups most convinced that the government should take some redistributive role, there is little desire for a policy setting a maximum amount that individuals can earn.

On the whole, the views of leaders and the public toward government redistribution of income parallel their more general philosophical attitudes. All leaders follow the ideal of equality of opportunity, as opposed to equality of result. That philosophical position is consistent with opposition to an income ceiling. Yet American leaders disagree in their perception of whether the American economic system actually provides equal opportunities. The more conservative leaders believe that it does, and that the poor have only themselves to blame for poverty. The more liberal leaders feel that it does not, and that the system itself is the main cause of poverty. The groups are split along the same lines over the extent to which they think the government should intervene to reduce the income gap. That connection carries some powerful and deep-rooted implications for the way equality issues are treated in America.

More specifically, the leaders are widely split over two propositions:

1. The poor have only themselves to blame for their unequal condition. The system gave them a fair chance to get ahead and they failed to take advantage of it.
2. The government should not take substantial steps to make income more equal and help the poor.

Generally, American leaders accept either both or neither of these propositions. The more a group believes the first proposition, the more likely it is to accept the second as well. The attitudes are parallel and consistent.

However, while the statistical link between the views is clear, the analytical link is much less clear. The views are not inseparable, since the second one need not follow from the first. The altruist, for example, might argue that even though the poor had the chance to succeed and failed through their own fault, society should be generous enough to share its bounty with them. This position is embraced by few of the American leaders surveyed. What ties the two propositions together in the minds of leaders—and what makes the saintly or altruistic position so foreign in America—is a pervasive and fundamental conception of desert, the same concept that animates the universal recognition of equal opportunity as the ideal of all American leaders. Given their allegiance to this ideal, even the most liberal challenging groups apparently agree that the second proposition follows if the first proposition is true. Otherwise, American leaders would express more support for equality of result. Instead, they justify government assistance only because they believe that the system *has* failed to give certain groups an equal chance.

Thus, American leaders on both the left and the right share the basic view that individuals may in fact deserve to be unequal in results, because of their own failures. The equality debate in America, therefore, is not over whether anyone really deserves to be at the bottom or whether the losers are always worthy of help from the government, but over whether those currently at the bottom are the ones who deserve to be there, and thus whether the government should assist them.

## Quotas and Affirmative Action

The most sensitive equality issue on the public agenda is the issue of affirmative action, quotas, and "numerical criteria." There is widespread debate over the meaning of affirmative action and the amount of effort that should be put into it. Insofar as affirmative action implies greater efforts to make sure that opportunities are equally open to all, such as by making sure that schools and employers open opportunities to all races, both sexes, and people of all sorts, there is little controversy about its desirability. Affirmative action becomes a subject of intense controversy only when it involves more extensive intervention by the government or other institutions to ensure equality of result across social groups.

In most cases, equality of result requires some kind of quota or guideline as to the number of people with specified characteristics who will be employed or will be admitted to a particular educational institution. Such guidelines or quotas imply that people who are otherwise less qualified might be given preference on the basis of sex or of race or other specific characteristics. In fact, numerical quotas have rarely been applied. Numerical quotas are used, if at all, as guidelines, the nonachievement of which puts the burden of proof on the employers to show that they did not discriminate. But even this more moderate form of quota generates great resistance.

Because quotas are one of the most controversial public issues, the leadership groups were presented with two pairs of alternatives, one applying to blacks, the other to women. In relation to blacks, the leaders were asked whether they supported "quotas in school admission and job hiring ... to ensure black representation" or whether they believed "school admission and job hiring should be based strictly on merit." A parallel question concerned job quotas for women. The questions could have been asked in such a way that one could favor quotas without explicitly rejecting merit selection, and this approach undoubtedly would have invited strong support for affirmative action among the leaders. However, the questions were deliberately phrased to require the leaders to confront directly the difficult choice between quotas and pure meritocratic criteria.

The leadership groups are polarized over the issue of quotas both for blacks, in relation to school admission and jobs, and for women, in relation to jobs (Table 4.4). The cleavage is between the black and feminist leaders and the other leaders. As for quotas for blacks, three out of four black leaders favor such a policy, and they are supported by a slight majority of feminist leaders. Among groups generally allied with blacks and feminists, though, there is little support for racial quotas. Only three out of ten Democratic leaders and college youths support such quotas, as does only one in four labor leaders.

Democrats, youth, labor, and intellectuals, who blame the system for black poverty almost as much as black and feminist leaders do, nevertheless deplore the use of racial quotas (Table 4.5). The same pattern extends to quotas for women, to which these groups give even less support. They agree with blacks and feminists on the problem but disagree with them on the solution.

It is not overly cynical to speculate that the reason for this difference is in part that these groups stand to lose more from the

**Table 4.4**
Support for Quotas (%)

| Group | Support quotas for blacks in school admissions and jobs | Support quotas for women in jobs |
|---|---|---|
| Business | 10 | 7 |
| Labor | 25 | 20 |
| Farm | 8 | 5 |
| Intellectual | 18 | 16 |
| Media | 22 | 16 |
| Republicans | 5 | 5 |
| Democrats | 31 | 29 |
| Blacks | 75 | 59 |
| Feminists | 53 | 56 |
| Youth | 30 | 25 |
| Public-at-large | — | 18 |

**Table 4.5**
Attitudes on Causes of Black Poverty and on
Racial Quotas (%)

| Group | Blame system for black poverty | Support quotas for blacks |
|---|---|---|
| Blacks | 82 | 75 |
| Feminists | 83 | 53 |
| Democrats | 73 | 31 |
| Intellectuals | 65 | 18 |
| Youth | 69 | 30 |
| Labor | 52 | 25 |

imposition of racial quotas than do blacks, who will gain from them, and women, who might suffer a little from racial quotas but would likely benefit more by support for quotas in general. College students might be thinking about competition for places in graduate school and jobs; intellectuals are worried about the paltry and declining number of teaching positions and tenure opportunities; labor leaders are nervous about job security; and Democratic leaders, concerned about contests for crucial delegate positions in their nominating bodies, fear that they will lose the support of the other liberal constituencies over the issue of quotas.

Quotas also fly in the face of these groups' general ideology toward equality, their preference for equality of opportunity rather than equality of result. Black and feminist leaders must overcome this ideological barrier in deciding to support quotas. It is likely, though, that in choosing a stance on how to solve a problem, they are motivated by self-interest. Indeed, self-interest probably shapes their preference for a solution more than it shapes their view of the nature of the problem. The solution is more tangible, immediate, and palpable. This is one of the reasons for the greater diversity among the groups over specific solutions than over general ideals or descriptions of the nature of problems. The immediacy of solutions forces self-interest to emerge more emphatically.

On the issue of job quotas for women, once again only black and feminist leaders give majority support. Even among the feminists only a small majority favors quotas. The near unanimity of feminist leaders on many other issues breaks down over quotas. Blacks contrast sharply with feminists on this issue (Table 4.6). Both black and

**Table 4.6**
Attitudes on Causes of Inequality and on Quotas (%)

| Group | Blame system for inequality of | | Support quotas for | |
|---|---|---|---|---|
| | Blacks | Women | Blacks | Women |
| Blacks | 82 | 67 | 75 | 59 |
| Feminists | 83 | 92 | 53 | 56 |

feminist leaders regard their groups as victims of discrimination, but they differ widely on the matter of solutions. Among black leaders, 82 percent see themselves as victims of discrimination, and 75 percent support quotas as a remedy. Feminists are a good deal more likely to see themselves as victims of discrimination (92 percent) but much less likely to support quotas for themselves (56 percent).

This difference reflects an attitude toward quotas *per se* and not just toward quotas for one's own group. Sixty-seven percent of black leaders see women as the victims of discrimination, and nearly the same proportion (59 percent) support the idea of quotas for women. Even more of the feminists think that blacks are victims of discrimination (83 percent), but only 53 percent support racial quotas. Both groups heavily blame the system for racial and gender inequality, but in both cases blacks are more likely to support quotas as a solution.

The explanation for this disparity may be that blacks are more resigned, perhaps justifiably, to the conclusion that through no fault of their own they are less well-educated and qualified for university admissions and jobs. In the short run, at least, affirmative action may be necessary to give them an equal chance. Feminists probably have a different conception of their situation. Women generally have been the victims, at least in recent decades, of a more attitudinal discrimination. They are not denied educational opportunities as much as blacks are. But feminist leaders claim that they are subjected to unfair competition for jobs and school admissions because of the irrational and erroneous attitude that they are poorly equipped for positions other than work in the home.

As a result, women might perceive that all they need to achieve equality with men is the elimination of biases which prevent schools and employers from considering their abilities and training objectively; if those barriers were removed, no special quotas would be necessary. In contrast, blacks might believe that quotas are necessary now because discrimination against them has been so pervasive that they are no longer as qualified as whites. Having been denied the chance to become equally qualified, they cannot be given the chance to compete effectively just by the removal of current discriminatory barriers.

Such an explanation for the difference between blacks and feminists on the issue of job quotas is consistent with the rhetoric used by the two groups. Modern feminists usually demand the right to be treated as they deserve, by which they mean "as equals." Their rallying cry is "Equal pay for equal work." Feminists argue that they are just as qualified as men. Yet black leaders campaign more vigorously for the right to become equal, not simply to be treated as equal. They call for better education from the ground up ("A mind is a terrible thing to waste").

This distinction helps to explain the lukewarm support of feminist leaders for quotas in contrast to their near unanimity on many other equality issues. The division among feminists on quotas might be tied to the self-image of individual leaders. They may feel that they are being treated unequally either because of other people's irrational prejudice or because of their own lack of qualification due to past inequality in their education or training. The group that blames prejudice would see no particular need for a quota; the less qualified group might be more sympathetic to quotas. A sizable number of feminist leaders and of women in general probably fall into each group. A much larger proportion of blacks presumably fall into the latter group.

Yet the main reason blacks solidly support affirmative action may not be that they recognize a lack of qualifications. It may be that they perceive racism to be embedded even in well-intentioned whites that only by imposing strong compensatory measures can blacks receive the same positions as equally qualified whites. "Qualification" is a slippery term, defined to benefit whites, according to some observers. Blacks may think that only by forcing the issue through affirmative action will employers be induced to reconsider outmoded, irrelevant, or partial measures of qualification.

On a number of policy issues, such as a moderate redistribution of income, the attitudes of American leaders suggest the potential for a fairly wide coalition in favor of greater governmental commitment to equality. However, on issues concerning affirmative action, at least the tough kind of action embodied in quotas, the stability of that coalition is called into question. Challenging groups like blacks and feminists are divided among themselves over these issues, though they still tend in the direction of government intervention. But they lack the support of other groups that would otherwise rally around egalitarian policies. Furthermore, the American public is hardly enamored of such policies. For example, only 18 percent of Americans favor job quotas for women, and there is little difference between men and women on this score.

EQUALITY is likely to remain a political issue for a number of reasons. First, a large and significant segment of leadership in the United States thinks that the system is unfair in the current distribution of rewards and would like to see the government intervene to create greater equality. The existence of such leadership groups ensures that the issue will remain on the public agenda. At the same time, the sharp differences in attitudes toward equality among leadership groups ensure that the issue will remain controversial. Despite widespread philosophical consensus favoring equality of opportunity rather than equality of result, American leaders disagree over both the extent to which equality of opportunity actually exists and the policies that should be pursued to expand it.

# 5

# A Common Language
# of Equality

Attitudes on different issues of equality in America vary considerably. Some issues generate widespread agreement, others sharp disagreement, across the leadership groups. Furthermore, where there is consensus, groups sometimes take the more egalitarian view and sometimes agree on the less egalitarian position.

However, people's views on specific questions about equality may yield an incomplete or even misleading picture. Where matters of equality are concerned, the leaders' opinions on specific issues, such as whether they approve or disapprove of hiring quotas, are less significant than their general attitudes or ideologies. Specific equality issues will appear on the political agenda in new and unexpected forms in future years. At the same time, some of the old, unsolved issues of equality will remain in the cauldron of public debate. Which disputes emerge and which positions people take will depend, as always, upon who stands to gain and who to lose in each instance. American leaders, though, hold fundamental views on equality that have an underlying structure; their opinions on particular issues follow coherent and meaningful patterns.[1]

## Attitude Structure

Social scientists have long been concerned with the subject of "issue constraint," the extent to which individuals' views on one issue are

---

This chapter was written with G. Donald Ferree, Jr.

consistent with their views on seemingly related issues. On some subjects, research has found remarkably little constraint in the public at large, with the position individuals take on one issue providing little indication of what they will say on a related matter. This inconsistency may suggest that people do not have "real" attitudes on such matters but merely offer random responses to questions about which they have not previously thought.[2]

Among American leaders, however, attitude structures are far more coherent. For one thing, the leaders are a highly educated group with extensive political involvement. Many studies have shown that the coherence of views increases as one moves from the less well-educated to the better-educated segments of society and from those less involved in politics to those more involved. More important, the coherence of one's attitudes is greater in those issue areas about which one cares most.[3] The average citizen may not have a coherent pattern of attitudes in relation to foreign policy, but the foreign policy specialist probably will. For many of the leaders in this study, the issue of equality is central to their daily work, particularly for leaders of black and feminist organizations whose main goal is to increase equality. Equality issues also appear in the ordinary work of labor leaders and business leaders and cannot be too far from the consciousness of leaders in the other spheres.

The assumption that these attitudes have a coherent structure in relation to equality is crucial to the significance of the study. If the leaders were merely responding to a set of discrete policies or, even worse, if they were responding randomly to questions about which they had not thought, an extended analysis of their views would be futile. The structure of these attitudes could be either unidimensional or multidimensional. If the former, all the leaders would be arrayed along a single dimension of preference for or opposition to equality. There would be egalitarians, antiegalitarians, and others in between. It seems clear, however, that equality is more complex than that. Equality is not a simple state that either exists or does not exist, nor does it exist in a single dimension. The complexity of equality as a subject is reflected in the complexity of the attitudes of American leaders on the subject.[4]

Since equality is multidimensional, any specific issue related to equality embodies a number of more general issues. Take, for example, the specific issue of whether the government should enforce quotas for blacks in higher education. The position one holds on the issue may reflect one's attitude on any of the following: the group involved (blacks), the particular means (quotas), the value being equalized (access to education), the degree to which the government should be involved in enforcing equality, and equality of result versus equality of opportunity. People can be expected to differ a great deal over the aspects of the proposal which strike them as most important. Political debates often turn on how a particular issue should be categorized. One's position on food stamps, for example, probably depends largely on whether one sees this issue as dealing with hunger, or welfare, or the federal deficit, or federalism, or farmers' surplus crops.

Our goal here is to identify which of these categories or dimensions are most important in shaping attitudes toward equality. If the racial aspect of an issue is the most crucial, people who feel a particular way about educational quotas for blacks are more likely to feel that way about other issues involving blacks, such as residential integration. If race is not an important consideration, the position on racial quotas in education is likely to be unrelated to positions on integrated neighborhoods. Likewise, if people feel strongly about quotas, their views on educational quotas for blacks and on job quotas for women will probably be related.

Measuring the coherence of an individual's positions on the basis of the interrelationship among attitudes assumes that a coherent set of related views can be identified in advance. Some combination of views that appears inconsistent or outlandish to one person may make sense to another. In-depth studies of the political ideologies of individuals reveal that a person's attitudes are often bound together by a remarkable array of idiosyncratic patterns. However, such patterns, though meaningful to the individual, are usually of little political significance. To be politically meaningful, a set of attitudes has to be shared, at least to some extent, with others. Otherwise, the weight of its impact on political affairs will be minimal. Therefore, the study did not address the particular attitude pattern for any single leader but rather the extent to which there is a shared pattern among many leaders.

The nature of the underlying structure of attitudes is crucial to comparisons among the leadership groups. People differ in both the extent to which their views have a well-defined structure and the extent to which that structure is shared. This is a question not of whether groups agree or disagree substantively on the issues but whether they agree on what is at stake. For instance, one group may prefer equality of result and another group equality of opportunity, but if both groups agree that the polarity between results and opportunity is significant, they share the same attitude structure toward equality. If one group does not see that distinction as important, the debate between them is less sharply focused.

The presence or absence of a common structure across groups is important for an understanding of equality as a political issue. If groups "speak a different language" about equality, the lines of opposition become blurred; one group is concerned with one aspect of the issue, another group with a different aspect. This may not make opposition any less intense, but it still makes it more difficult for one group to understand the position of the other. The same holds for alliances. If groups are concerned about different dimensions of equality, alliances based on common views are difficult to arrange and even harder to maintain. On the other hand, alliances based on logrolling, where groups cooperate though they may not share the same goals, might be easier if different aspects of the equality issue are salient to different groups.

In sum, digging for the underlying dimensions of equality serves several purposes. The first is to show that the equality attitudes of American leaders are in fact structured in a predictable and meaningful way. The second is to identify the underlying dimensions that organize attitudes toward equality. The third is to show that the same general structure is shared by all of the leadership groups. And the last is to make it possible to distill many specific issue questions into a manageable number of summary measures which will help to compare the positions of the leadership groups.

## A Factor Analysis

To uncover the dimensions along which equality attitudes are organized, traditional factor analysis was used. This statistical technique takes the interrelationships among responses to many specific questions and reduces them to a limited set of underlying dimensions or "factors."[5] To identify a common attitude structure, factor analysis was applied to the leaders as a whole rather than to each leadership group separately. Twenty-two items from the questionnaire, all dealing in one way or another with the issue of equality, were entered into the analysis (see Appendix B).

The first analysis produced a four-factor solution, that is, four underlying dimensions (Table 5.1). Fortunately, most of the issue questions are related to only one of the four dimensions, and the

**Table 5.1**

Underlying Dimensions of Equality: Four-Factor Solution

| Issue question | I | II | III | IV |
|---|---|---|---|---|
| | Factors[a] | | | |
| Government should reduce income gap | .68 | | | |
| Government should guarantee jobs | .70 | | | |
| Fault of system that poor are poor | .67 | | | |
| Private enterprise system not fair | .47 | .39 | | |
| Laws mainly favor the rich | .57 | | | |
| Fair to tax the rich to help the poor | .73 | | | |
| Female workers as reliable as men | | .43 | | |
| Wives with working husbands should not be laid off first | | .67 | | |
| ERA should be passed | | .43 | | |
| System discriminates against women | | .53 | | |
| Women should have careers | | .65 | | |
| Put top limit on income | | | .47 | |
| All should receive equal pay | | | .60 | |
| Equality of result preferable | | | .57 | |
| Favor busing | .46 | | | .33 |
| Racial integration not going fast enough | .49 | | | .33 |
| Support quotas for jobs for women | | | | .71 |
| Support quotas for jobs and school admissions for blacks | | | | .84 |
| System discriminates against blacks | .42 | | | |
| Government should help blacks get jobs | .57 | | | |
| Integrate housing | .44 | | | |
| Government should provide welfare | .52 | | | |

a. Loadings shown are those above .30. See Appendix B for exact wording of the issue questions and details of the methodology.

dimensions are fairly easily identified.[6] The first combines attitudes on economic matters with attitudes on racial issues. The second contains various attitudes on the role of women. The third deals with redistribution and equality of results—whether a ceiling should be imposed on income, whether all should receive equal pay, and whether equality of result or equality of opportunity is more desirable. The question about the fairness of the capitalist system is related to the third factor, as well as to the first. The fourth dimension is less clear. It includes attitudes toward quotas for blacks and quotas for women, plus views on racial integration, whether it is going too fast and whether busing is a good way to achieve it. The last two issues are not nearly as strongly tied to the factor as attitudes toward quotas.

Two sets of attitudes stand out clearly: those on gender equality and those on redistribution and equality of result. Other results are quite puzzling. The first dimension combines attitudes on economic matters with attitudes on race, and the last dimension is mixed as well. More surprising, perhaps, is the absence of a cluster of attitudes specifically associated with racial equality, one of the most intense issues of the politics of equality.

A six-factor solution was therefore developed, the dimensions of which partially overlap with the previous four factors (Table 5.2). The first category emphasizes welfare state issues: whether to lessen the income gap between rich and poor, whether the government should guarantee citizens jobs, whether poverty is the fault of the system rather than of the poor themselves, whether capitalism is a fair system, whether the laws favor the rich, and whether it is fair to tax the rich to help the poor. These issues lie at the heart of the conflict that dates back to the struggles of the New Deal over governmental responsibility for economic welfare. It seems appropriate to label this a New Deal dimension.

This dimension comprises a disparate set of economic issues that have in common a critique of laissez-faire capitalism coupled with a commitment to government intervention to reduce inequities in the economy. The factor taps a general split over the New Deal economic policies which has long divided mainstream Democrats from mainstream Republicans. Inasmuch as it lumps together a variety of social policies and values, this factor is not analytically neat. Its complexity, however, makes it an appropriate summary of the New Deal critique of free enterprise America, which was quite varied and at times ambiguous and inconsistent, leading to a mixture of government programs. This dimension is relevant even today, embracing issues that have not yet been settled. Though many of the New Deal policies, such as social security, seem secure against abolition, programs that extend beyond the basic New Deal reforms have always stirred debate, and even the basic "unassailable" programs often face budgetary uncertainty. The Democratic and Republican platforms traditionally differ on economic issues, and the advent of the Reagan administration in 1981 demonstrated that the issues of the New Deal are far from settled.[7] The New Deal factor explains the highest proportion of variance in the data and contains the most items.

**Table 5.2**
Underlying Dimensions of Equality: Six-Factor Solution

| | Factors[a] | | | | | |
|---|---|---|---|---|---|---|
| Issue question | New Deal | Gender | Redistri-bution | Quotas | Causes of inequality | Race |
| Government should reduce income gap | .61 | | | | | |
| Government should guarantee jobs | .56 | | | | | |
| Fault of system that poor are poor | .45 | | | | | |
| Private enterprise system not fair | .55 | | | | | |
| Laws mainly favor the rich | .56 | | | | | |
| Fair to tax the rich to help the poor | .41 | | | | | .32 |
| Female workers as reliable as men | | .41 | | | | |
| Wives with working husbands should not be laid off first | | .68 | | | | |
| ERA should be passed | | .48 | | | | |
| System discriminates against women | | .40 | | | .38 | |
| Women should have careers | | .61 | | | | |
| Put top limit on income | | | .44 | | | |
| All should receive equal pay | | | .53 | | | |
| Equality of result preferable | | | .72 | | | |
| Favor busing | | | | .33 | | .32 |
| Racial integration not going fast enough | | | | .33 | | .30 |
| Support quotas for jobs for women | | | | .83 | | |
| Support quotas for jobs and school admissions for blacks | | | | .92 | | |
| System discriminates against blacks | | | | | .71 | |
| Government should help blacks get jobs | | | | | | .37 |
| Integrate housing | | | | | | .41 |
| Government should provide welfare | | | | | | .42 |

a. Loadings shown are those above .30. See Appendix B for exact wording of the issue questions and details of the methodology.

The second set of attitudes pertains to gender equality. It includes questions of whether women are less reliable workers than men, whether women with employed husbands should be laid off before other workers, whether the Equal Rights Amendment should be ratified, whether women are the victims of discrimination, and whether it is appropriate for women to hold jobs instead of staying home and restricting themselves to more traditional roles. The issues of gender equality are very old, but they have emerged recently with a new scope and form. Gender equality was high on neither the New Deal agenda nor the agenda of the civil rights movement. Many who are concerned with New Deal-type reforms or with racial equality are much more hesitant in their commitment to equality between the sexes. This is clearly a separate issue.

The third group of issues includes views on whether incomes should be limited, whether all people should earn approximately the same income, and whether equality of opportunity is preferable to equality of result. This factor is labeled the redistribution factor since it contains items tapping attitudes toward a radical equalization of incomes. This set of issues is distinguished from the New Deal factor by the greater extent of its social reforms. The policies of the New Deal and subsequent legislation have provided a base of social services for the needy but have not aimed at radical income redistribution. In this sense, the New Deal was conservative, and many who support its reforms would wince at more radical change. By no coincidence, the legitimacy of taxing the rich to help the poor falls on the New Deal factor, while the more radical notions of limiting or equalizing income falls on the separate redistribution factor. The New Deal factor apparently involves programs that create a floor of social welfare, a safety net, and the redistribution factor involves programs that place a ceiling on income.

The fourth category subsumes attitudes on busing, the speed of racial integration, quotas to increase the number of blacks in good jobs, and quotas for women. Although the first three issues relate to race, this does not appear to be the unifying theme. The two issues most strongly related to this dimension are quotas for women and blacks. Attitudes toward quotas for women appear here and not on the feminism dimension. This set seems to deal more with the use of affirmative government programs, particularly in the more radical context of quotas, to improve the conditions of previously disadvantaged groups. The fact that items dealing with affirmative action separate off from the group-oriented dimensions—namely gender, the second dimension, and race, the sixth—indicates that quotas represent a special issue not encompassed by people's general concern with gender or racial equality. In some sense, quotas are to race or gender what redistribution is to the New Deal. Quotas and redistribution of income are more radical policies than are those around which most debate takes place, since they mandate a floor and a ceiling for access to a particular benefit. They are supported by a smaller minority than the social programs of the New Deal or the liberal programs for blacks and women. In this sense they stand apart from the other dimensions.

The fifth underlying dimension links two questions on the causes of inequality for blacks and women, whether inequality is their fault or the fault of an unjust society. This dimension reflects perceptions of the causes of inequality.

The sixth dimension taps attitudes toward the use of taxes to help the poor, busing, welfare, the speed of racial integration, whether the government should ensure the fair treatment of blacks in employment, and whether people should be able to discriminate on the basis of race in selling their homes. This category has a racial stamp, though attitudes toward the poor also appear here, more than on the first dimension. Many studies have found that race and welfare are closely related in the minds of Americans. The dominant theme of this sixth dimension is clearly race. Some of the specific issues encompassed in the race factor, such as busing or fair housing, are explicitly linked to race, while others, such as welfare, are implicitly linked to race in the minds of many. Equality for blacks is clearly related to issues of the New Deal and of redistribution: blacks benefit disproportionately from New Deal social programs because of their lower socioeconomic status and would enjoy a net gain from income redistribution. However, the New Deal did not frontally attack racial inequality. Only since the New Deal has the issue of equality between the races been the focus of much organized activity in the United States. Accordingly, some issues of racial equality are separate from, though not totally unrelated to, economic issues, such as school integration, busing, and fair housing laws. Clearly the race factor picks up a central and separate issue of contemporary politics.

It is difficult to say which analysis, the one with four factors or with six, better captures reality.[8] The six-factor analysis is used here because it is less ambiguous and it makes distinctions, especially where racial attitudes are concerned, that are not possible with the four factors.

Attitudes on gender equality, the gender dimension, exhibit a stronger coherence than do attitudes on racial equality in both the four- and six-factor solutions. The four-factor solution shows racial attitudes intermingled with attitudes on economic welfare. And even the six-factor solution, which more effectively isolates a dimension associated with race, produces a factor that combines racial and general welfare issues. This difference suggests that attitudes toward equality for women have a more distinctive component than do attitudes toward equality for blacks. Gender attitudes are more closely related to each other and less closely related to other attitudes than is the case for racial attitudes.[9] Gender equality, even more than racial equality, has a life of its own, separate from the general economic reforms of the New Deal. The question of racial equality is associated in the minds of many leaders with other characteristics, such as poverty and welfare. As a result, racial equality has in large part become merged with other equality issues, such as economic equality and the role of the government in alleviating inequality, whereas gender equality stands out as an issue unto itself.[10]

A number of social factors, universally understood but inadequately appreciated, help account for the fact that the leaders' attitudes on gender issues are less correlated with economic matters than are their racial views. Whatever economic deprivations women have suffered are less well-perceived than the problems of the black community. For several reasons white women have never been as completely separated from the "ruling white male class" as blacks have been. The closer emotional and social connections between the sexes, through marriage or family ties, have operated to conceal the economic disadvantages of women. Furthermore, female disadvantages are less visible to society and the public consciousness because, unlike poor blacks, poor women are not as trapped in segregated areas of American life.

This underlying structure of attitudes found among the full set of leaders also characterizes each of the various leadership groups. Conceivably the six-dimensional structure common to all the leaders might mask group-specific differences. However, as several statistical tests show, this common structure of equality attitudes does not vary appreciably from group to group (see Appendix C). For example, the racial and gender questions do not cluster together more noticeably for blacks or feminists than for other groups. Conversely, that which other groups see as economic issues, blacks and feminists do not see in racial or gender terms.

In addition, the six identifiable and separate dimensions of attitudes toward equality are by no means unrelated. In fact, it is possible to predict the position of individual leaders on one dimension from their positions on the others; hence, the factors are fairly closely connected (Table 5.3). In most cases, more than half of the variance in any one factor can be explained by the position that leaders take on the other factors. For the New Deal factor, 70 percent of the variance is explained by the other factors. The single dimension most weakly related to the others is gender. Though it is related to the others, a substantially smaller proportion of its variance is explained by the other factors. Thus, in two ways the gender dimension stands out from the rest: it appears most clearly on both the four- and the six-factor solutions, suggesting that it is quite a robust set of attitudes, and it is least well explained by the other factors, suggesting that it is relatively independent.

THESE DIMENSIONS of equality attitudes capture some of the major political issues associated with equality. Indeed, they provide almost a capsule history of the evolution of equality since the 1930s: a set of attitudes toward the innovative New Deal policies which created a social welfare floor, a set of views covering the issue of income redistribution that was left unresolved by the New Deal, two attitude dimensions relating to the newly mobilized black and female demands for equality, and one dimension touching on the extension of minority demands into the controversial area of quotas. These dimensions, though by no means exhaustive, help to locate the sources of conflict over equality.

They also help to identify what American leaders hold in common. There is a common language of equality. American leaders

**Table 5.3**
Variance in Each Factor Explained by the Other Factors

| Factor | Variance explained ($r^2$) |
|---|---|
| New Deal | .69 |
| Race | .62 |
| Quotas | .59 |
| Causes of inequality | .56 |
| Redistribution | .52 |
| Gender | .43 |

from a wide range of sectors respond to equality issues in terms of the same underlying dimensions. Of course, these dimensions are not the only possible ones. Since the dimensions found depend on the questions asked, an entirely different set of questions might yield a different underlying framework. But within the universe of issues defined by the survey, which encompasses most of the major issues, a common structure exists. Each of the dimensions—the two separate economic dimensions (New Deal-type attitudes and views toward radical redistribution), the race and gender dimensions, the quota dimension, and the dimension that assigns blame for inequality—highlights a significant component of the equality debate.

# 6

## Group Positions

That the various leadership groups share a way of organizing their thoughts about equality around such issue areas as gender, race, and economic redistribution does not mean that they agree with each other on those issues. In fact, the nature of the dimensions of equality suggests that the various groups have distinctive positions. Several of the equality issues are crucial to particular groups. Consider the two major economic groups. Disputes between business and labor are at least as old as the commercial and industrial revolutions. The lines of the current dispute in the United States, however, were drawn largely by the battles fought during the New Deal era, when the modern labor movement was formed and its success was assured by federal legislation. The issues of the New Deal era that cleaved labor from management have since dominated the political agenda in the United States. Business and labor are thus likely to be at opposite poles on the New Deal issues of equality. The polarization between these two groups on other dimensions of equality is not nearly so obvious.

The views of business leaders are fairly predictable. It is expected that they would take a conservative stand on the issue of income redistribution. And they would just as likely be uneasy about racial and gender equality. Should the government seek to achieve racial equality, it would have to develop social welfare programs that might

---

This chapter was written with G. Donald Ferree, Jr.

prove costly 'for business. Furthermore, special employment treatment for blacks or women reduces business autonomy. Thus, business would also tend to be conservative on the racial, gender, and quota dimensions, even though these issues do not cut as close to the heart of business interests as do the more strictly economic issues.

The position of labor on issues outside the New Deal dimension is likely to be more mixed. The American labor movement has fought hard for many liberal social reforms but never very strongly for income redistribution. Labor unions have often been found in a liberal coalition with civil rights and feminist groups when dealing with broader social issues, but the issues of gender and racial equality split the labor movement, as well as cut it off from potential allies. Job quotas or special treatment for blacks and women might be seen as a challenge to the established positions of unionized workers, who are predominately white and male. Thus organized labor leaders would be expected to diverge on equality issues other than those of the New Deal.

Feminist and black leaders would presumably show the most cohesiveness on the equality dimension directly related to their own constituent groups, but would be quite liberal on other issues as well. Black leaders would take strongly liberal positions on economic issues, which materially affect their constituency. Where they stand on the gender dimension is less clear. On the one hand, they might empathize with fellow victims of discrimination; on the other hand, they might perceive feminism as a middle-class white ideology that interferes with their attempt to achieve social justice. The position of feminists is similarly uncertain. Their largely middle-class background suggests somewhat conservative views on economic or racial matters. Moreover, in its early history the feminist movement experienced a rocky relationship with the New Left. Women were often given inferior positions in civil rights groups and the student movement, causing resentment among some women and perhaps a lack of sympathy for blacks. Yet feminist leaders, despite their middle-class origins, are generally liberal or radical. As a result, women would be expected to manifest a left point of view on matters of race.

A certain amount of ambivalence seems likely among farm leaders as well. They probably represent a socially conservative group that takes little interest in racial or gender equality. On economic issues, however, their position should be mixed. The circumstances of the farm sector are quite heterogeneous. But many farmers, along with their organizations, share a concern for government support, coupled somewhat inconsistently with a tradition of fierce individualism. All this combines with a populist hostility to bigness.

Just how much the leadership groups agree or disagree on equality issues can be determined only by comparing their views. To simplify this task, the leaders' responses to a large number of survey questions were reduced to six composite attitude scales, one for each of the dimensions of equality identified by the factor analysis: New Deal issues, gender, income redistribution, quotas, perception of the causes of inequality, and race (See Appendix D). The scales are "standardized," which means that, for each scale, the average, or mean, is zero and the standard deviation for all leaders together is one. For any particular group, however, the mean and the standard deviation can themselves deviate.

This standardization establishes the position of each group relative to the other groups. Each attitude scale shows which groups take distinctive positions to the left or the right of the mean of all groups and how each group's position relates to that of others. It is impossible to say, in an absolute sense, whether a group is left or right on an issue, since the distribution on each scale depends upon the questions asked and, more important, on the groups questioned. If, for instance, more conservative groups had been included, such as right-to-lifers or the Moral Majority, the anchoring point of each equality scale, or the average, would lie further to the right.

Nevertheless, the ten groups chosen—business, farming, unions, Democrats and Republicans, intellectuals, media members, feminists, blacks, and youth—cover a wide spectrum of attitudes. Comparison of the relative positions of these groups across the several dimensions of equality shows where there is a greater spread among groups and where there is more consensus, or which dimension most clearly distinguishes a particular group.

### Individual Versus Group Attitudes

The attitudes of individuals toward equality are structured by the leadership group to which they belong. Leaders are both significant political actors as individuals, and representatives of segments of society that have distinctive positions on matters of equality. This is particularly true of the major contending groups in America, namely business, farmers, labor, feminists, blacks, and party leaders, but it is true perhaps of all groups.

One way of assessing the distinctiveness of the positions on equality held by the various leadership groups is to consider the variance in attitudes both within groups and across groups. For example, disagreement between two business leaders may be less likely than between the average business leader and the average labor leader. The clearest conflict among groups occurs when all leaders of one group take a certain position on equality issues while all leaders of another group take a different position.

Attitudes within the groups are compared to those across the groups on the six dimensions of equality by use of analysis of variance techniques (Table 6.1). The first two columns of the table compare the variance within groups with that between the groups. The third column reports a statistical test, an *F* test, which shows that the attitudinal differences across the groups are all statistically significant and thus not simply the result of chance. The last column shows the extent to which groups differ in their views on the various issues by comparing the variance within groups to the variance among all the groups, using the Eta$^2$ statistic.[1]

The groups are most clearly distinguished on New Deal issues. This means that the basic economic issues of government responsibility for jobs and for helping the poor, as well as the issue of whether the capitalist system is fair, are matters that continue to be hotly debated between groups. The issue that comes next in terms of differentiating among groups is a much newer one: quotas and affirmative action. The issue on which there is least difference among groups is the redistribution of income. This is not merely a reflection of the relatively high consensus on this issue. The statistic we use

**Table 6.1**
Analysis of Variance of Equality Attitudes

| Issue | Variance within groups | Variance between groups | *F* ratio | *Eta*$^2$ |
|---|---|---|---|---|
| New Deal | 1298.8 | 884.1 | 192.9 | 0.41 |
| Gender | 1391.8 | 541.2 | 110.2 | 0.28 |
| Redistribution | 1532.7 | 286.7 | 53.0 | 0.16 |
| Quotas | 1548.1 | 781.6 | 143.0 | 0.34 |
| Causes of inequality | 1528.1 | 430.6 | 79.8 | 0.22 |
| Race | 1278.9 | 577.1 | 127.9 | 0.31 |

tells us that any differences of opinion are largely differences among individuals within groups rather than across the groups themselves.

These results clarify the nature of conflict over issues of equality. They show that there are real group differences on these issues, which go beyond individual differences of opinion. On some issues, conflict between groups is particularly sharp. Examples are the older economic issues associated with the New Deal and the newer economic issue of quotas. An issue like income redistribution, in contrast, is less likely to stir conflict, since attitude differences are more generally distributed within the population and are not connected to group affiliation.

**Group Differences**

The spread among the ten leadership groups on equality issues varies from one issue area to another (Figure 6.1). The most widely dispersed pattern is found on the New Deal scale; the most highly concentrated is found on the scale for the other economic issue, redistribution. However, the relative position of each group on the various dimensions is generally the same. Business, Republican, and farm leaders anchor the less egalitarian, or "conservative," end of the scale. Feminist, black, and Democratic leaders monopolize the more egalitarian, or "liberal," end. The other groups consistently fall in between.

The most striking feature on the conservative side is the proximity of business and Republican leaders. On every issue, they are practically cheek to cheek. Indeed, no other pair of groups is so closely allied. Farm leaders are also usually on the conservative end of the spectrum, but their conservatism varies from issue to issue. On economic issues, such as New Deal policies and income redistribution, farmers are more liberal than the business and Republican leaders.[2] Their stand on the redistribution issue reflects farm leaders' general dissatisfaction with the current income distribution in America, as well as their populist heritage. However, on issues involving social equality and racial equality, farm leaders are the most conservative group, often by a substantial margin. This tendency is most pronounced on the gender issue. The farm group is characterized by social conservatism coupled with a more ambivalent position on economic matters.

The feminist and black leaders dominate the liberal end of the spectrum. On economic issues they are far to the left, as they are

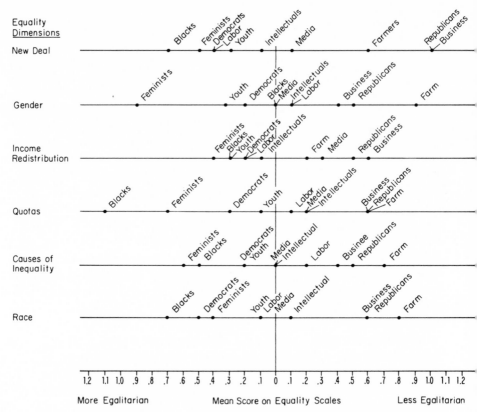

**Figure 6.1**
Attitudes on Equality Issues by Group

on the issues of quotas and the causes of inequality, both of which refer specifically to their own groups. On the gender issue, the feminist leaders, as one might expect, are the most liberal group. Indeed, they have a rather isolated position on that subject: the gap between them and the nearest group, youth, is larger than the distance between adjacent groups on any other issue. Furthermore, on this issue the feminists' usual allies on the left, the Democrats and especially the blacks, take positions quite far from the feminists, closer to the average for all leaders. Youth and Democratic party leaders are more liberal than blacks on matters of equality between the sexes. More than any other group on any other issue, however, the feminists are off on their own on issues of gender equality.

The position of black leaders is most distinctive on the issue of racial equality. They are farthest to the left, but not nearly as far from their potential allies as are the feminists on gender issues. Blacks are also the most liberal group on the New Deal and quotas, and they are quite liberal on income redistribution and the causes of inequality. Only on gender equality do they stray far from the liberal end. Feminist leaders are much closer to blacks on race issues than blacks are to feminists on gender issues.

Organized labor is the group that swings most widely from scale to scale. Labor falls on the liberal side on three of the issues and on the conservative side on the other three. Toward the New Deal, labor leaders are fairly far to the left, quite close to the Democratic party leaders. And they cluster with a number of other groups on the liberal side of income redistribution. On the race issue as well they lean toward liberalism, though not by much. However, they take a conservative stance toward gender equality, quotas, and the causes of inequality. In a sense, their position parallels that of the farm leaders, though it tilts farther toward the left. They are liberal on economic issues, especially those of the New Deal, and more conservative on social issues. The parallel does not hold, however, when it comes to race. Here farmers are the most conservative, labor relatively liberal.

The media leaders and intellectuals fall close to the center of most of the scales. There is no evidence of a leftward tilt on the part of the media relative to the other groups.[3] On four of the issues they are located almost exactly equidistant between the most liberal and the most conservative groups. On the two issues where they are off-center, income redistribution and quotas, they are closer to the conservative end than to the liberal groups, suggesting a meritocratic orientation on their part.

On average, relative to the other groups, the media and intellectuals occupy a position consistent with their intermediary status. These two groups, and to a lesser extent college youth, occupy more centrist positions because their group affiliations exert a much weaker grip on their attitudes toward equality. The institutional groups occupy positions that reflect strong ideological commitments on equality issues. Blacks and feminists are professional advocates of the need for racial or gender equality. Labor, business, farm, and especially party leaders are expected to have views toward equality that are closely linked to their roles. Intellectual and media leaders are less the actors on the stage than the critics and the audience.

The centrist position can also be the product of substantial variation within each of the intermediary groups. That is, a group can be composed of a mixture of pro- and antiegalitarian leaders who "cancel each other out," causing the group to appear moderate on average. This is partly true for the intellectuals but is not the case with the youth and media leaders. Of course, the media leaders may be centrist in the context of the particular groups included in this study and yet stand to the left in the context of all groups in American society. The mid-point for the leaders in the study probably lies somewhat to the left of the public and perhaps of all "leaders." Nonetheless, it is noteworthy that on all of the equality issues, youths, Democrats, feminists, and blacks are more liberal than the media, and on two of the issues they are joined by labor and intellectuals.

These results generally confirm the polarity of groups on the New Deal issues. Business and Republican leaders anchor the conservative side, while farmers are a bit more moderate. The liberal side, though more spread out, includes all the expected groups: blacks, feminists, Democrats, and labor. This set of issues illustrates most clearly the traditional liberal-conservative split in America. The issue of quotas, over which there is also substantial controversy, illustrates a different pattern of polarization. The conservative side is even more tightly knit, with farm leaders close to business and Republicans. On the other side, however, only feminists and black leaders are decidedly liberal. Democrats are quite close to the center, and organized labor is somewhat to the right of center. Clearly the issue of quotas produces more division among liberals than does the older set of New Deal issues. The gender and race issues resemble the quota issue, with a greater split among the liberal groups. On gender equality, feminist leaders are fairly isolated on the left, with other groups either in the middle of the spectrum or off to the right. On racial equality, Democratic leaders and feminists stand close to black leaders. Finally, income redistribution produces the least polarization, since leaders are united in their opposition to such a radical change.

The overall pattern reflects accurately the nature of equality conflicts in American politics. The issues of the New Deal era continue to split groups along the major fault lines formed in the 1930s. On radical income redistribution, however, although the groups are ordered from left to right much as they are on the New Deal issues, the weight of opinion in all groups is toward a consensual position opposing such a measure. On the noneconomic issues of race and gender equality, especially quotas, the New Deal coalition appears more fragmented, with labor quite far from feminists and blacks.

### Racial and Gender Equality

In many important respects, racial and gender equality are similar issues. In each case, a portion of the population has been discriminated against historically in both formal and informal ways. In each case, the discrimination has been ostensibly justified by elaborate belief systems, sometimes shared by the "victims." In each case, the discrimination has been challenged through political and legal means. And in each case, debate continues over the extent of the remaining inequalities, the principal causes of these inequalities— whether continued discrimination, the aftermath of past discrimination, or differences in motivation or ability—and the proper role of the government in overcoming these inequalities.

Yet in equally important respects, racial and gender equality are dissimilar issues. One of the most significant differences between them is the greater isolation of gender equality as an issue and of feminist leaders as a group. Equality between the sexes has not been incorporated into other equality issues to the same extent as racial equality. Feminist leaders are less likely than black leaders to attribute poverty in general to a discriminatory system. This is partly because women are less likely than blacks to see themselves as poor. The gender dimension stands out most clearly in both the four- and the six-factor analysis solutions, while racial equality is more intertwined with economic issues.

The isolation of gender equality means that the issue is less likely to be part of the general political views that leaders bring to politics. This is shown by the relationship between the leaders' views on the various issues of equality and their ideological descriptions of themselves (Table 6.2). The leaders' ideological identity is most closely related to their attitudes on economic issues, and it is related more closely to their attitudes on racial equality than to their attitudes on equality between men and women. This is true for the leaders as a whole as well as for each of the leadership groups: attitudes on gender are not so well predicted by ideology as are attitudes on the other issues. There are two minor exceptions. Among blacks, gender attitudes are tied a little more closely to their ideological positions, but the relationships are extremely low for all aspects of equality. Among intellectuals, gender attitudes are also more closely linked

**Table 6.2**

Effect of Ideology on New Deal, Race, and Gender Attitudes

| | Variance explained[a] | | |
|---|---|---|---|
| Group | New Deal | Race | Gender |
| All | .49 | .40 | .25 |
| Business | .16 | .21 | .12 |
| Farm | .29 | .18 | .00 |
| Labor | .21 | .24 | .14 |
| Intellectuals | .45 | .19 | .34 |
| Media | .34 | .35 | .16 |
| Republicans | .22 | .26 | .12 |
| Democrats | .32 | .20 | .10 |
| Blacks | .04 | .01 | .06 |
| Feminists | .36 | .27 | .14 |
| Youth | .41 | .35 | .21 |

a. The New Deal, race, and gender factors were each regressed on self-described ideology. The figures reported are $r^2$ statistics.

to ideology than are racial attitudes. In general, however, one's views on gender issues are not nearly so close to the heart of one's self-definition as liberal or conservative as are racial views.

This finding parallels the finding that one's egalitarianism in general tells less about one's position on gender matters than on racial matters. In confirmation of this observation, attitudes toward economic, racial, and gender equality are each predicted by attitudes on all the other equality issues (Table 6.3).[4] The first column of the table indicates to what extent variance in the New Deal attitudes is explained by the other five equality issues, and the next two columns report race and gender. Attitudes on economic equality and racial equality are much more accurately predicted by other equality attitudes than are attitudes toward women's rights. When all leaders are taken together, their positions on the several equality issues account for 69 percent of the variance in New Deal attitudes and 62 percent of the variance in racial attitudes, compared with only 43 percent for the gender scale. This pattern is replicated in each of the leadership groups. The differences among the equality issues are particularly striking for the three established groups: business, farmers, and labor. For business and farm leaders, about twice as much of the variance in economic or racial attitudes can be predicted from other equality attitudes as can be predicted in gender attitudes. For labor the margin is even greater.

That gender attitudes should bear essentially no relation to the other attitudes is ironic, since the issues of gender equality permeate all aspects of life, both public and private, and intimately involve matters of economic, social, and political hierarchy. Income, job opportunities, access to education, legal and political rights—these are the substantive values around which issues of gender equality revolve. Yet, while racial equality tends to be subsumed under economic, political, or social equality, gender equality has remained isolated.

One explanation is that gender equality is an especially sensitive issue which cuts perhaps most closely to the heart of the assumptions and habits of day-to-day life. The demands for greater gender equality seriously challenge ingrained ways of thinking and acting. Thus the issue of inequality between women and men in earnings implicates much more general concerns about the relationship between the sexes than just concerns about equal economic rewards.

Another explanation for the isolation of gender issues is that they

**Table 6.3**

Effect of Other Equality Attitudes on New Deal, Race, and Gender Attitudes

| | Variance explained[a] | | |
|---|---|---|---|
| Group | New Deal | Race | Gender |
| All | .69 | .62 | .43 |
| Business | .52 | .50 | .27 |
| Farm | .58 | .49 | .24 |
| Labor | .50 | .53 | .05 |
| Intellectuals | .66 | .58 | .45 |
| Media | .62 | .59 | .35 |
| Republicans | .64 | .53 | .41 |
| Democrats | .58 | .36 | .28 |
| Blacks | .41 | .30 | .27 |
| Feminists | .64 | .46 | .38 |
| Youth | .72 | .52 | .36 |

a. The New Deal, race, and gender factors were each regressed on the remaining five factors. The figures reported are $r^2$ statistics.

have emerged only recently. When a new challenge to established patterns arises, it needs some time to be incorporated into people's established political and social views. Attention to the new issue focuses on ways in which it differs from other issues rather than on ways in which it relates to them, especially when the new issue challenges habitual ways of life. In this respect, the struggle for gender equality resembles the struggle for racial equality in the American South at the beginning of the civil rights movement. Every demand, from those for access to schools or jobs to those for access to public facilities, was seen as a racial issue, not as an educational, economic, or social issue. Perhaps attitudes toward gender issues are in just such a stage of development. Only when racial or gender demands are recognized as legitimate do they become part of larger social issues involving other aspects of equality. This acceptance has gone further in relation to race than to gender.

Yet another factor that helps account for the isolation of gender issues is that many feminist leaders have not conceived of their movement and its agenda in economic terms, certainly not as much as black leaders have. This difference partly reflects the relative priorities that feminist leaders assign to economic, social, or political goals; it also reflects the fact that gender cuts across class lines more than race does, making it far more difficult for feminist leaders to appeal to women in unambiguous economic class terms.

There are signs, however, that this state of affairs may be changing rapidly. The growing feminization of poverty, for example, has strengthened the link between issues of gender discrimination and issues of economic equality. In recent years feminist organizations have placed greater emphasis on economic issues in their demands.[5] This shift is reflected in the attitudes of women. Although data on leadership attitudes for the early 1980s are not available, some evidence from the population at large suggests that a closer relationship has emerged between gender issues and other issues.

Public opinion data for the years 1976 and 1980 show the relationship among views on three gender issues—the proper role of women, the extent of sex discrimination, and the Equal Rights Amendment—and two more general political indicators—a liberal or conservative ideology and attitudes toward a government guarantee of jobs (Table 6.4). Little change took place between 1976 and 1980 in the relationship between gender issues and a liberal or conservative orientation. In both years, ideology was strongly related to support for the ERA and moderately related to the more general

**Table 6.4**

Correlation Between Gender Issues and Other Political Views,
1976 and 1980[a]

| Gender question | Self-described political ideology | | Attitude toward government job guarantees | |
|---|---|---|---|---|
| | 1976 | 1980 | 1976 | 1980 |
| Proper role of women, "in" versus "outside" the home | .25 | .24 | .07 | .11 |
| Presence of sex discrimination | .28 | .24 | .13 | .08 |
| Support for Equal Rights Amendment | .46 | .50 | .13 | .35 |

a. Based on public opinion data from the University of Michigan, Center for Political Studies, 1976 and 1980 American National Election Studies. The correlations reported are gamma coefficients.

issues of an equal role for women and the degree of gender discrimination. A change took place, however, between 1976 and 1980 in the relationship of gender issues to the economic issue of jobs. In 1976 all three gender issues were unrelated to the jobs issue. In 1980 the issue of the ERA was related to the jobs issue, although the other two gender issues remained separate. This suggests some movement toward integrating gender with other issues.

This recent trend, which adds an important qualification to the relatively weak historical correlation between gender and economic issues, leads directly to a final explanation for the isolation of gender issues. The specific change in relation to the ERA probably stemmed from the positions taken by the political parties in 1980, when the ERA first lost its bipartisan support and thus became a party issue. The manner in which political issues typically are raised enhances the likelihood that they will remain distinct while they are still new, rather than becoming subsumed under other issues. A new issue, such as gender equality, is usually advanced by an interest group which concentrates on that single issue. The very goal of single-issue groups is to keep their claims pure and separate from other concerns. In contrast, political parties are multi-issue organizations which attempt to package disparate issues into a more general agenda of concerns. Parties are reluctant to take a firm stand on new issues like gender equality, for fear that the newly developing controversies might disturb their fragile coalitions. Only gradually do new issues work their way, and sometimes force their way, onto party agendas.

Not only do feminist issues stand out from other issues but the feminist leaders stand out from the other leaders. They are more likely than any other leaders to call themselves liberals and are more likely to hold views on equality that are consistently egalitarian. Furthermore, they are more cohesive than are other leadership groups on the equality issue that most affects their group. That is, feminist leaders are more cohesive on gender equality than black leaders are on civil rights issues or labor leaders are on economic issues.

The degree to which the position of feminist leaders on the issue of gender equality differs from the positions of other leadership groups on the equality issue that most concerns them is also demonstrated by the fact that feminists are considerably more liberal on gender issues than might be predicted from their stands on other issues (Table 6.5). The "constants" from the equations used to predict views on the New Deal, gender, and race issues based upon views on the other equality issues as well as self-described ideology reveal

**Table 6.5**

Comparison of New Deal, Race, and Gender Attitudes with Expected Attitudes Based on Other Political Views

| | Constants from equations[a] | | |
|---|---|---|---|
| Group | New Deal | Race | Gender |
| Business | −.48 | .07 | −.13 |
| Farm | −.06 | −.14 | −.60 |
| Labor | .27 | .09 | −.08 |
| Intellectuals | .07 | .00 | .00 |
| Media | .05 | .06 | −.01 |
| Republicans | −.31 | −.05 | −.12 |
| Democrats | .13 | .25 | .07 |
| Blacks | .08 | .32 | −.24 |
| Feminists | .04 | .16 | .65 |

a. The New Deal, race, and gender factors were each regressed on the remaining five factors and self-described ideology. The figures reported are the constants from each equation. Positive numbers indicate that a group is more liberal on the particular issue than expected from its scores on other issues. Negative numbers indicate that a group is more conservative than expected.

the extent to which a group is more liberal or conservative on a particular issue than one would predict on the basis of its position on the other issues and its ideological leanings. If a group's position on a particular issue is completely consistent with the position it takes on other issues, the constant is close to zero. This is the case for two groups, intellectual and media leaders. On each of the equality issues, the positions of these two groups are quite close to what one would expect from their positions on the other issues. Yet other groups show substantial deviations from the expected position. On New Deal economic attitudes, business leaders are substantially more conservative, as indicated by a negative constant, than would be expected from their other attitudes, as are Republican leaders, though to a lesser extent. In contrast, labor leaders hold somewhat more liberal New Deal attitudes than one would expect on the basis of their other positions.

The comparison between race and gender shows that blacks are more liberal on race than one would predict from their other positions. However, blacks are less distinctly to the left on race issues than feminists are on gender issues. Indeed, the most substantial deviation from a predicted score occurs among feminists on the gender issue; they are a full .65 units more liberal on the gender issue than one would predict. In other words, though they are a generally liberal group, feminists are much more liberal on the issue of gender than their other views would suggest. The evidence confirms two other conclusions. Farm leaders are not only conservative on issues of gender equality but also more conservative than one would predict from their other views. Furthermore, feminist leaders are somewhat more liberal on the race issue than one would predict, whereas black leaders are somewhat more conservative on issues of gender equality than their other positions would suggest.

The special nature of gender as an issue and of feminists as the group most attuned to that issue are really two sides of the same coin. Gender's distinctiveness may be closely related to its newness on the political agenda. Feminist leaders are distinctive less in terms of their socioeconomic characteristics than in terms of their political positions. And the political position on which they are most distinctive is that of equal rights for women.

## Sources of Different Attitudes

American leaders of various groups have quite distinctive views on equality. Their views can be linked to their leadership positions either by selection or by socialization. In the case of selection, those who have particular views choose, or are chosen, to enter a particular institutional context. Those who strongly favor racial equality are more likely to become leaders of civil rights groups. Similarly— though the link is not as strong—those who oppose changes in the capitalist system are more likely to choose a business career than are those who favor such changes. Socialization within the institutional setting also plays a role. Those who occupy a particular position, such as a civil rights leader or a business executive, are gradually influenced by their exposure to the dominant ideology of the group.

Another possible, though not probable, source of the groups' distinctive ideologies toward equality is their varying demographic composition. However, when the effects of demographic variables are eliminated and everything else is more or less equal, the groups still differ from each other in terms of their views toward equality (Figure 6.2). The top line in the figure shows the placement of each of the leadership groups on three of the equality issues. For purposes of uniformity, intellectuals are arbitrarily placed at the zero point on each issue, a choice that does not affect the results for any of the groups. The second line presents the average liberalism score for each of the groups after the effects of such demographic variables as family income, education, age, and religion are taken into account.[6] The group differences in ideology, reported in the third line, are also controlled for party affiliation in addition to demographic characteristics. When demographic factors are taken into account, the groups are quite distinct from each other on the New Deal, race, and gender issues. Indeed, there are relatively few changes in the average group attitudes when demography is eliminated. The groups do not converge to any appreciable degree, as they would have if the demographic characteristics of the leaders rather than their institutional position determined attitudes on equality.[7] When the effects of party affiliation are also removed from the attitudes of the leaders, the differences among the groups shrink somewhat. The most conservative groups appear less conservative, and the most liberal groups appear less liberal, at least on the New Deal and race issues. With respect to the gender issue, partisanship is unrelated to the positions of the two extreme groups, feminists and farmers. For business, however, party affiliation does make a difference. Apparently, Democratic business leaders are more liberal on matters of women's rights than are Republican business leaders.

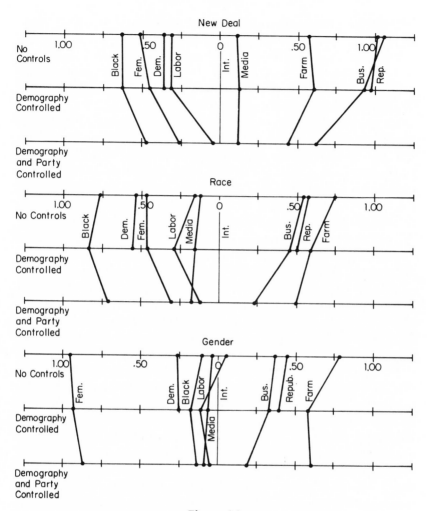

**Figure 6.2**
Equality Attitudes Controlling for Demography
and Party Affiliation[a]
a. Positions shown are averages for each group.

It comes as no surprise that party affiliation should diminish these group differences. Among the leaders, Democrats are predictably more liberal on the New Deal issues, and Republicans are more conservative. Since black, labor, and feminist groups are largely Democratic, while business and farm leaders are largely Republican, the groups converge toward the middle when one eliminates party.

Yet feminists and farmers remain solid on the issue of gender equality regardless of their party affiliation.

However, even after taking partisanship into account, the groups still differ markedly in their equality attitudes. Furthermore, it is hard to know which comes first, group affiliation or partisanship. That business leaders are more likely to be Republican could be either because Republicans are more likely to go into business or because business leaders are more likely to vote Republican.

Group affiliation, in short, is closely related to the leaders' views on equality. The distinctive positions of leaders in different groups are linked to their institutional roles. In this sense, the potential conflicts over equality may be understood as being structured by the various sectors of society reflected in the leadership groups.

Demographic characteristics do not explain away the attitudinal differences among the groups. However, this does not mean that background factors are totally unrelated to attitude. Specific demographic factors are still important within certain groups. Indeed, since some demographic factors can push a group in the liberal direction while others push it in the conservative direction, the demographic characteristics of a given group can be quite potent without changing the average position of the group.

The impact of demography on attitude position is shown by inverting the analysis and eliminating, or "controlling for," the impact of group membership (Table 6.6). Party identification is the best predictor of views on most of the issues. This is particularly true of the New Deal issues. It is natural that party effects are greatest on the set of issues that has long formed the major cleavage between the two parties. The only issue on which party is not the best predictor is gender equality. Party is important there, but age and, to a lesser extent, education strongly affect one's position on gender issues. These results further reinforce the distinctiveness of the various sets of equality issues. Gender equality is strikingly different from the New Deal issues. It is the least partisan issue. Party makes the most difference on the most partisan of issues, the New Deal. In addition, age is important only on gender equality, as might be expected for the newest issue.

Religious differences seem relatively unimportant. Catholics are a bit more conservative than are other religious groups on gender equality; Jews are somewhat more liberal, especially on the New Deal factor. Income and education differentiate between economic and social issues. Higher income is associated with more conserv-

**Table 6.6**

Effects of Social Background, Party, and Group Membership on Equality Attitudes[a]

| | Equality issue | | | | | | | | | | | |
|---|---|---|---|---|---|---|---|---|---|---|---|---|
| Social trait | New Deal | | Gender | | Redistribution | | Quotas | | Causes of inequality | | Race | |
| Family income | -.09 | (31.6) | .08 | (20.4) | -.14 | (49.7) | -.03 | (2.2) | .03 | (2.3) | .03 | (3.7) |
| Age | -.03 | (2.6) | -.19 | (76.3) | -.00 | (0.0) | -.07 | (12.6) | -.08 | (12.2) | -.06 | (7.1) |
| Education | .01 | (0.5) | .11 | (33.4) | -.01 | (0.1) | .06 | (10.8) | .09 | (21.6) | .10 | (28.9) |
| Protestant | -.06 | (7.5) | -.01 | (0.2) | -.03 | (1.6) | -.01 | (0.1) | -.02 | (0.6) | -.05 | (3.7) |
| Catholic | -.01 | (0.3) | -.08 | (10.9) | .01 | (0.1) | -.02 | (0.9) | -.03 | (1.6) | -.03 | (2.1) |
| Jewish | .06 | (10.6) | .03 | (2.8) | .03 | (1.4) | .01 | (0.2) | .04 | (3.3) | .05 | (7.0) |
| Partisanship | .41 | (462.9) | .17 | (58.8) | .27 | (102.9) | .28 | (168.5) | .29 | (158.1) | .33 | (231.5) |
| $r^2$ | .50 | | .37 | | .21 | | .38 | | .28 | | .37 | |

a. The six equality factors were each regressed on social background characteristics, party, and group membership. The coefficients for group membership are not reported. The figures reported are beta coefficients with $F$ ratios in parentheses.

ative positions on New Deal-type issues and income redistribution, but with more liberal positions on gender equality. Higher education corresponds more generally to a liberal position on social issues, but it has no bearing on economic issues. Status clearly relates differently to social and economic issues. The higher one's income, the more conservative one is on economic issues, but the impact of income on social issues is either liberal or neutral. More education, in contrast, leads to social liberality; it has no effect on economic attitude.[8]

**National Priorities**

Equality is a dominant value in American life; few claim to oppose it. Indeed, since there are so many "equalities," no one is obliged to express outright support for inequality. One simply prefers one type of equality to another. People do not so much oppose equality of result as favor equality of opportunity, allowing those who have more talent or skill, or who work harder, to receive their just deserts. Nor do Americans explicitly oppose equality for women or blacks. Few individuals are willing to say that they favor gender or racial inequality. The issue turns on whether that equality should be secured by government intervention or by individual effort. One way in which people choose among equalities is by assigning priorities. Equality of one sort or another may be desirable, all else being equal. But all else is never equal, and the real issue is the importance of achieving equality, given the other needs and problems facing the nation.

American leaders give different priorities to equality as a national goal, particularly to equality for women and for blacks, two of the most recent movements for equality, both of which are jockeying for position on the national agenda (Figure 6.3). In ranking ten national goals in terms of their importance, American leaders confirm the existence of differences among the various groups.[9] Gender equality appears at or near the botom of the ratings more often than any other goal. Half of the groups place it last, and everyone but feminist leaders, who rank it first, and youth place it among the three lowest categories. Equality for blacks does not fare much better. Six of the ten groups place it in the bottom three categories. Only blacks rate it near the top, considering unemployment a touch more important. For most groups, economic matters rank near the top—inflation above all, but jobs and energy too.

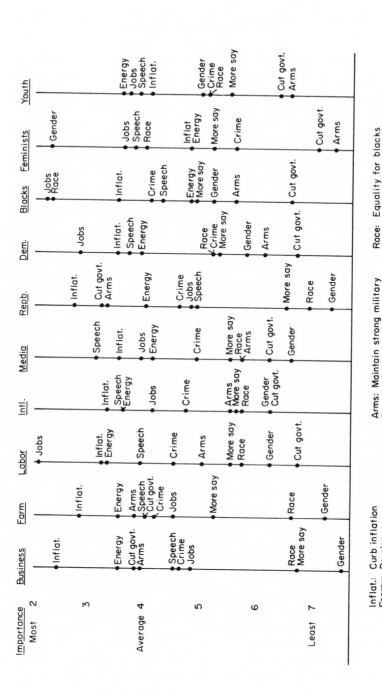

**Figure 6.3**
National Priorities by Group

When demands are made for a new form of equality, leaders of established groups are likely to offer resistance, assigning it a low priority. Business, farm, and Republican leaders rank equality for blacks and for women accordingly. But other groups place these issues low as well. Labor leaders rank the goal of cutting government last, but equality for women and blacks next to last. The low priority among labor leaders is a clear indication of the way the issues of gender and racial equality can fragment the New Deal coalition. Intellectuals and media people are similar to labor in their priorities.

Another pattern emerging from the leaders' rankings is the contrast between blacks and feminists. For blacks, unemployment is the top priority, rated slightly above racial equality. In third place they put another economic issue, inflation. Issues of race and economics are closely related to each other. These results give further evidence that black leaders see the question of racial inequality in an economic light. Yet the leaders' attitudes on gender equality are independent of their economic views. For feminists, who attach more weight to gender equality than does any other group, economic issues are less important. Curbing unemployment is rated in second place, but far below equality for women, and inflation comes even farther down the list. Feminists, it seems, are less apt to evaluate equality from an economic perspective than is the other challenging group.

The leaders of the two political parties also have contrasting views. For Republican leaders, the major issues are controlling inflation, cutting government, and building national defense. Curbing unemployment is very low on their list, and equality for blacks and women is at the bottom. Democrats reverse this order, at least in part. Reducing unemployment comes first by a wide margin. On the Democratic wish list, the Republicans' second and third priorities—cutting government and strengthening the military—come last. The Democrats, like their partisan opposites, are concerned about inflation, but they do not elevate it above the need for fuller employment. Nor do they rank equality for blacks and women at the bottom. The two parties overlap considerably in their views on income redistribution; there is a consensus against radical income leveling. However, when it comes to policy preferences on matters of equality, the parties are less like identical twins than like distant relatives.

In some sense, each of the leadership groups places most emphasis on those issues which best serve its own interests. The economically oriented groups focus on economic priorities. For business and farm groups the concern is inflation and energy. Labor attaches the highest priority to jobs. The media leaders deem free speech most crucial, and intellectuals rank it second only to stemming inflation. Blacks are most concerned with jobs and racial equality, feminists with gender equality.

Finally, youth generally favor gender and racial equality, but these are not their highest priorities. Their views are more mixed, as shown by the fact that no single goal ranks very high. If they agree on anything, it is a combination of four issues: energy, reducing unemployment, free speech, and curbing inflation. Though they lean to the left on some equality issues, their basic orientation is toward the creation of a sound economy where basic freedoms are protected—a society of opportunity, not of radical equality.

Each group has a distinctive position on the various aspects of equality, reflecting its own personal interests. There may be common ground among all groups, especially when it comes to the rejection of radical income redistribution or strong affirmative action. But the views of American leaders on specific issues show that there is much room for disagreement on policies and priorities within that framework.

# Political Parties

In America, as in most democratic nations, the parties are the principal instruments in the political struggle over equality. Though they differ from their counterparts in a number of other countries—as in having no rigidly ideological positions or intimate ties to particular groups—the American political parties have traditionally staked out divergent positions on issues of economic equality and, to a lesser extent, on other aspects of equality. The differences between the parties are real and crucial. So are the differences within the parties. American parties are complex coalitions of groups with different positions and priorities. Hence, a diversity of views is found within each party.

Although American parties diverge on matters of equality, the fact that they are broad coalitions shapes and limits that divergence. For one thing, the parties' differing views on equality are bounded by the American ideology of equal opportunity. Furthermore, the multiplicity of groups within each party—each group with a somewhat different equality issue at the top of its agenda—moderates not only the differences between parties but also to some extent the views of the groups themselves. If there was only one basic equality issue derived from a single underlying dimension—say a conflict over distribution between workers and the owners of the means of production—the unification of many groups into one party struggle might heighten the clarity and intensity of the conflict. But since there are many distinct equality issues, the uniting of interests into parties can mute the conflict.

The representation of multiple equalities in the parties has strong historical roots. Six sets of issues underlie the attitudes of American leaders on equality. This chapter will highlight three of them: economic, racial, and gender issues. These three equality issues entered the arena of partisan dispute at different periods. The oldest issue, less a bone than a fossil of contention, is economic equality. From the origins of the American party system, conflicts over the distribution of wealth have shaped the contrasting character of the two major parties and have summoned into existence many minor parties as well.[1] Indeed, on the issue of economic equality the American system has most closely resembled a strong party system offering a clear policy choice tied to pledges of sharply different government action. This was especially true during the New Deal, particularly in the years surrounding the election of 1936.

The New Deal had three crucial consequences for equality, each of which has influenced today's political parties. First, though the New Deal involved no commitment to wholesale redistribution, it had a major impact on economic equality by creating a variety of social measures that placed a floor under income. Second, the New Deal created a structure of influence in which labor acquired political power commensurate to that of business. And third, the New Deal was largely silent on several equality issues that later emerged forcefully, in particular the issues of gender and racial equality.

The New Deal era created the party system and public philosophy that dominated American politics for a generation and still play a role today. The key issue that propelled the New Deal was economic equality, in particular the legitimacy of government intervention to regulate the economy and to increase social welfare. The egalitarianism of the New Deal did not seek the redistribution of income so much as the redistribution of political power by altering the bargaining authority and status of employees vis-à-vis employers. But even though the main struggle was over political power, that power was related to economic issues. The disputants were business and labor; the dispute, which hinged on control over economic decisions and the benefits thereof, became the main cleavage of the New Deal party system: Democrats and Republicans divided along economic lines, between the interests of business and labor. The New Deal and the depression of the 1930s gave the partisan division the cast it has today. The New Deal cemented the ties of the working class to the Democratic party and placed the two parties on opposite sides on the issues of social welfare and government intrusion into the economy. In so doing, it may have deterred the conflict over equality from taking a more radical turn. The New Deal commit-ment to equality lay fully within the American ideological tradition. It concentrated on welfare and ignored redistribution as a goal in itself.

The political contest of the 1930s did not include the race and gender dimensions of equality. The New Deal Democratic party nimbly sidestepped the issue of racial equality. Not until the 1960s, after a long period of uncertainty and division, did the Democratic party become the champion of racial equality, and it was rewarded with the overwhelming support of black voters. Today the incor-poration of racial issues into the party system is almost complete. Yet the incorporation of gender issues, which began only in the 1970s, has a long way to go. Although the parties now differ in their positions on gender issues, with the Democrats again on the egali-tarian side, these differences are less pronounced. Furthermore, though women now lean in a Democratic direction, the gender differential between the parties is still minor compared with the differences on economics or race.

Gender equality, however, like race equality earlier, seems grad-ually to be gaining a stronger footing in partisan politics. As long as extrapartisan interest groups take the lead in presenting the issue, it will be seen as unconnected with the other major issues of the day. Conversely, as it is taken up by political parties, this previously isolated issue will become part of a larger political framework.

**Differences Between Parties**

The American party system is distinguished by its lack of sharp ideological contrast. Unlike parties in many other countries, the two major U.S. parties are broad coalitions without will-defined political world views. Yet despite the familiar complaint that these parties play Tweedle-dum and Tweedle-dee, they are by no means so vague as to be indistinguishable, as shown by the attitudes of party leaders. The progressive polarization of the two parties on economic, racial, and finally gender equality can be seen in many contexts, especially in their platforms, the support for the parties among interest groups, and the attitudes of Democratic and Repub-lican partisans.

Party platforms are often dismissed as meaningless artifacts, knocked together out of lavish, righteous, and vague pronounce-ments that are likely to be forgotten after the election, if not sooner.

But platforms are neither vacuous nor useless for gauging party differences. They are the face that each party aims to show the public. Their content reflects the alignment of forces within each party. Nor are they ignored by candidates once elected.[2] Party platforms on matters of equality are thus a good sign of the differences between the parties.

On the issue of economic equality, the Democratic platform in 1976 contained three times as many references to matters of distribution as did the Republican platform. A similar difference appeared in relation to unemployment. As far back as the 1920s, there was a consistently higher level of concern with unemployment in the Democratic platform than in the Republican.[3]

Indeed, the party differences on economic equality date back further. Comparison of platforms reveals that leaders of the major parties have consistently diverged in their stance toward equality in reference to a wide range of issues, including taxation, government spending, and civil rights.[4] The thrust of party rhetoric reflects two fundamentally different approaches to equality. For the Republican party, the recurrent theme from 1856 to the present has been the citizens' equal rights to liberty. The phrase "the equality of all individuals in their right to life, liberty, and the pursuit of happiness" rings out again and again in Republican platforms. The party has consistently interpreted the defense of equality as the protection of equality of opportunity. Its stress is more on the opportunity than on the equality—more on the freedom from restraint than on equality of result.

Democratic party leaders echo this concern for equal opportunity, but with a different rhetorical emphasis. Since 1848 the party has declared itself the opponent of privilege. Adopting Thomas Jefferson as its patriarch, the Democratic party has frequently declared its adherence to "the Jeffersonian maxim, 'equal rights to all; special privileges to none.' " The party's opposition to privilege first arose as part of its defense of states' rights and its criticism of the favored treatment accorded to some states by the federal government. Eventually this opposition evolved into a general repudiation of economic privilege. The parties are thus not far apart in their abstract notions of the ideal form of equality. As close as the parties may be in principle, however, the distinction between their concrete approaches to equality is more than a matter of nuance. While both parties honor the concept of equality of opportunity, the Democratic party places its stress on the word *equality*. The different emphases and interpretations of the two parties lead to distinctly different forms of government intervention.

This difference is revealed most clearly and consistently in relation to economic equality, as opposed to racial or gender equality. The two parties have long been at odds over the issue of government economic assistance. Since the New Deal, Democrats have vigorously promoted social welfare programs. Their party platforms have bulged with proposals for slum clearance and low-rent housing, urban renewal, a lower retirement age for women, a higher minimum wage, jobs programs, and extended social security and welfare benefits. The Republicans have generally pledged to extend benefits to the aged, handicapped, and unemployed. Yet these commitments have always been couched in terms considerably more equivocal and less aggressive than those of the Democrats and have generally extended to proposals that, if they did not help the poor, would certainly not hurt the rich. For example, the Republicans have claimed that the best way to protect social security benefits is to stop inflation, and they have continually chastised the Democratic party for neglecting the potential of free enterprise measures to reduce poverty.

Taxation is, in theory, one of the principal government instruments for altering the distribution of income. The Democratic party's commitment to limitations on privilege is reflected in the centrality of taxation issues in its platforms. Since 1916 the party has demanded tax reform in order to equalize the tax burden, called for the elimination of tax loopholes that favor special groups, opposed regressive sales taxes, and denounced tax breaks for dividend income and capital gains. The party's most radical economic pronouncement appeared in its 1972 platform, which called for a restructuring of "economic relationships throughout the entire society in order to ensure the equitable distribution of wealth and power." Other platforms have been somewhat more muted, but the same themes have appeared. Taxation issues have not figured prominently in Republican party platforms. When they do appear, they take the form of opposition to tax policies that destroy incentives to work and of support for policies that encourage capital investment. Their platforms have generally put more emphasis on economic growth, including a trickle-down theory to foster it, than on economic redistribution. Tax measures of this sort were prominent in the 1980 Republican platform.

In contrast to economic issues, racial and gender issues have historically inspired more convergence in party platforms. Although the Republican party was the earliest champion of civil rights, supporting black emancipation and enfranchisement long before the Democrats, who did not make an unequivocal commitment to racial equality even during the New Deal, the platforms of the two parties gradually came to sound quite similar in civil rights policy. The parties began to go their separate ways only in the 1960s and 1970s. Republicans declared unyielding opposition to school busing for achieving racial balance, while Democrats refused to rule out the policy. The Republicans forthrightly opposed the use of racial quotas in universities; the Democrats favored them.

With regard to women's rights, too, the two parties have until recently expressed similar views in their platforms. Both favored the extension of suffrage to women by 1916; both came to oppose job discrimination based on sex by the 1940s; both favored a constitutional amendment on equal rights for women by 1940; and both used the slogan "Equal pay for equal work" by the 1950s. Differences emerged only in the 1970s, when the Republican party made clear its distaste for affirmative action programs. In 1980 these differences sharpened when, in a controversial move that stirred a small revolt within the party, the GOP rescinded its support for the Equal Rights Amendment.

The party platforms trace a pattern of gradual incorporation of the three equality issues into the party system. By the 1980s, the two parties presented themselves to the electorate on the opposite sides of economic, racial, and gender issues. The gradual change has also occurred in the voter support for the two parties. At roughly the same time that the party positions were clarified on economics in the 1930s, on race in the 1960s and 1970s, and on gender in the 1980s, differences appeared in the partisan identification of the poor, minorities, and women. In the 1930s blue-collar workers mounted the Democratic bandwagon; in the 1960s black Americans did the same. The discovery of the gender gap in the 1980s signaled a similar, though not nearly so complete, migration of women toward the Democrats.[5]

This historical pattern emerges clearly in the positions of adherents of the two parties. Consider the correlation between the party allegiance of citizens and their views on economic, racial, and gender issues (Figure 7.1). Higher correlations signify greater distinctiveness between the policy positions of Democratic and Republican partisans. Clear partisan differences in economic attitudes, which first appeared in the 1930s, have since been fairly constant. But Demo-

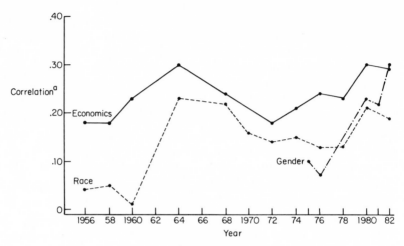

**Figure 7.1**
Correlation Between Party Allegiance and Opinion on Economic, Racial,
and Gender Equality, 1956–1982
a. Correlations are gamma coefficients. The correlations between party identification and attitudes toward job guarantees and minority aid were calculated from National Election Study surveys conducted by the Center for Political Studies, University of Michigan; the correlations between party identification and attitudes toward the ERA are based on Gallup surveys, *Gallup Opinion Index.*

crats and Republicans were by no means distinct on racial issues in the 1950s. Only in the 1960s, beginning most clearly in 1964, did differences appear between party supporters on matters of race.[6] Nor did these differences merely reflect the racial composition of the support groups for the two parties, because differences were apparent among white party supporters as well. The parties remained similar on gender issues much longer. Partisan differences on these issues were a phenomenon of the late 1970s. Indeed, some of the gender issues first appeared in 1980.

The contrast with the way gender issues were incorporated into partisan politics in another democracy, Sweden, is most revealing.[7] The Swedish Social Democratic Party worked deliberately and successfully to make gender equality a subset of the general issue of equality and not a separate, isolated set of demands. In particular, this meant getting feminists to focus on issues related to the status of women in the marketplace—in other words, economic issues. Neither party in the United States was able to recast feminist demands in terms that followed the traditional lines of party cleavage.

Instead, feminism became associated most closely with issues like abortion, quotas, and the ERA, which undercut and disrupted traditional party support, especially among the Democrats. In Sweden, such issues never became central to political debates over feminism, and the Social Democrats shaped feminist demands; in the United States, feminist demands transformed the Democrats. Since 1980, in an effort to capitalize on the "gender gap"—the preponderance of female support enjoyed by Democrats, largely because of opposition to Reagan's cuts in social programs and his hawkish foreign policy—the Democrats have moved quickly to solidify and expand their support among women. This effort culminated in the nomination of a woman for Vice President. It remains to be seen whether Democratic efforts to woo female support and the party's stands on gender-related issues will increase the partisan differences in gender equality which first appeared in 1980.

## Divisions Within Parties

Although the two parties have become more polarized on the issues of equality, they have not internally become more homogeneous. If the social disadvantages of economic, racial, and gender inequality concerned the same populations, the party positions could be straightforward. However, the older and newer equality issues do not coincide neatly. Some political groups demand that inequality be redressed in all three areas; other groups are concerned about only one. This pattern has caused severe strains and dislocations within the parties, requiring adjustments in the positions of their leaders and shifting alignments among the voters at large. In short, the interplay of the old and new equality issues has created unstable party coalitions.

The metamorphosis of the equality issue into a multidimensional conflict has affected the divisions within the parties. At the heart of each party is a triangular relationship among party leaders, leaders of allied interest groups, and rank-and-file supporters. Party leaders include both the leaders of the party as an organization, such as party officials on national, state, and county committees, and the leaders of the party in government, such as officials elected under the party labels. Allied elites are the leaders of organized interests that associate with one or the other of the parties. The leadership study contains several such groups: labor, black, and feminist leaders, who generally ally with the Democratic party; business and, to a lesser extent, farm leaders, who usually ally with the Republican party. The rank-and-file supporters of the two parties are made up of two groups: the large number of people who regularly vote for or identify with one or the other of the parties and the smaller number who are active in campaigns and in party organizations. Neither group is homogeneous.

In choosing what position to take on equality issues, the party leaders may be moved by their reading of the voters whose votes they seek, by their perception of the interest group leaders whose support they also want, and by their own personal views. To complicate matters, the party leaders themselves are by no means a homogeneous group. Local leaders may differ from national leaders, elected leaders may differ from nonelected, and any of those categories may itself be torn by dissent. To add one more complication, the causality is not all in one direction. Party leaders may respond to their mass or interest group constituencies, but they may also influence the positions that these constituencies take.

The views of party leaders affect and are affected by the views of those affiliated with them. The flow of influence governs the way in which the equality issues emerge in American politics. These issues are potentially polarizing, because where one group gains equality, another loses privilege. The polarization can stem from any of three places: from the public itself, with members of the affected population groups taking clearly opposing stances on the issues, such as black voters versus white, men versus women, rich versus poor, and workers versus management; from the party leaders, who present more distinct alternatives than the positions held by the public; or from the interest group leaders, who take more extreme positions than either the mass of voters or the party leaders. Under the first and last possibilities, the party leaders might take centrist positions while surrounded by more extreme voters and interest groups. As vote maximizers, the party leaders would choose the middle as a way of gathering the largest vote even if the public were more polarized. Under the second possibility, the party leaders might occupy the extremes on equality issues, presenting clear ideological alternatives, perhaps at the risk of losing votes. In fact, however, the leaders are presented with an even more complex situation. They usually stand between their allied interest groups and their mass supporters. Each of the allied groups is more extreme in advancing its particular equality issue than are the party leaders. The party leaders, in turn, outflank their mass support base, whose position is more moderate.

This situation places the party leaders squarely in the middle of the conflict over equality. They are caught between special interest groups with distinct positions on equality and their own rank-and-file supporters, who hold less extreme views. This is especially true of the Democrats, but it applies to the Republicans as well. The party leaders are thus in a position to link those who push for distinctive equality policies to their potential supporters in the public.

The situation is rendered still more complex by variations among the several equality issues. The different configurations of commitments and attitudes pose more of a problem for the Democrats. Republican adherents line up quite consistently from issue to issue; not so for the Democrats.

The variation over time is also crucial. This variation takes two forms. In the short run, there is the distinction between what party leaders believe on an issue and how they present that issue during a primary election or general election campaign. The leaders of the two parties may hold polar positions but present more moderate positions in the election. In the long run, there is variation from election to election. The party leadership changes, often in response to the rising and falling stars of presidential candidates from various wings of the parties. And even if the composition remains the same, leaders may change their views. Such changes have taken place in both parties over the past two decades. But these shifts may really reflect a change in the salience of the various equality issues, such as the addition of race and gender to the equality agenda.

The sources of division within and between the parties on the three issues of equality may be the rank-and-file supporters, the special-interest support groups, or the party leaders. In other words, parties may respond to the pull of voters, to the push of members of their coalition of special interests, or to the sway of the leaders themselves. The configuration, furthermore, may vary from issue to issue.

On the whole, party differentiation is sparked more by the leaders than by the push or pull of supporters; that is, the party leaders are more apt to lead than to be led. Studies have shown these leaders to be more ideological than their followers and more likely to out-flank their followers on political issues, with Democrats to the left of their supporters and Republicans to the right of theirs.[8] Yet party leaders remain political power brokers, eager to create and maintain coalitions. They are not likely to choose outlying positions if to do so would endanger mass support. Any move to a position far from their supporters is likely to be made in response to pressure from those more intensely committed to one equality issue or another, the special interest groups allied to each party. Thus, party leaders are situated rather uncomfortably between their voting base and their allied interest groups.

How uncomfortable the position is depends on the issue involved. For the older issue of economic equality, the various components of the party coalition have had time to converge. For the two newer issues, there may be more tension between leaders and followers. Furthermore, the allied interest groups may be divided among themselves. The addition of the new equality issues to the party agenda may create the kind of strain within the party coalition, especially for the Democrats, that had previously been worked out in the economic sphere.

### Democrats Versus Republicans

In terms of party position as reflected in platforms, the Democrats and Republicans have been divided most unequivocally and for the longest time on economic equality, followed by racial equality, and then by gender equality. A similar ordering of party differences marks the attitudes of the party leaders. The distinctions between the two sets of party leaders are greatest on economic issues, somewhat narrower on racial matters, and narrower still on gender equality—despite a sharp party difference in all three equality issues. This is true not only for the party leaders but also for all the leaders when they are divided according to their own party affiliations (Figure 7.2). The data for black, feminist, and labor leaders who are Republican must be viewed with caution since these categories are small. On all three equality issues, Democrats are generally more liberal than Republicans. Party differences exist in all three domains of equality, the differences are sharper in economic than in racial equality and are in turn greater in racial than in gender equality, and the party distinctions are sharper between the party leaders themselves than between the adherents of the two parties in the other leadership groups. The only exception is gender equality, where Democratic and Republican labor leaders differ more than do Democratic and Republican party leaders, but since only four percent of the labor leaders are Republican, the number of cases is too small to confirm that distinction, plausible though it may be. These partisan differences across the three equality issues are real and robust. Even after taking other demographic characteristics and group membership into

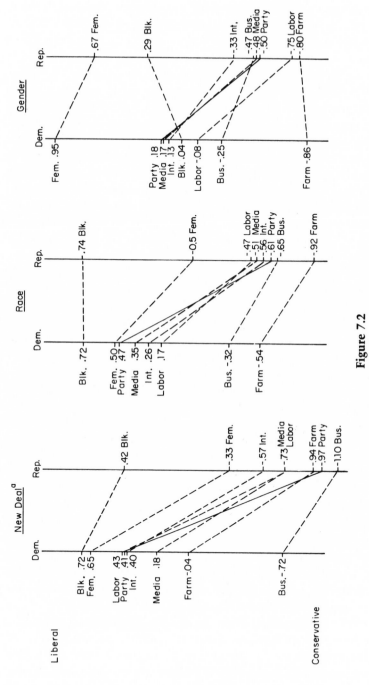

**Figure 7.2**

Attitudes on Equality Issues by Party

a. Figures are average factor scores for each group. Note that only 8 percent of black leaders, 10 percent of feminist leaders, and 4 percent of labor leaders are Republicans.

account, Democrats differ from Republicans within each of the leadership groups.[9] The parties clearly are smack in the middle of the equality debate.

### Party Leaders and Supporters

There are two possible ways in which party leaders might conduct themselves in relation to equality issues. They could assume either a passive role, simply mirroring the polarities within the general public, or an active role, stoutly posing choices for the public. In other words, the differences between the Democratic and Republican parties could reflect a polarization within their separate support groups or could mean that the party leaders themselves are more polarized than their followers.

Studies by Herbert McClosky and others on the relationship between party leaders and party supporters on a wide range of issues, some related to equality, found that in the late 1950s Republican and Democratic convention delegates outflanked rank-and-file party supporters. Democratic leaders were more liberal than Democrats at large; Republican leaders more conservative than their Republican supporters. The evidence suggested that party leaders were in the vanguard; they exhibited a sharper polarization than existed in the public. In addition, both Democratic and Republican supporters were closer in attitude to Democratic leaders than to Republican leaders.[10]

Jeane Kirkpatrick found that in 1972 party leaders still outflanked party supporters, but both Democrats and Republicans in the public were closer in outlook to Republican party leaders than to Democratic. This change was thought to reflect the growing liberalization, if not radicalization, of Democratic leaders, especially McGovernites in the "New Politics" wing of the party.[11]

To compare attitudes of party leaders and their rank-and-file supporters, four measures are used here: economic attitudes, racial attitudes, feminist attitudes, and overall equality attitudes. The measures are somewhat different from the scales used thus far, since some questions were omitted from the mass survey (see Appendix D). The leaders are also divided into their local and national components to allow for finer comparisons.[12]

On the overall equality measure which combines issues from all three domains, both components of the Democratic leadership outflank their party's supporters by a mile, but the Republican leaders display a less simple pattern (Figure 7.3). Republican national leaders are actually slightly closer to the center of the attitude spectrum than are the Republican rank-and-file. The pattern is closer to 1972 than to 1956; that is, supporters of both parties are closer to Republican leaders than Democratic. The Republican supporters fall between the national and local Republican leaders. Democratic supporters, in contrast, are situated between the Democratic and Republican leaders, but somewhat closer to the Republican. The Republicans are impressively cohesive in their attitudes toward equality; the Democrats are significantly more divided.

These results are somewhat misleading, however, since they combine three different sets of equality attitudes. The positions of the public and leaders on the separate equality issues provide a better key for reconciling the findings for 1956 and 1972 (Figure 7.4). Economic issues stand out strikingly from the race or gender patterns. Here data line up much as in the 1956 pattern: the party leaders outflank their rank-and-file; Democratic supporters are much closer to their own leaders, and Republican supporters, while not closer to

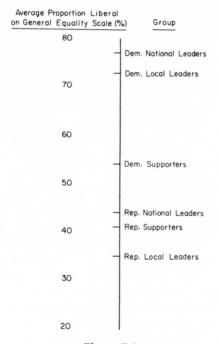

**Figure 7.3**
Attitudes of Party Leaders and Supporters on General Equality

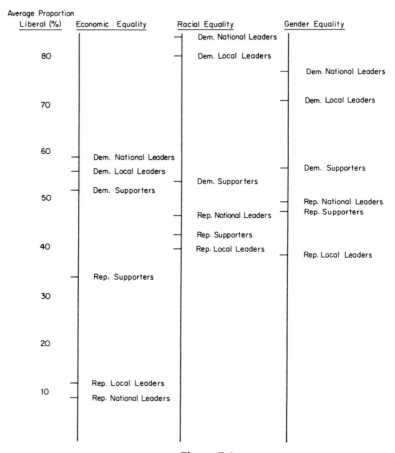

**Figure 7.4**
Attitudes of Party Leaders and Supporters on Economic,
Racial, and Gender Equality

Democratic leaders, are about halfway between the two sets of party leaders. On race and gender issues, however, the 1972 pattern pre-vails: Democratic supporters are farther away from their own party's leaders than they are from Republican leaders, and the Democratic leaders stand out. The swing from the 1956 pattern to the 1972 pattern appears to reflect the shifting focus of the political agenda, namely the growing salience of social issues and the eclipse of eco-nomic issues at that time. The relationship between leaders and supporters varies, depending on which type of issue is prominent. Since race and gender are relatively recent additions to the equality commitment of the Democratic party, these issues are more apt to split party leaders from supporters than is the more established issue of economic equality.

In sum, the distance between the public at large and the party leaders varies from issue to issue. On matters of economic equality, the public, regardless of party affiliation, is closer to the Democratic leaders; on matters of racial and gender equality, the views of Republican leaders are more representative. This difference emphasizes the importance to the parties of the evolution of equality issues since the New Deal. Democratic party leaders are close to their rank-and-file on the economic issues that created the New Deal alignment but are far more liberal than their public on the newer racial and social equality issues.

## Party Coalitions

On most equality issues, Democratic and Republican party leaders display wide differences in attitude. These are not the result of underlying differences between party supporters at large. Not only do the leaders differ from their supporters in attitude, but in nearly every case the party rank-and-file is much closer to the middle of the road. If leaders hoped to mirror the positions of their followers, they would act as an ideologically uniting rather than a dividing force. If they were seeking mass support, they would be even more moderate than their own constituents; each party's leadership would attempt to maximize its attractiveness to the entire electorate and compete for support in the center. Indeed, regular and periodic elections serve as a constant reminder of the need to moderate views to win votes. However, as persuasive as this electoral logic might be in an a-priori sense, it does not fit the facts.[13] By and large, party leaders hold more extreme views than do their followers.

One reason for this discrepancy might be that Democratic and Republican party leaders are different "kinds of people" with different social backgrounds. In America's first party system, the social origins of the Federalist and anti-Federalist leaders were strikingly dissimilar.[14] Yet while today's party leaders differ somewhat in their social background—Democratic leaders, for example, are more likely to have attended graduate school—the contrast is slight. A more likely reason for the extreme attitudes of party leaders lies in the nature of the coalitions of groups associated with each party. The leaders of these allied interest groups take positions that pull party leaders away from the center.

The positions of the party leaders and their group coalitions can be mapped (Figure 7.5). The distance between the Republican and Democratic leaders is greatest on the issue of the New Deal, followed by race. On the former issue the party leaders and interest groups cluster most tightly, with the Republican, farm, and business leaders fairly close on one end of the scale, the Democrat, labor, feminist, and black leaders on the other end, and a good deal of space in between.

The two parties stand in the middle of their coalitions on each issue. Republicans are always flanked by business and farmers. On most issues the clustering around the Republican leaders is tighter than it is around the Democratic leaders. However, the coalition nature of the Democratic party is also clear. The Democratic leaders consistently occupy the center of their coalition, surrounded by labor, feminists, and blacks. In all cases, labor is to their right. Blacks and

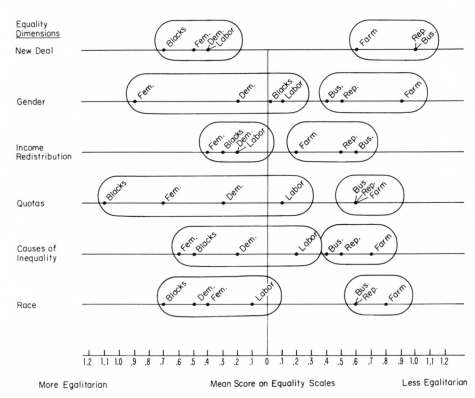

**Figure 7.5**
Party Coalitions on Equality Issues

feminists are to their left, except that on the issues specific to those groups the Democrats are outflanked only by the group for whom that issue is more relevant: feminists on gender and blacks on race.

The political position of the Democratic leaders is more delicate than is that of the Republicans. On noneconomic issues, the Democratic coalition is far-flung. The Democrats walk a tightrope between labor and the other interest groups. On three of the issues—gender, quotas, and the causes of inequality—labor falls on the conservative side, while feminists and blacks fall far to the liberal side. And even on the race issue, which has labor, feminists, blacks, and Democratic leaders all on the liberal side, there is a substantial gap between labor and blacks. The gender issue puts the Democratic leaders in the most difficult position. They are still in the middle, but much closer to blacks and labor than to the feminists. These findings are consistent with the notion that the Democratic party can rally around issues of economics but is more fragmented by newer racial and especially gender issues.[15] The Republicans and their allies, on the contrary, seem more cohesive on social issues and slightly more dispersed over economic matters. On economic issues, such as the New Deal and income redistribution, business and Republican leaders lean in equal measure to the right, but farm leaders are substantially closer to the middle of the road. When it comes to the social issues, such as gender, quotas, race, and the causes of inequality, the groups on the conservative side are generally close-knit.

The position of the Democratic leaders is, again, not enviable. They are in accord with labor on economic matters but are substantially more liberal on social issues. Unfortunately for them, that position still does not bring them very close to blacks or feminists. Democratic leaders are not as liberal as either blacks or feminists on economic matters. Nor are they as liberal as blacks on race or as feminists on gender. Their dilemma is that they cannot move closer to one group on any of the three issues without moving away from the others.

On any issue, the amount of attention that party leaders pay a group depends not only on the views of the group but also on the proportion of that group which supports the party. Labor, black, and feminist leaders are strongly identified with the Democratic party, while business and, to a lesser extent, farm leaders align with the Republican party (Table 7.1). Each group believes that the party it identifies with helps it more. Yet the percentage of business leaders who identify with the Democrats exceeds the percentage who think that the Democratic party helps business. Nearly all business leaders acknowledge that the Republican party helps business more, but some lay aside their self-interest as business people and vote Democratic for other reasons. Still, business leaders as a whole are overwhelmingly in the Republican camp.

Several kinds of information can be used to illustrate the complex position of the Democratic party leaders in relation to their leadership allies and mass support groups (Figure 7.6). These include the position of the Democratic leaders themselves on each of the three equality dimensions; the positions of both those interest-group leaders who identify as Democrats and the rank-and-file Democratic supporters; the position on the relevant equality scales of Democratic union members, Democratic blacks, and Democratic women; and the percentage of each group that supports the Democratic party. This information locates the Democratic leadership amid the various elite and mass groups that might pull it one way or the other. On each of the equality issues, the Democratic leaders fall between the relevant public and most of their more supportive leadership groups. On economic issues, the Democratic leaders are outflanked in a liberal direction by labor, feminist, and black leaders, while the mass of Democratic supporters and Democratic union members take more moderate positions to their right. On the race issue, the Democratic leaders are outflanked on the left by black and feminist leaders. Democratic supporters and even black Democratic supporters are more moderate, as are labor leaders. A similar pattern appears

**Table 7.1**
Democratic Support among Leaders (%)

| Group | Identify themselves as Democrats[a] | Regard Democratic party as helping their group more |
|---|---|---|
| Business | 16 | 6 |
| Farm | 39 | 34 |
| Media | 59 | 53 |
| Intellectuals | 53 | 59 |
| Feminists | 80 | 80 |
| Blacks | 84 | 84 |
| Labor | 90 | 91 |

a. Includes Independents who say they are closer to the Democratic party.

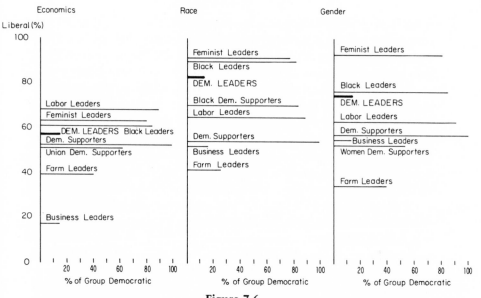

**Figure 7.6**

Democratic Coalition of Leaders and Supporters by Equality Issue[a]

a. Only leaders and supporters who consider themselves Democrats are included. The positions of these Democrats on three equality issues are arrayed along the vertical axes. The length of each horizontal line indicates the proportion of each group which identifies with the Democratic party.

on the gender issue. The relevant groups in the mass are generally more moderate than the Democratic leaders. Among the leaders, the feminists are far to the left of the Democratic leaders, and the blacks are less so, while labor is more moderate. On all three issues, Democratic business and farm leaders are more conservative than their party leaders.

In short, the Democratic leaders take more extreme positions compared with their supporters in the public. Relative to their allied leadership groups, they generally take more moderate positions. They are pulled in a more liberal direction on the economy by all allied leadership groups; on race, by feminists and blacks; and on gender, by feminists. Their position jibes with the role of parties as intermediaries between groups with specific interests and the more amorphous and centrist public. The position in which the party leaders find themselves involves too many disparate pressures to permit them often to take clear and unambiguous positions.

The position of Republican leaders as shown by parallel data is simpler (Figure 7.7). Republican voters and the leadership groups supporting the Republican party are more tightly clustered on most equality issues. On economic issues, the Republican leaders' position is similar to that of the Democrats: Republican leaders are to a certain extent outflanked by their main allied group, business, while Republican voters are more moderate. On the race issue, the Republican-supporting leadership groups are somewhat more conservative; on gender issues, the farm leaders outflank Republican leaders and the rank-and-file. Only on the economic issue must Republican leaders serve as intermediaries between a moderate base of rank-and-file supporters and a more extreme leadership group.

Democrats have to perform a more complicated juggling act. On the issues of equality Republican leaders are fairly close to their staunchest ally, business, and are not far from another ally, farm leaders. And except on the economic issues, they are close to rank-and-file Republican supporters. Their distance from the black, feminist, and labor leaders who identify with the Republican party should

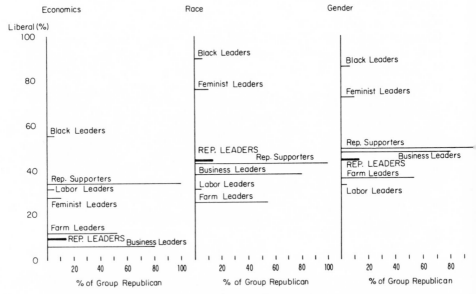

**Figure 7.7**
Republican Coalition of Leaders and Supporters
by Equality Issue[a]

a. Only leaders and supporters who consider themselves Republicans are included. The positions of these Republicans on three equality issues are arrayed along the vertical axes. The length of each horizontal line indicates the proportion of each group which identifies with the Republican party.

cause them little strain, because so few leaders of these groups are in their camp. Democrats, in contrast, are allied with several leadership groups, each representing one of the equality issues. Thus, they find themselves caught not only between elite and rank-and-file supporters but also between their elite allies. On issues of race and gender they are to the right of blacks and feminists but to the left of labor. Not only do they find themselves treading a precarious path between their allied interest groups and their mass supporters, but they also must strike a balance among the differing allied interest groups.

The awkward position of Democratic leaders vis-à-vis their coalition of allied interest groups is shown by the relative priorities that the various leadership groups assign to equality issues when asked to rank them (Figure 7.8). The Democratic coalition holds together quite nicely on the economic issue; labor, feminist, and black leaders all rank unemployment higher than inflation, and all place it at or near the top of their priorities. The coalition holds together less well in regard to racial and gender equality. Blacks rank racial equality high, but that view is not seconded by feminists or by labor, which put the issue fairly far down on their list. The feminist commitment to gender equality also receives little support from the other groups, including the Democratic leaders.[16] Indeed, the party leaders align with blacks and feminists less closely on the priority of race and gender equality than on the race and gender scales. This may reflect an effort to reduce the strain of their position by downplaying the issues. The problem may be that blacks or feminists will deny Democratic leaders the luxury of neglecting the issue. In contrast, the Republican leaders and their allied interest groups—business and farm leaders—are neatly lined up on their priorities. Inflation is more important to them than jobs, and gender and racial equality rank quite low.

In sum, party leaders variously sharpen issues by taking positions distant from the views of the electorate and assuage conflict by taking centrist positions. Compared to the parties' mass supporters, the leaders take positions that are more polarized. But these positions are less extreme than are those of the relevant allied leadership groups, which lie even further from the center of the issue spectrum. In such cases, the party leaders play intermediary roles, softening the sharp alternatives championed by these groups.

THE DEMOCRATIC and Republican parties are not Tweedle-dum and Tweedle-dee. Their leaders differ substantially in their positions on

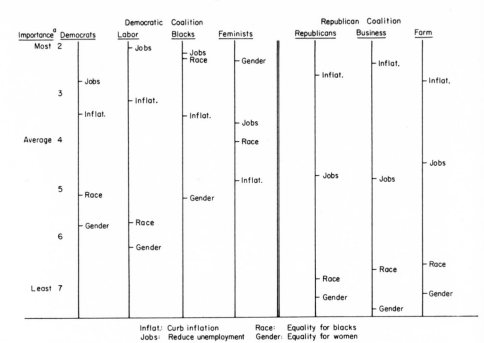

Inflat.: Curb inflation      Race:    Equality for blacks
Jobs: Reduce unemployment    Gender: Equality for women

**Figure 7.8**
National Priorities by Party Coalition
a. The average ranking of each goal by each leadership group.

equality issues, in contrast with the more centrist views of the public at large. Moreover, there are crucial differences between party leaders' attitudes on economic issues and on racial or gender issues. The New Deal coalition was glued together by economic adversity and dispute over economic policy between richer and poorer segments of society. American politics has never been class-based in the European sense, but in the New Deal era it came closer than it has come since. The Democratic party coalesced around issues of economic class. The newer issues of race and gender were bypassed by the New Deal for the good political reason that no effective forces were pushing them onto the political agenda. Furthermore, if they had been placed there, they would have been divisive. Now that these issues have been placed on the agenda, they are divisive.

Historically, equality issues appeared on the party agenda in the order of economics, race, and then gender. That is also the order of the issues in the degree to which they divide the parties one from another, as well as in the extent to which the Democratic party is internally united.

The function of the parties in structuring political issues is both polarizing and mediating. From the standpoint of the general public, the parties pose fairly clear alternatives. The Democratic leaders manage to provide alternatives across all issues, while the Republican leaders do so mainly in the economic sphere. From the standpoint of particular interest groups with a stake in the equality issue, the party leaders are a mediating force. Thus, political parties serve two different functions. First, the parties oppose one another by offering alternative policy positions. This is an ideological function, which is necessary to preserve the loyalty of activists and hence to maintain the parties as organizations. Second, the parties emphasize uncontroversial and undivisive issues to compete for votes. This is a coalitional function, which is necessary to win elections. There is a constant tension between these two competing roles, between the parties' organizational need to oppose each other ideologically and their electoral need to attract a large public following. The complaint that there is no real difference between the political parties is at once true and false, depending on the perspective from which they are viewed.

# Equality of Income

Americans agree on an ideal of equal opportunity, but not on how closely the United States approximates this ideal or how vigorously the government should pursue it. Just how much equality American leaders deem appropriate can be determined precisely for one of the most important and valued concepts of equality: income equality. American leaders differ in their views on the existing distribution of income across various occupations, as well as on the distribution they believe ought to exist.

There are many attributes with which individuals can be equally or unequally endowed, of which money is only one. Cash income, though an important ingredient of general well-being, is by no means the only measure of a person's welfare. Income in kind—the receipt of goods and services in lieu of cash—is important to a range of individuals, from the poorest vagrant, who gets free medical care, to the most affluent executive, who enjoys free use of the company yacht. Yet levels of income and levels of well-being do not always coincide. On this score, songwriters and statisticians agree. The correlation between income and satisfaction with income is modest. And there is evidence that as a measure of general happiness income is less significant than are leisure activities and family life.[1]

Even if money is not everything, it is certainly something. Money has a substantial effect on satisfaction both directly and indirectly, through its effects on leisure, health, and other requisites for a happy life. As humorist Fred Allen used to say, there are many things in life more important than money, and they all cost money. Money may not guarantee happiness, but a perceived lack of it clearly creates unhappiness. A national sample of people who were dissatisfied with their lives mentioned financial limitations before all other problems as standing in the way of fulfillment.[2] Money may not buy happiness, but happinesss apparently cannot be had for free.

Economic equality is also closely linked to political and social equality. For example, income seems to be the main criterion by which people evaluate the status of others. As Lee Rainwater and Richard Coleman put it, "Money, far more than anything else, is what Americans associate with the idea of social class."[3] Attitudes toward income equality therefore map out the contours of Americans' beliefs about equality in general.

Equality of earnings has at least two meanings. Earnings may be considered equal if people of comparable skill or productivity are rewarded alike. Under this conception of equality, equal wages for two different jobs might constitute unequal treatment. As used here, however, the term means simply numerical equality of reward: two individuals have equal earnings if they receive the same amount of money for full-time performance of their jobs. The meaning of equality in this context is purely algebraic; it is not offered as a normative conception of ideal distribution. There is no assumption that such a reward structure exists, is feasible, or is necessarily fair. Numerical equality is merely a benchmark by which to compare American leaders' conceptions of what is a just distribution of income. This benchmark can be compared with three others: the actual earnings of various occupations as disclosed by objective income statistics, leaders' perceptions of those earnings, and leaders' views of what fair earnings ought to be. A comparison of these views and perceptions across the leadership groups reveals how much consensus there is on what constitutes a fair income distribution and how close the American system comes to the ideal of fairness.

In the conflicting assessments of how much income inequality exists, the currency of the debate is itself a point of contention; there is no one appropriate and practical measure of income. Tax subsidies and transfer payments are difficult to take into account or accurately estimate. Fringe benefits are hard to quantify, yet much income takes the form of perquisites rather than money. And the individual's income differs from the family's. The time span is another variable. Two individuals—one younger, the other older—who have different incomes at a given point may have similar incomes when these are aggregated over their life spans. In addition, collective measures of inequality are by no means unambiguous, whether it be the Gini index, which summarizes the entire income distribution, or the income shares measure, which focuses on those at the top or bottom of the income hierarchy.[4]

Yet these variables are largely irrelevant to the goal of the leadership study, which is neither to determine how much income inequality there actually is nor to settle the thorny question of the degree to which income has become equally distributed. The estimates of income made by American leaders are compared with actual earnings in various occupations in order to see how they perceive the income distribution and how they would like that distribution to change. Because the earnings are those typical of particular occupations, the study avoids in part the issue of "whose income." And the occupations are those of relatively mature adults, thereby eliminating the time-span problem of low-income earners who are just beginning their careers.

The leaders' views about how income is and ought to be distributed are related to their general values about equality. They also have a bearing on the reality of income inequality in America. Though differences in income can be explained by the functional worth or marginal productivity of various occupations, such explanations hardly account for the full range of variation across occupations. Inequality of earnings also reflects what people believe occupations ought to earn. And the beliefs that count most are the leaders'. As actors in the formation of public policy, they define the limits of the debate over the government's proper function in income redistribution. And in the private sector the leaders play an even more important role. As Jan Pen points out, "the top incomes in business are set by what top executives themselves consider right and proper." Business leaders value themselves highly and pay themselves accordingly. That high self-valuation is not shared by other leadership groups. Thus the conflict over fair income, though representative of a larger and more abstract conflict of values, shapes the actual distribution of wealth in American society.[5]

Disputes among economists over the proper distribution of social benefits such as personal income commonly concern issues of both efficiency and equity. The efficiency issue hinges on the relationship among income distribution, investment and work incentives, and productivity.[6] Nearly all people agree that some income disparity is necessary to maintain efficiency. Societies that have undertaken radical measures to eliminate disparities have wound up with stagnant economies in which all suffer.[7] However, the question remains as to how much disparity is needed. According to Lester Thurow, "current inequalities are much larger than those necessary to produce and expand the current Gross National Product."[8] According to other economists, growth requires that a larger proportion of income be left in the hands of the affluent, who are more likely to invest it.[9] Data from the leadership study show that the leaders' attitudes largely parallel the dispute among economists: they agree on the desirability of income differentiation but disagree on the proper amount.

Amid the differences of opinion are a few tenets common to all. One is that some income variation is both desirable and appropriate. American leaders of all ideological stripes agree that income should be based upon skill and effort. Few believe that equal pay for all is an acceptable ideal; those in favor range from one percent of business executives and Republicans to 16 percent of blacks. And only a tiny minority accept the notion that the government should impose a ceiling on income; only two percent of business people and Republicans support such a limit, and even among feminists, the group with the most radical view on this issue, only 23 percent are in favor. These attitudes mirror the general rejection of radical redistribution in American politics. The New Deal introduced social programs but steered clear of a substantial income redistribution. The succeeding reform movements, such as the Great Society, have been equally chary of redistributive schemes. Since the 1930s the public has consistently supported income differentiation and opposed radical attempts to flatten that distribution or to set a ceiling on incomes. The consensus against an income ceiling is even greater now than in the 1930s.[10]

How high a floor the public wants is less clear. In 1960, 59 percent of Americans thought that the government should see to it "that every person has a job and a good standard of living," a belief shared by only 17 percent of the public in 1978.[11] Yet a "good" standard of living lies well beyond "adequate" or "minimal"; it is therefore likely that even in 1978 a sizable percentage of the population favored some kind of income floor. Indeed, when the Reagan administration took office in 1981, it proposed to cut spending on social programs substantially but promised to provide a "safety net" for the "truly needy."

The general opposition of Americans to a radical leveling of income and their support of some government protection for the least well-off defines the outer boundaries of income equality. Within those boundaries, however, there is considerable latitude for disagreement. Most concur that income differences across occupations are legitimate. The disagreement involves how much income inequality there actually is in the United States, how much there ought to be, and how to rank occupations in terms of earnings.

## Measuring Attitudes

The measurement of attitudes toward income inequality poses the same requirements as does the estimation of actual income inequality: defining income and selecting a yardstick of equality. Furthermore, the limited patience and economic expertise of American leaders constrains what they can be asked. Questions have to be fairly simple and straightforward, although the issue is neither simple nor straightforward. Leaders cannot be asked to make complex calculations of income before and after taxes or to estimate Gini coefficients for the United States.

The leadership study therefore asked simply what the "average annual earnings before taxes" for people in different occupations actually are and what these earnings should be (Figure 8.1). The presentation of a wide variety of occupations makes it possible to see how large a gap individuals think should separate occupations near the top of the income distribution and those near the bottom. Both public and private jobs are included, as well as white- and blue-collar work. The occupational categories are precise enough that the actual income variation within each cannot be great.

The specific occupational categories give a concrete referent for the leaders' responses. They would likely have found it far more difficult to come up with hard figures for more abstract categories like "the bottom 5 percent of families." In addition, the question asks about the salary and wages of the occupation itself, not the total income of someone in that occupation, including other jobs or investments. The question pertains to equality of pay more than to equality of total earnings, since the study's main concern is the distribution of rewards for work. The results obtained might have been quite different if the question had dealt with assets or unearned income rather than earnings: the distribution of wealth in the United States is more highly skewed than is the distribution of earnings.[12]

The question is about earnings before taxes. This simplification

**Figure 8.1**

Income Question

Some occupations are listed below. In the first column, please indicate what you think the average annual earnings are for someone in that occupation before taxes. In the second column, please indicate what you think someone in that occupation should earn, again before taxes. (Most people do not have precise information on salaries in other occupations, but we would like your best estimate.)

|  | Average Annual Salary is | Fair Annual Salary would be |
|---|---|---|
| A grade school teacher with five years' experience in a midwest school. | $_____ | $_____ |
| President of one of the top hundred corporations. | $_____ | $_____ |
| A semi-skilled worker in an auto assembly plant. | $_____ | $_____ |
| Star center, NBA basketball team. | $_____ | $_____ |
| A bank teller. | $_____ | $_____ |
| U.S. Cabinet member (Secretary of Commerce, Labor, HEW, etc.) | $_____ | $_____ |
| An elevator operator. | $_____ | $_____ |
| A policeman in a midwest city with five years' experience. | $_____ | $_____ |
| An aeronautical engineer. | $_____ | $_____ |
| A college professor. | $_____ | $_____ |
| A doctor in general practice in a large city. | $_____ | $_____ |
| Someone at your level in your own occupation. | $_____ | $_____ |
| A plumber. | $_____ | $_____ |

would cast suspicion on the validity of the findings if the study were concerned mainly with Americans' ultimate purchasing power and that power differed a lot after taxes. However, because the overall tax system in the United States has little if any redistributive impact, the results would probably have been similar for earnings after taxes.[13]

The use of pretax earnings is necessitated by the limitations of the method. Normally Americans think about earnings in terms of pretax income; a question about earnings after taxes would therefore have required the leaders to think in unfamiliar numbers. In addition, a question about income after taxes, or about both pre- and post-tax income, would have been too burdensome. For one thing, income tax schedules are too complicated to allow citizens to calculate the tax bite on different occupations. For another, there are many complex taxes that must be considered. To have asked about income after federal income taxes alone would have given a poorer idea of actual net income distribution, since the progressivity of the federal income tax is counterbalanced by regressive taxes in other areas.[14]

Finally, the question is laid out as a matrix comparing the various occupations in terms of what is thought to be earned and what ought to be earned. The leaders thus had in front of them the full list of occupations, as well as the distinction between actual and ideal income. This format made the task an explicitly comparative one, between actual and ideal, and among occupations. Appropriately, the leaders were forced to make relative comparisons.

### Perceptions and Values

The leaders' estimates of actual income for each occupation come surprisingly close to the mark (Table 8.1). Their average estimates are fairly close to the actual earnings for most occupations.[15] There is only one disagreement in the ranking, the relative position, of the occupations: bank tellers are estimated to rank above elevator operators, whereas they actually earn slightly less. In addition, the earnings of a plumber are greatly exaggerated, though the ranking of that occupation is objectively correct, and the incomes of top executives and professional athletes are underestimated.

There are plausible explanations for these inaccuracies. The high estimate for the income of a plumber probably reflects a social stereotype as well as a misperception based on the contact that most Americans have with plumbers. The average middle-class citizen meets a plumber only in connection with home repairs, and the fees are high. But most plumbers are not independent journeymen and do not keep those fees. The misplacement of the elevator operator is of greater methodological concern. This occupation was included in order to anchor the bottom of the income distribution, in the belief that such unskilled workers were in fact the worst paid of the

**Table 8.1**

Perceived and Objective Income of Occupations ($)

| Occupation | Perceived income[a] | Objective income |
|---|---|---|
| Top executive | 206,200 | 230,000–333,000[b] |
| Professional athlete | 159,300 | 325,000[c] |
| Doctor | 86,300 | 53,900[d] |
| Cabinet secretary | 50,400 | 60,000[e] |
| Engineer | 26,700 | 24,600[d] |
| Professor | 21,000 | 24,400[c] |
| Plumber | 20,000 | 13,800[d] |
| Automobile worker | 12,600 | 12,600[f] |
| Police officer | 12,300 | 12,500[g] |
| Teacher | 10,700 | 12,100[g] |
| Bank teller | 9,500 | 8,300[g] |
| Elevator operator | 7,200 | 8,400[f] |

a. Figures are average estimates by the leaders for each occupation.

b. *Business Week*, May 23, 1977. The larger figure includes bonuses.

c. *Time*, "A Random Sample of Pay," June 13, 1977. Data for NBA basketball star, not necessarily a center.

d. *Occupational Outlook Handbook* (Washington, D.C.: Bureau of Labor Statistics, 1978).

e. *World Almanac and Book of Facts* (1976).

f. 1970 U.S. Census, extrapolated to 1976.

g. *Current Wage Developments* (Washington, D.C.: Bureau of Labor Statistics, 1977, 1979), extrapolated back to 1976.

occupations. That belief is shared by American leaders, even though the bank teller actually earns slightly less.

Sex differences may account in part for the unexpected wage differences between these two occupations. Elevator operators are likely to be men, while bank tellers are mostly women. But it may be that bank tellers are predominantly female because the pay is so low, rather than vice versa. Another factor is technology. Now that self-operated elevators are ubiquitous, operators are typically a luxury retained by expensive hotels and old government office buildings. The operators are often civil service workers or members of strong unions. In contrast, technological advances in banking have not made tellers obsolete yet, but they have made the position increasingly "unskilled," requiring no prior training or expertise. The mathematical and accounting aspects of the teller's work are now fully automated.

It is also unclear whether the top executive belongs at the head of the list. Top executives outrank professional athletes only if the executives' bonuses are included. The corporate boards that set executive salaries assume that bonuses are integral to an executive's take-home pay. Notwithstanding these ambiguities, the executive and the elevator operator are treated here as the highest- and lowest-paid occupations, since that is how they were ranked by each of the leadership groups. The ranking of these two occupations is a good measure of the maximum income gap considered appropriate in a fair society.

Perceptions of what earnings actually are differ from views on what earnings should be (Table 8.2).[16] Americans do not find the present income distribution, as they see it, entirely fair. In general, they want to slash the earnings at the top of the hierarchy and boost the earnings at the bottom. Corporate executives are on average perceived to earn almost twice what they ought to receive, and professional athletes are thought to earn more than twice what is proper. Doctors, in the upper reaches of the income hierarchy, and plumbers, in the middle, should also lose income under prevailing views. Those in the public and nonprofit sectors are deemed un-

**Table 8.2**
Perceived and Fair Income of Occupations ($)[a]

| Occupation | Perceived income | Fair income | Difference |
|---|---|---|---|
| Top executive | 167,070 | 95,230 | − 71,840 |
| Professional athlete | 112,703 | 42,612 | − 70,091 |
| Doctor | 74,374 | 52,798 | − 21,576 |
| Cabinet secretary | 48,062 | 48,119 | +    57 |
| Engineer | 24,916 | 24,705 | −   211 |
| Professor | 20,268 | 22,766 | + 2,498 |
| Plumber | 18,845 | 15,575 | − 3,270 |
| Automobile worker | 12,102 | 12,045 | −    57 |
| Police officer | 12,012 | 14,385 | + 2,373 |
| Teacher | 10,474 | 12,812 | + 2,338 |
| Bank teller | 9,083 | 10,454 | + 1,371 |
| Elevator operator | 6,877 | 7,954 | + 1,077 |

a. Logged income is reported in this table and those following. The figures here are averages for all the leaders.

derpaid. Cabinet secretaries, teachers, policemen, and college professors should all receive more. So should the two lowest paid
occupations, the bank teller and elevator operator.

Since the data are averaged for all the leaders, they mask wide
variations among groups. The leadership groups disagree on how
much the earnings of a particular occupation should be raised or
lowered. To compare the changes in income that groups would favor,
the ratio between proposed (fair) and perceived earnings, or the "ought/
is" ratio, is used. The ratios for a group are based not on the ratio
between the mean income that an occupation ought to earn and the
mean income it is perceived to earn but on an average of the individual ratios for each leader within a group. If all members of a group
agree that income for an occupation should stay the same, the average ratio is one. If 50 percent of a group wants to double earnings
and 50 percent wants to cut them in half, the ratio is also one. If
all group members want to increase an occupation's earnings by 50
percent, the ratio is 1.5. If they wish to triple earnings, the ratio is
three. If all group members want an occupation to earn one-third of
what it does, the ratio is .33.

The leadership groups differ on the fairness of current earnings at
the top and bottom of the hierarchy, as shown by their attitudes
toward the incomes of business executives and elevator operators
(Table 8.3). On balance, all groups except business would slightly
raise the income of the elevator operator. The ought/is ratio for this
occupation is highest among the feminists, because they estimate
the elevator operator's earnings to be lower than do other groups
and they desire a higher income for the occupation. Among the other
groups there is a good deal of variation. Business and Republicans
consider the earnings of the elevator operator roughly appropriate.
Labor and blacks would raise the earnings of such an occupation
more than most other groups, though only by about 25 percent.[17]

A mirror image appears in the perceived and fair earnings of top
business executives. In this case, all of the groups opt for a reduction
in earnings. The proposed reductions are in general more substantial
in both absolute and ratio terms than are the suggested increases
for the lowest-paying occupation. The variation among the groups,
however, is sizable. Business, at one extreme, would reduce executive earnings only a little, apparently considering them just. And
within this group, the national business leaders, themselves top
executives of major corporations, do not regard their own earnings
as any greater than they should be.

The other leadership groups seem to have no qualms about cutting

**Table 8.3**

Perceived and Fair Income of Top and Bottom Occupation.[a]

| Group | Elevator operator | | | Executive | | |
|---|---|---|---|---|---|---|
| | Perceived income ($) | Fair income ($) | Fair/perceived ratio | Perceived income ($) | Fair income ($) | Fair/perceived ratio |
| Business | 7,137 | 6,990 | 0.98 | 199,295 | 187,314 | 0.94 |
| Farm | 7,096 | 7,643 | 1.08 | 138,325 | 87,855 | 0.63 |
| Labor | 6,959 | 8,627 | 1.25 | 173,907 | 90,612 | 0.51 |
| Intellectuals | 7,101 | 8,261 | 1.16 | 189,151 | 94,741 | 0.50 |
| Media | 7,124 | 7,861 | 1.10 | 179,410 | 107,322 | 0.60 |
| Republicans | 6,969 | 7,201 | 1.03 | 164,776 | 130,223 | 0.81 |
| Democrats | 7,008 | 8,209 | 1.18 | 181,754 | 99,484 | 0.56 |
| Blacks | 6,739 | 8,121 | 1.21 | 130,074 | 79,761 | 0.61 |
| Feminists | 6,197 | 8,527 | 1.37 | 172,128 | 69,650 | 0.41 |
| Youth | 6,794 | 8,026 | 1.18 | 152,168 | 70,615 | 0.47 |

a. The figures are averages for each group.

those earnings. Again feminists are at the opposite pole from business. They would reduce executive earnings by more than half. Labor, intellectuals, and youth also support substantial cuts. In fact, no group would leave executive income at its present level.

The attitudes of the two political parties toward the earnings of the elevator operator and the executive are symmetrical. Each would raise the earnings of the elevator operator, but the Democrats would raise them much more than would the Republicans. Each would cut the executive's salary, but the Democrats would cut it much more. The party differences in more general attitudes toward equality reappear in these estimates of the ideal.[18]

Attitudes toward the incomes at these two occupational extremes of executive and elevator operator reveal a number of attitudes toward income differentials in general. First, there is a general desire to see a smaller gap between the top and the bottom of the income scale.[19] All groups except one would pay more to the elevator operator and less to the executive. Second, groups differ widely on how much smaller the gap should be. Business and, to a lesser extent, Republicans consider the boundaries of the current earnings gap to be equitable. Feminists and, to a lesser extent, labor and intellectuals consider the earnings gap the most unfair. Third, despite differences among the groups on how extensively earnings ought to be changed, no group would completely eliminate the income gap. Though many groups want to see greater equality, each group believes on average that elevator operators ought to earn substantially less than executives. In this sense, the findings are consistent with the American consensus that income need not be fully equal but should reflect differences in talent and effort. And finally, the common ideal is to equalize income by lowering the ceiling rather than raising the floor. Executive income is in general reduced—in absolute and relative terms—more than an elevator operator's is raised. The asymmetry is most apparent among intellectuals and youth, who would lower executive salaries substantially but would raise the earnings of elevator operators only marginally.

A fuller picture is portrayed in the fair/perceived ratios by leadership groups for each occupation (Table 8.4). The profiles of the groups' views of the occupations show that the leaders basically agree on the general direction of change in income for each occupation but disagree on the magnitude of that change. This schism shows up in relation to the earnings of the top executive: all groups agree executive incomes are too high but differ in the size of their

## Table 8.4
### Proposed Change in Income for Occupations by Groups (fair/perceived ratios)[a]

| Occupation | Business | Farm | Labor | Intellectuals | Media | Republicans | Democrats | Blacks | Feminists | Youth |
|---|---|---|---|---|---|---|---|---|---|---|
| Top executive | 0.94 | 0.63 | 0.51 | 0.50 | 0.60 | 0.81 | 0.56 | 0.61 | 0.41 | 0.47 |
| Professional athlete | 0.39 | 0.39 | 0.45 | 0.30 | 0.37 | 0.41 | 0.42 | 0.59 | 0.32 | 0.33 |
| Doctor | 0.85 | 0.65 | 0.69 | 0.62 | 0.72 | 0.86 | 0.69 | 0.85 | 0.60 | 0.68 |
| Cabinet secretary | 1.31 | 0.87 | 1.00 | 1.03 | 1.08 | 1.17 | 1.12 | 0.97 | 0.92 | 0.80 |
| Engineer | 1.03 | 0.90 | 1.04 | 0.97 | 1.00 | 1.03 | 0.99 | 1.03 | 0.96 | 0.97 |
| Professor | 1.06 | 0.96 | 1.13 | 1.20 | 1.19 | 1.01 | 1.18 | 1.14 | 1.20 | 1.10 |
| Plumber | 0.79 | 0.79 | 0.97 | 0.75 | 0.81 | 0.83 | 0.84 | 0.90 | 0.85 | 0.81 |
| Automobile worker | 0.91 | 0.91 | 1.09 | 0.97 | 0.97 | 0.94 | 1.03 | 1.04 | 1.08 | 1.04 |
| Police officer | 1.13 | 1.15 | 1.26 | 1.18 | 1.25 | 1.17 | 1.21 | 1.14 | 1.28 | 1.21 |
| Teacher | 1.11 | 1.09 | 1.27 | 1.24 | 1.27 | 1.10 | 1.25 | 1.22 | 1.38 | 1.24 |
| Bank teller | 1.09 | 1.07 | 1.26 | 1.15 | 1.12 | 1.11 | 1.14 | 1.16 | 1.31 | 1.13 |
| Elevator operator | 0.98 | 1.08 | 1.25 | 1.16 | 1.10 | 1.03 | 1.18 | 1.21 | 1.37 | 1.18 |

a. Figures are averages for each group. Key:

― occupation seen by the group as the most underpaid

═ occupation seen by the group as the second most underpaid

.... occupation seen by the group as the most overpaid

:::: occupation seen by the group as the second most overpaid

proposed reductions. They also agree that the next two high-income occupations, professional athlete and doctor, have inappropriately large earnings. This is particularly true for the athlete, whose income each group would cut the most. The decrease is substantially more than that for the top executive, although the executive is perceived to earn more than the athlete. Intellectuals, feminists, and youth would reduce the athlete's income more than the other groups would. Blacks, though they would slash the earnings of the athlete substantially, are less severe than any other group, perhaps because minority groups see a sports career as a road to advancement.

The relationship between perceived and fair income for a given occupation makes clear that size of earnings is not the only criterion the leaders apply. Although all groups perceive that executives earn more than sports stars, everyone would take more away from the athletes. Whether executives are believed to deserve more because they have more valuable skills, make a greater contribution to society, or control more resources is not known.[20]

The leadership groups are unanimous in their desire to cut the income of two other occupations, doctors and plumbers. Business and Republicans would cut the earnings of plumbers more than the earnings of doctors; the other groups would do the opposite. Only labor would leave the plumbers with roughly their current earnings, but even this reflects a negative view of plumbers relative to other blue-collar occupations, which labor would raise. Although plumbers are not seen near the top of the income hierarchy, the groups agree that they are overpaid. The basis for this agreement is doubtless a combination of direct experience and social stereotype.

The perceived earnings of engineers and automobile workers are roughly appropriate. Not surprisingly, business would cut the earnings of auto workers and labor would raise them, though in neither case is the change substantial. Other groups would change the incomes of those occupations even less. Mainstream workers in the private sector are thought to earn about what they ought to earn.[21]

Attitudes differ toward bank tellers and elevator operators, the two lowest-earning occupations. Although the leadership groups would raise the income of bank tellers, usually by more than 10 percent, they break ranks over the income of the elevator operator. With the single exception of business, which would slightly lower the income for this occupation, all other groups would raise it, once again by more than 10 percent in most cases. Business leaders apparently make a distinction between the more and less deserving among the lowest occupational groups. They view elevator operators, the stereotypical unskilled job, as getting their just deserts, while bank tellers are seen as underpaid.

Both ideology and self-interest clearly influence how groups would alter current income shares, as shown by those occupations that each leadership group considers the most underpaid and overpaid and the second most underpaid and overpaid. Business and Republican leaders, two relatively conservative groups, think the Cabinet secretary and police officer are the most underpaid occupations. Curiously, no other group singles out the Cabinet member for special income improvement. The reason may be that the survey was conducted during a Republican administration with a Republican, largely business cabinet. But beyond the immediate self-interest of Republican loyalists, business and Republicans probably display greater deference for established authority in any sphere, in this case political executives. The agreement between business and Republicans that police officers are among the most underpaid may tap some conservative law-and-order sentiment.

A similar uniformity appears at the other end of the ideological scale. Feminists and blacks both see teachers and elevator operators as the most underpaid occupations. Although they share with other groups that view toward teachers, just as business and Republicans share with others a concern about police officers, feminists and blacks stand alone in identifying elevator operators as the most underpaid occupation. Perhaps predictably, intellectuals see college and grade school teachers as the most underpaid. Virtually everyone agrees about the grade school teachers, but intellectuals alone see college professors as one of the most underpaid jobs. Every group but farmers would raise the income of a college professor, but only slightly.

Aside from these five groups, there is striking consensus across the sectors as to which occupations are most underpaid: teachers and police officers. All groups would raise the earnings of these two public sector jobs, in most cases by more than 25 percent, despite recent controversy over the earnings of municipal workers and the cost of municipal services.

At the top of the earnings hierarchy there is more consensus. All groups find the professional athlete most overpaid. All groups but business find the executive the next most overpaid.

The groups' overall dissatisfaction with the structure of earnings is shown by how much on average they want to change earnings either by adding or by subtracting (Table 8.5). The higher a group's average fair/perceived ratio, the more it would change the present income distribution as it sees it. For example, a group that would not change the income of any occupation has a score of 1.0. A group that would on average double or halve the income of each group has a score of 2.0. Business is most satisfied with the earnings situation in the United States. The least satisfied group are the feminists, followed by youth and intellectuals. The dissatisfaction of feminists is probably linked to their generally liberal ideology and to their unhappiness over both gender discrimination in pay within occupations and with the assignment of high prestige and pay to supposedly "male" occupations. The dissatisfaction of intellectuals also probably stems in part from their liberal tendencies and in part from the discrepancy between their income and their general social standing.[22] Blacks have the second lowest average score, indicating that they are a good deal more satisfied than other groups with which they usually share egalitarian views. This is partly because blacks would not cut the salary of the professional athlete as much as would other groups. If blacks were as dissatisfied with the high earnings of the sports star as are intellectuals or feminists, their average ratio

#### Table 8.5
Amount of Desired Change in Income by Group

| Group | Average fair/perceived ratios[a] |
|---|---|
| Business | 1.24 |
| Farm | 1.31 |
| Labor | 1.33 |
| Intellectuals | 1.44 |
| Media | 1.34 |
| Republicans | 1.23 |
| Democrats | 1.33 |
| Blacks | 1.22 |
| Feminists | 1.51 |
| Youth | 1.42 |

a. For ratios under 1.0 (desired decreases in income) reciprocals are used. Figures therefore show the average deviation from 1.0 in either direction, both increases and decreases in income.

would be about 1.34, lower than that of intellectuals and feminists but close to that of labor.

### The Income Gap

The size of the income gap that Americans accept as legitimate is shown more clearly in their attitudes toward two contrasting pairs of occupations, an executive vis-à-vis an automobile worker and an executive vis-à-vis an elevator operator (Table 8.6). The comparison between the head of a major corporation and an ordinary worker represents a typical disparity of income found within a large organization. The comparison between the executive and an elevator operator reflects the largest income gap found within society's hierarchy of earnings. Rather than relating what a single occupation is perceived to earn to what people think it ought to earn, the ratios relate what an executive is perceived to earn to what an auto worker is perceived to earn and what an executive ought to earn to what an auto worker ought to earn. Similar ratios are reported for the executive/elevator operator pair.

In general, all groups agree in perceiving a substantial and consistent income gap between an executive and an auto worker. The

**Table 8.6**
Perceived and Fair Income Ratios for High and Low Earners by Groups[a]

| Group | Executive vs. auto worker | | Executive vs. elevator operator | |
|---|---|---|---|---|
| | Perceived (real/real) | Fair (ideal/ideal) | Perceived (real/real) | Fair (ideal/ideal) |
| Business | 15.1 | 15.6 | 27.9 | 26.9 |
| Farm | 11.1 | 7.9 | 19.4 | 11.7 |
| Labor | 14.8 | 7.2 | 24.9 | 10.6 |
| Intellectuals | 15.1 | 7.9 | 26.6 | 11.4 |
| Media | 14.1 | 8.7 | 25.1 | 13.6 |
| Republicans | 13.2 | 11.3 | 23.6 | 18.0 |
| Democrats | 15.4 | 8.2 | 26.0 | 12.1 |
| Blacks | 10.8 | 6.4 | 19.1 | 9.7 |
| Feminists | 15.2 | 5.7 | 27.5 | 8.2 |
| Youth | 13.4 | 6.0 | 22.6 | 8.9 |

a. Figures are averages for each group.

groups differ in what gap they consider fair, ranging from business, which favors an income ratio of 15.6 between the executive and the assembly line worker, to feminists, who prefer an income ratio of 5.7, about one-third that of business. The other groups favor earnings ratios of about 7 or 8, with the exception of Republicans, who prefer a ratio of 11.3. These ratios suggest how much inequality leaders think is justified and how much the leaders would change income differences. Business is the only group that prefers an income gap larger than that which it believes to exist. Feminists would reduce the income gap between two occupations to less than half of what they perceive it to be; other fairly egalitarian-minded groups, such as labor, intellectuals, blacks, Democrats, and youth, would cut the gap approximately in half.

Nevertheless, the fact that each group, however egalitarian, considers a fairly substantial gap acceptable shows that their commitment to income equality is limited. This is reflected in the perceived and fair income ratios between the top business executive and the elevator operator. Groups vary in how big they perceive the gap to be, but all groups agree that it is wide. All groups, furthermore, would reduce the gap. The amount of reduction proposed varies more widely than does the perception of the gap. Business leaders would reduce the gap hardly at all. Other groups would narrow it significantly. Most of the more egalitarian groups would reduce the gap to about half of what they perceive it to be; the feminists would reduce it to less than one-third. But these groups still consider a gulf between the two occupations fair. Most of the more egalitarian groups have ideal ratios ranging from 9 to 12—the lowest ratio, that of feminists, being 8.2. Thus, groups critical of the current distribution of earnings display an ambivalent commitment to greater equality or, to put it differently, a strong belief in unequal rewards for unequal ability, effort, or marketability of skills. These groups would reduce the income gap, but they would leave substantially unequal earnings after the reduction.

Given that these groups cover a broad ideological spectrum, the unanimity with which they uphold wide disparities in income as just or somehow desirable is striking. The lack of egalitarian impulse is all the more impressive considering that the question posed to the groups was a relatively easy test. Those who endorse a more equal income distribution in the abstract might be far less enamored of the idea if it entailed tough trade-offs, such as producing undesirable side effects or precluding other favorite goals, or if it were difficult or impossible to accomplish. Some leaders probably thought about these trade-offs, but the survey question did not explicitly raise them. Even though the leaders were not forced to weigh the possible costs of creating a more equal income hierarchy, they still express relatively little favor for the idea.

Full income equality among all occupations might seem to be an unrealistic benchmark. Only the most radical egalitarian would consider such an arrangement fair or desirable. However, a society that is more egalitarian than America—but hardly so egalitarian as to make comparisons silly—provides corroboration that much smaller earnings ratios are realistic. In Sweden similar leadership groups have ratios much smaller than the ones reported for the more liberal groups in the United States, in the 2 to 3 range rather than the 9 to 12 range.[23]

### Leaders' Own Income

American leaders' own earnings can be placed on the earnings hierarchy alongside the earnings of various occupations. The leaders were asked what they believe "someone at your level in your own occupation" earns and ought to earn. The leaders' jobs vary. In business and the media the organizational position which qualifies the individual for inclusion in the leadership study is also that person's full-time occupation. In farm, labor, party, black, and feminist organizations, the organizational position may not be the leader's main job. Furthermore, intellectuals cover a wide range of occupations. These variations among leaders do not prevent them from placing themselves on an income hierarchy with other occupations. Where they place themselves on the scale of fair earnings reveals how much income they feel justified in earning in relation to other occupations.

The leaders' report of what they themselves earn and ought to earn may be compared with what they believe executives and elevator operators earn and ought to earn (Table 8.7). There are wide differences from group to group in the distance between what the leaders earn and what they believe an executive earns. There is remarkable agreement across the groups, however, in the desired ratio between the two. Each group on average believes that an executive ought to earn about 3½ times what the group members believe they ought to earn. Business leaders deviate slightly from this, since many are themselves top executives.[24]

The similarity across groups in their desired position in relation

**Table 8.7**

Perceived and Fair Income Ratios for Self and Others by Group[a]

| Group | Executive vs. respondent | | Respondent vs. elevator operator | |
|---|---|---|---|---|
| | Perceived (real/real) | Fair (ideal/ideal) | Perceived (real/real) | Fair (ideal/ideal) |
| Business | 3.1 | 2.8 | 9.1 | 9.6 |
| Farm | 7.1 | 3.7 | 2.7 | 3.1 |
| Labor | 7.7 | 3.7 | 3.3 | 2.9 |
| Intellectuals | 8.3 | 3.6 | 3.2 | 3.2 |
| Media | 7.0 | 3.7 | 3.6 | 3.7 |
| Republicans | 5.4 | 3.8 | 4.4 | 4.7 |
| Democrats | 6.7 | 3.4 | 3.8 | 3.5 |
| Blacks | 6.7 | 3.5 | 2.9 | 2.8 |
| Feminists | 11.0 | 3.9 | 2.5 | 2.1 |

a. Youth are omitted because a question on self-earnings was inappropriate. Figures are averages for each group.

to the executive is all the more striking in view of the fact that it is based on a wide disparity in what groups believe executives ought to earn as well as in what they believe they should themselves earn. For example, labor and Republicans are almost identical in the ratio they regard as fair between their own earnings and those of an executive. However, they differ substantially on the amount they think a leading executive ought to earn. Labor and Republicans can have similar ratios, despite the difference between their views on fair executive income, because labor has a lower average desired income for itself than do Republicans: labor averages $24,600; Republicans average $32,800. The groups also differ in the actual incomes they report: $22,400 and $30,100 respectively. An even clearer contrast is between Republicans and feminists. Both agree that top executives ought to earn about four times what they themselves ought to earn. But this similarity is achieved by different-size cuts on the part of each group. The feminist ratio for executive earnings is .41; the Republican ratio for executives is .81. In other words, feminists want a cut in executive salaries that is twice as great as that desired by Republicans. But the result of these different reductions is to bring the executives into the same relative position vis-à-vis each group.

The position of the groups with respect to the elevator operator

varies in both the perceived and the desired ratios. The desired income ratios range from business, which believes it ought to earn
nearly ten times what an unskilled worker earns, to feminists, who
believe they ought to earn only twice as much. There are, however,
two striking uniformities across the groups. All groups believe, regardless of occupation, that they should earn several times more
than an unskilled worker. Furthermore, they all consider the gap
that now separates them from the unskilled worker more or less
correct.[25]

Despite the wide divergence in the absolute amounts that the
three positions—an executive, an elevator operator, and someone
in one's own occupation—are perceived to earn and the wider divergence in what they are thought to deserve, all groups wind up in
a similar relative position in their ideal scheme of income distribution. All groups would consider it fair if the highest-paid individuals earned about three-and-a-half times what they themselves earn
and if, in turn, they themselves earned as many times the lowest
income as they currently do. In other words, each group, wherever
it stands in the income hierarchy, favors a uniform ceiling above it
as a ratio to its own earnings, though absolute differences vary.
Others can earn more, but only so many times more. This "ceiling"
on earnings is consistent with the earlier data on the opposition of
all groups to a top limit on income set by the government. The belief
that a certain income is fair for an executive and anything higher is
unfair does not translate into endorsement of a government-imposed
ceiling. Nor do the leaders object to earning several times more than
those at the bottom of the scale. Again the uniformity of the gap
can best be understood in ratio terms. The desired ratio of one's own
earnings to the earnings floor varies across groups, but they agree
that the existing ratio is about right.

### The Income Hierarchy

This complex mix of attitudes is reflected in what the leadership
groups consider an overall fair income hierarchy, as shown when
the income that the groups see as fair for each occupation is related
to the fair income for an elevator operator (Figure 8.2). The ranking
of the occupations is almost identical across groups. Although some
groups differ from others in the distances they would create between
occupations, the ordering is consistent. In each case the executive
is placed at the top of the hierarchy by a substantial amount. Next

come the doctor, Cabinet secretary, and professional athlete, usually in that order. The engineer and professor follow, always close together. Next come the plumber, police officer, teacher, and auto worker together, usually in that order. Then comes the bank teller. All place the elevator operator on the ground floor. There is a consensus on the income ranking of occupations, although the desired income gap varies across the groups. A similar ideal ranking of occupations is found in other nations, despite a good deal of variation across nations in the size of the income differentials among occupations.[26]

What the leaders consider to be a fair income hierarchy can also be looked at from the perspective of their own income (Figure 8.3). The average income a group desires for itself is set at zero, to show the income gaps for other occupations. For the business group, only responses of local business are included, since national executives would be forced to compare themselves with themselves otherwise. There is a good deal of uniformity in where each group places itself in relation to other groups. The executive is a similar distance above the self-location for each group, while the elevator operator is a similar distance below. Every group but business places itself closest to the engineer/professor pair. Americans differ in how much more equality they want, but they agree that it is proper to earn more than some occupations and less than others. Again the pattern is mixed: the consensus that full equality is not desirable is coupled with differences in the amount of inequality that is considered legitimate.

The ideal ranking of occupations is strikingly similar to the actual perceived ranking. In almost no case do groups want to change the income ranking of other occupations relative to themselves. Those groups that perceive certain occupations to earn more than they themselves do would maintain that ranking. The only exceptions are farmers, who see professors as earning a bit more than they do and would have them earn a bit less; intellectuals, who feel the same way about engineers; and feminists, who feel the same way about plumbers. But these changes are among occupations perceived as very close in earnings. Otherwise, the hierarchies remain the same.

Even more significant, no group would elevate any occupation it perceives as below it to a rank above. The groups would generally like to reduce the income gap by raising those below them and lowering those above them. All the groups want greater equality, but not at the cost of relinquishing their present rung on the ladder.

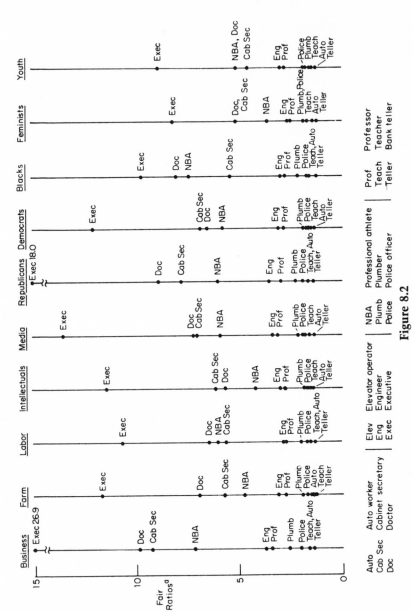

**Figure 8.2**

Fair Income Hierarchy by Group

a. Fair ratios relative to elevator operator (set at 1): 10 = 10 times elevator operator. Logged income.

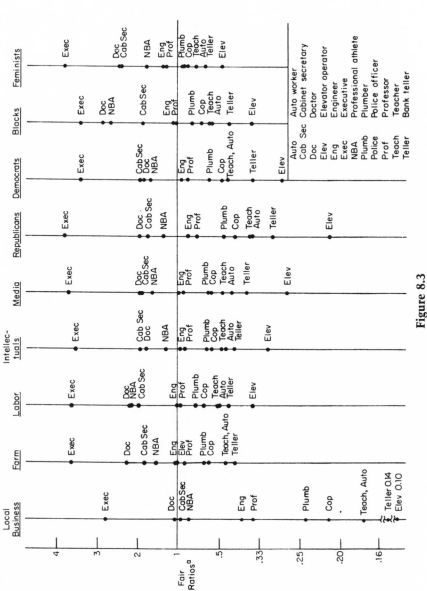

**Figure 8.3**

Fair Income Hierarchy from Perspective of Self Income

a. Preferred "Self" income = 1. Logged income.

It is probably no coincidence that Americans believe that they deserve more than those below them. This belief is intimately connected to the way income differences are prized as a source of status.

### Job Status as Source of Attitudes

The general attitudes we found toward equality of opportunity and result parallel the more specific attitudes toward a fair income distribution. But how closely they are linked is unclear. Evaluations of the propriety of a particular occupation's earnings may reflect general equality attitudes, such as commitment to a meritocratic system of reward; attitudes toward the significance of particular occupations, such as the skill or effort needed for a job, its impact on the economy, and its scope of control over others; or attitudes toward assumed characteristics of the people who are likely to fill the positions, such as their race, gender, and family needs.

A national study of the public's judgment of income fairness, which focused on the criteria used in deciding "who should get what," found a specific income effect. If an income is high, the public wants it to be lowered; if it is low, the public thinks it should be raised.[27] This pattern is reflected as well in the leadership data. Leaders would lower earnings at the top of the scale and raise earnings at the bottom. However, there is more to the story. The groups would cut the professional athlete much more than the executive and would adjust the pay for other occupations in ways that are not obviously linked to the level of income. Two additional criteria are used by the public. They assign fair income on the basis of both need and merit. Presumably leaders, too, would consider need but, being largely upper-status, would focus more on merit.

That this is the case is seen by comparing the leaders' occupation rankings with the prestige Americans assign to occupations. Another national study obtained ratings from the public on the "general standing" of various occupations, based on the prestige or respect accorded to someone in those occupations.[28] Not surprisingly, its ranking of occupational status is quite similar to the leaders' ranking of both perceived and fair income (Table 8.8). Income is a good predictor of an occupation's general standing. Furthermore, desired change in the income of an occupation is related to the extent to which the income ranking of the occupation is out of line with its prestige. Two examples are professors, who are perceived to earn less than engineers but are ranked higher in prestige, and teachers,

**Table 8.8**
Perceived and Fair Income and Status of Occupations

| Occupation | Perceived income according to leaders ($) | Fair income according to leaders ($) | Status according to public[a] |
|---|---|---|---|
| Top executive | 167,070 (1)[b] | 95,230 (1) | 583 (1) |
| Doctor | 74,374 (2) | 52,798 (2) | 324 (1) |
| Engineer | 24,916 (3) | 24,705 (3) | 165 (4)[c] |
| Professor | 20,268 (4) | 22,766 (4) | 264 (3) |
| Plumber | 18,845 (5) | 15,575 (5) | 114 (6) |
| Automobile worker | 12,102 (6) | 12,045 (7) | 80 (8)[d] |
| Teacher | 10,474 (7) | 12,812 (6) | 131 (5)[e] |
| Bank teller | 9,083 (8) | 10,454 (8) | 104 (7) |
| Elevator operator | 6,877 (9) | 7,954 (9) | 62 (9)[f] |

a. Richard P. Coleman and Lee Rainwater, *Social Standing in America* (New York: Basic Books, 1978), pp. 58–59.
b. Rankings appear in parentheses.
c. Civil engineer.
d. Machine operator in truck factory.
e. High school teacher.
f. Marginal blue-collar and service jobs (mid-point of range for those occupations).

who are perceived to earn less than plumbers and auto workers but are also ranked higher on the prestige scale. In each case, the changes would bring income more into line with perceived social standing: engineers are lowered a bit, and professors raised; similarly, plumbers and auto workers are lowered, and teachers raised.

Although the changes bring social standing and income closer together, they are not sufficient to remove the inconsistencies in rank. In the ideal world, professors are closer to engineers in earnings but still earn less than engineers, despite their higher rating on general standing. Also in the ideal world, teachers move only marginally ahead of auto workers in earnings but remain behind plumbers, despite teachers' substantially higher social standing. This suggests that income is not the only factor that contributes to the status of some professions. In the case of professors and teachers the main factor is probably the status attached to intellectualism.

The large reduction in earnings of the professional athlete may derive from the fact that a major determinant of social standing is the educational level needed for the occupation. Professors and teachers have a higher standing than their income would warrant. The athlete fully merits the high income in one sense, for in few other fields is skill so constantly tested and so vital to success. Yet the merit is of a special sort, unconnected with formal education. At least in this respect, the groups may consider the high income to be unearned.

The reason that ideal income and general social standing do not correspond perfectly may simply be that the two sets of ratings are made by different groups, leaders and the general public. However, it is more likely that the leaders, though they think income ought to come close to social standing, are also influenced by the established claims that occupations have on particular income levels. The current income distribution creates claims that people may not want to violate even if earnings are out of line with social standing. In other words, people's ideal preferences are bound by their perceptions of reality. Americans' imagination about how much income an occupation ought to receive is anchored by the status quo, the current income. In addition, they may feel that in some cases social standing and income are appropriately out of line. On the one hand, there are cases where an individual earns respect for taking a low-paying job for the good of society, as in the case of teaching. On the other hand, an individual may get more pay to compensate for the low prestige of a job, such as garbage collection and other "dirty work."

### Ideology as Source of Attitudes

American leaders' assessments of fair income appear to reflect general norms of equality as well as the attributes of each occupation. This can be investigated more closely by turning back to the six underlying dimensions of equality attitudes. If the leaders' attitudes toward a proper income distribution are part of a general equality ideology, those views should be correlated with their views on the six scales. In particular, attitudes toward the earnings of occupations should be related to positions on the income redistribution scale.

This supposition is confirmed by the impact of demographic characteristics, including income, age, education, and religion, as well as of party allegiance, self-described ideology, attitudes toward the six equality scales, and group membership on how much the leaders would like to reduce the income gaps between an executive and an automobile worker and between an executive and an elevator operator (Table 8.9).[29] The strongest influences on the preference for income gap reduction are beliefs, particularly about redistribution and New Deal-type issues. Ideological position is also significant. In contrast, actual income, age, education, and partisanship have little effect. This means that attitudes toward income differentials are closely connected to an individual's general belief system about equality but are not so closely connected to a person's life circumstances. The issue is one of ideology rather than personal circumstances.

**Table 8.9**

Effect of Social Background, Party, and Political Views on Desired Income Gap Reduction Between High and Low Earners[a]

| ·cial background party, and political views | Income gap reduction between executive and auto worker | | Income gap reduction between executive and elevator operator | |
|---|---|---|---|---|
| | Beta | F ratio | Beta | F ratio |
| ·mily income | −.02 | (1.5) | −.05 | (7.9) |
| ·ge | −.02 | (1.1) | −.03 | (2.1) |
| ·lucation | .01 | (.2) | .03 | (2.0) |
| ·atholic | −.01 | (.0) | −.01 | (.1) |
| ·otestant | −.01 | (.1) | −.01 | (.2) |
| ·wish | .01 | (.1) | .01 | (.2) |
| ·rty identification | .02 | (.1) | .04 | (2.4) |
| ·lf-defined ideology | .09 | (10.3) | .06 | (5.1) |
| ·ew Deal attitudes[b] | .24 | (98.9) | .25 | (51.5) |
| ·ender attitudes | .00 | (.0) | .04 | (2.7) |
| ·distribution attitudes | .29 | (138.1) | .31 | (158.1) |
| ·uota attitudes | .00 | (.0) | .00 | (.0) |
| ·uses of inequality attitudes | .06 | (5.1) | .06 | (5.2) |
| ·ace attitudes | −.03 | (1.4) | −.04 | (1.6) |
| | .63 | | .65 | |
| | .39 | | .42 | |

a. Desired reduction in the income gap between high and low earners (e.g., executive to auto ·rker "is" ratio divided by executive to auto worker "ought" ratio) was regressed on social ·ckground, party, ideology, equality attitudes, and group membership. The coefficients for group ·mbership are not reported.

b. Attitudes on the six equality issues are measured by factor scores.

The importance of attitudes toward redistribution further validates the earlier analysis of equality dimensions. The redistribution scale is the dimension that one would expect to be most closely related to specific attitudes toward income adjustment. Since the redistribution scale and the attitudes toward the income hierarchy are based on independent sets of questions, the close relationship corroborates the view that attitudes toward equality fall into separate dimensions.

The analysis can be taken a step further by comparing the pattern across occupations. If general attitudes toward equality are differentially related to attitudes toward the income of the various occupations, other criteria may be found to underlie the earnings evaluations. The redistribution factor and, to a lesser extent, the New Deal factor are related to attitudes toward the income gaps between the executive and auto worker and the executive and elevator operator. These examples represent a high income versus a low one, but they also represent the major poles of contention in economic policy: big business and labor. If the earnings of particular occupations are evaluated largely on the basis of whether they are high or low, without consideration for other aspects of the occupations, general equality attitudes toward all high- or low-paid occupations should be similarly related. Those who are liberal on redistribution or the New Deal should want to cut the income of the high earners and raise the income of the low earners. In contrast, those who evaluate occupations according to factors other than earnings levels should have a more differentiated pattern. For instance, they may take into account the idiosyncrasies of a particular occupation, or the extent to which the occupation reflects the traditional economic conflict between management and labor.

That the groups do make such differentiated evaluations is shown by a series of equations which summarize the effects of demographic characteristics, party affiliation, group membership (included in the equation but not shown on the table), and attitudes toward the equality scales on the desired change in the income of each occupation (Table 8.10). The effects of the equality scales are the key concern. They vary substantially across different occupations. Attitudes toward the income of an executive appear to be most heavily affected by an individual's general equality ideology. Views on the New Deal and redistribution have a significant impact on estimates of the executive's income. Judgments of the income of three other occupations—an automobile worker, a bank teller, and an elevator operator—are affected by one's equality ideology, in particular by one's view on redistribution. For a number of other occupations, ideology is only marginally connected to income judgments. For judgments of the income of a teacher, engineer, professor, doctor, and plumber, redistribution has a weak effect. And for two occupations, the professional athlete and police officer, ideology plays no role at all.

Judgments of how incomes should be changed are differentially related to general equality ideologies. Attitudes toward the earnings of those occupations that have traditionally formed the polarities for social and economic conflict are most affected by such ideologies. These occupations form the core of the traditional labor-management conflict: executive posts at the top; blue-collar industrial jobs (auto worker) and low-status service occupations (elevator operator) at the bottom. Attitudes toward the income of professionals or sports stars—whose class positions have often been unclear—are not closely related to general ideology.

Judgments of one's own income are affected not by ideology but by personal circumstances. This is not surprising, since the leaders keep what they think they should earn reasonably within the range of their present earnings. What is more intriguing is the weak effect of education and general ideology. The groups support, in theory, an equal opportunity meritocracy where the skilled, which presumably means the better-educated, get ahead. Yet individuals define their own deserts not in terms of their educational attainment, for even age exerts a stronger effect, but in terms of what they now earn, which is always seen as a little too low. People have no difficulty convincing themselves that they deserve at least as much as they now earn.

AMERICAN attitudes toward a fair earnings distribution fit well with their more general attitudes toward equality. The leaders agree that the gap between the top and bottom earners should be wide, but they differ on how wide. They agree that the top earner deserves about four times their own earnings, but since they earn radically different amounts, the result is a wide disparity in what would be the fair income for a top earner. Similarly, they accept as fair the existing ratio of their own earnings to the lowest-earning occupation, even though that ratio also varies widely, depending on their own income. And they agree that the ranking of occupations in terms of earnings is about what it ought to be. They share a belief that income

**Table 8.10**

Effect of Social Background, Party, and Political Views on Desired Income Change for Each Occupation

| Social background, party, and political views | Desired income change for[a] | | | | | | | | | | | |
|---|---|---|---|---|---|---|---|---|---|---|---|---|
| | Executive | | Professional athlete | | Cabinet secretary | | Doctor | | Engineer | | Professor | |
| | Beta[c] | F ratio | Beta | F ratio | Beta | F ratio | Beta | F ratio | Beta | F ratio | Beta | F ratio |
| Family income | .06 | (6.5) | .01 | (.1) | .16 | (52.2) | -.00 | (.0) | .11 | (19.0) | .10 | (16.8) |
| Age | .01 | (.2) | -.01 | (.0) | .01 | (.1) | -.01 | (.1) | .05 | (3.6) | .00 | (.0) |
| Education | -.04 | (2.6) | -.07 | (8.3) | .06 | (5.9) | .02 | (.9) | .02 | (.9) | .05 | (4.5) |
| Party identification | -.05 | (4.0) | -.03 | (.7) | .02 | (.4) | -.02 | (.5) | -.01 | (.2) | .07 | (5.8) |
| New Deal attitudes[b] | -.28 | (55.2) | -.11 | (6.7) | -.13 | (10.7) | -.07 | (2.7) | -.10 | (5.3) | .11 | (7.2) |
| Feminist attitudes | -.02 | (.5) | -.04 | (1.3) | .04 | (2.1) | -.04 | (1.6) | -.05 | (3.1) | .04 | (1.9) |
| Redistribution attitudes | -.16 | (35.8) | -.01 | (.2) | -.11 | (15.4) | -.09 | (8.6) | -.11 | (12.5) | -.15 | (25.0) |
| Quota attitudes | .01 | (.1) | .02 | (.3) | -.03 | (.9) | .04 | (1.1) | -.03 | (.9) | -.02 | (.2) |
| Causes of inequality attitudes | -.06 | (4.7) | -.04 | (1.4) | .00 | (.0) | .04 | (1.4) | -.03 | (.9) | .05 | (2.9) |
| Race attitudes | .03 | (1.0) | .09 | (6.4) | .16 | (25.1) | .00 | (.0) | .08 | (4.9) | .03 | (.9) |
| r | .52 | | .23 | | .42 | | .18 | | .27 | | .33 | |
| r² | .27 | | .05 | | .17 | | .03 | | .08 | | .11 | |

**Table 8.10** *(continued)*

| Social background, party, and political views | Desired income change for[a] | | | | | | | | | | | | | |
| --- | --- | --- | --- | --- | --- | --- | --- | --- | --- | --- | --- | --- | --- | --- |
| | Police officer | | Plumber | | Teacher | | Auto worker | | Bank teller | | Elevator operator | | Someone in own occupation | |
| | Beta | F ratio | Beta | F ratio | Beta | F ratio | Beta | F ratio | Beta | F ratio | Beta | F ratio | Beta | F ratio |
| Family income | .05 | (3.8) | −.01 | (.2) | .06 | (7.0) | .02 | (.6) | .01 | (.1) | −.04 | (3.1) | .31 | (210.5) |
| Age | −.10 | (13.3) | −.04 | (1.9) | −.06 | (4.3) | −.01 | (.2) | −.03 | (1.1) | −.04 | (1.8) | .11 | (20.5) |
| Education | −.06 | (5.0) | −.00 | (.0) | .04 | (3.1) | −.01 | (.1) | .01 | (.2) | .03 | (1.1) | .04 | (3.1) |
| Party identification | .10 | (10.5) | .01 | (.1) | .03 | (1.2) | .01 | (.2) | −.00 | (.0) | .04 | (1.5) | .00 | (.0) |
| New Deal attitudes[b] | −.02 | (.1) | −.07 | (2.6) | .08 | (3.8) | .07 | (3.3) | .07 | (3.0) | .01 | (.0) | .02 | (.2) |
| Feminist attitudes | −.02 | (.3) | −.02 | (.5) | .08 | (7.1) | −.06 | (4.1) | −.00 | (.0) | .04 | (1.5) | −.03 | (1.2) |
| Redistribution attitudes | .06 | (3.5) | .11 | (12.3) | .10 | (11.7) | .18 | (36.0) | .17 | (35.0) | .25 | (73.8) | −.02 | (.4) |
| Quota attitudes | −.06 | (2.6) | −.03 | (.9) | −.05 | (2.3) | .02 | (.5) | −.00 | (.0) | .00 | (.0) | .00 | (.0) |
| Causes of inequality attitudes | .06 | (3.2) | −.01 | (.2) | .07 | (6.2) | .05 | (2.8) | .09 | (8.7) | .03 | (1.3) | .01 | (.2) |
| Race attitudes | .01 | (.1) | .11 | (10.2) | .07 | (4.2) | .03 | (.6) | −.03 | (.8) | .06 | (3.1) | .04 | (1.8) |
| $r$ | .23 | | .27 | | .38 | | .34 | | .36 | | .38 | | .58 | |
| $r^2$ | .05 | | .07 | | .14 | | .12 | | .13 | | .15 | | .34 | |

a. Desired income change for each occupation ("is" rating divided by "ought" rating) was regressed on social background, party, equality attitudes, and group membership. The coefficients for group membership are not reported.
b. Attitudes on the six equality issues are measured by factor scores.

ought to vary across occupations. They do not favor equality of result. Yet there are substantial differences in what is considered an equitable income gap, and consequently, there are substantial disagreements over the fairness of the current distribution.

Attitudes toward the income hierarchy reflect specific characteristics of occupations. Yet they also reflect something more general. Earnings attitudes parallel attitudes toward equality. And the two sets of attitudes form part of a general ideology of equality. This ideology, however, concerns more than just equality. Views about a fair income reflect not only the amount that occupations earn but also the position of those occupations in traditional economic and political conflicts. The equality ideology is thus close to the heart of basic political conflicts in America.

These attitudes underscore the importance of beliefs and values of equality. People's views of a proper income distribution in America are little affected by their own personal economic and social traits. Leaders' attitudes on income are unrelated to their own income or education level. Their views on the fairness of their own income are shaped by their personal economic condition, but their views on general income equality derive rather from their general ideology as well as from their own institutional position. Once again, equality beliefs are seen to be autonomous and not merely the ideational manifestation of one's economic self-interest. What is deemed a fair income distribution depends not on narrow self-interest but on one's beliefs about equality in general and about where one's group stands in relation to competing groups.

Attitudes toward the distribution of income make clear that Americans do not support radical egalitarianism. On the contrary, a substantial income gap is considered fair by all the leadership groups. These findings confirm the general view of American political culture. The ideology of individual achievement remains potent. These findings also have important implications for matters of policy and politics. The income values of leaders set a boundary on acceptable income policies. Thus, sharp income differentiation is likely to remain central to American life.

# 9

# Equality of Influence

The United States is unique among nations in terms of equality. In economic matters it is a relatively unequal society with public policies that sustain a wider disparity of income than is found in most comparable nations. In political matters the United States has taken a strong lead in policies creating equal political rights, as have the American citizenry in the use of those rights. Americans' views toward economic stratification were found to be quite compatible with the substantial income differentiation that characterizes the United States. Their views on the stratification of political influence are similar in some ways, but quite different in others.

Political stratification refers to differences in the amount of influence or power wielded by individuals or groups over government policy.[1] Political and economic stratification are not easily compared, since there is no common metric. Indeed, political stratification has no acceptable yardstick at all. Hence, while there are many measures of the equality of income distribution from nation to nation, there are no parallel measures of the equality of political influence. Indicators of the distribution of political participation are indirect at best. The difficulty of measuring political stratification not only poses a methodological problem but bears heavily on the substance of political conflict.

As with income, what individuals believe to be the actual influence hierarchy in America is not the same as what they believe to be a fair distribution. The norm of equal citizen influence—one person, one vote—has greater appeal and is more fully reflected in public policy than the concept of equal citizen income. The government has attempted to put a ceiling on political influence in a way that finds no analogy in the economic sphere. And government has been more vigorous in providing a floor under political rights than it has been in providing an economic floor. The ideal of equal monetary reward for each occupation, though a useful numerical benchmark for comparing leadership groups, is both unrealistic and unsupported; equal political influence for individuals and groups is a less outlandish standard.

From another perspective, political influence is even more hierarchical than is economic position, for someone must influence someone else. All societies have distinctions between the rulers and the ruled. But for determining how influence over the rulers is distributed among the ruled, equality, though not expected, is a useful benchmark, denoting a society in which all nongovernmental actors have roughly equal influence over decision-makers. The mere fact that public policy supports equal political rights for all citizens does not mean that all citizens use those rights equally or that all leaders agree that all segments of society should have equal political influence.

The struggle for equal political rights—including the right to vote, the right to form political organizations such as parties, the right to petition the legislature, and the general right of equal access to the government and equal voice over what the government does—has been as long and at least as virulent as the struggle over economic and social equality. Its goal is not only the provision of abstract rights but the equalization of citizen influence over governmental decision—an equality derived from the basic democratic norm that the preferences of all adult citizens are of equal worth. Such influence over governmental activities is desirable both for its own sake and for the sake of the other rights it protects.

The ability to influence the government, to speak up and be heard, is a fundamental democratic right. Without some such influence, at least through suffrage, one does not enjoy full citizenship. The ability to participate in decisions affecting one's life confers dignity; the absence of the right to participate is a severe deprivation. Political influence is also valuable because it can be converted into other desirable goods, such as economic and social benefits. Groups that have been disadvantaged socially and economically have sought political influence in the hope that it can be used to improve their circumstances. Indeed, some leaders of disadvantaged groups argue that acquiring more political influence is the prime goal for the economically disadvantaged, since that is the only way to ensure the stability and security of any economic gains they may obtain. If the poor simply lobby for stronger welfare laws without attempting to secure more equal political influence, those benefits might evaporate after the next election. Since "the hand that gives can also take away," disadvantaged groups must see to it that they have a hand themselves in the distribution of benefits.

As the scope of governmental activity expands, more aspects of the issue of equality become politicized, and the political arena becomes the field of battle. Some issues, such as use of the tax system for redistribution, are inevitably political, but even those issues that could be left to the private sector, such as jobs or education, are likely to be resolved within frameworks set by legislation and regulation. Even issues concerning the division of family responsibility, which deeply affect equality between the sexes, are likely to be affected by governmental action in relation to day-care facilities, divorce and custody law, and medical benefits. Indeed, even by taking no action on such issues, the government is taking a position.[2] Equal political influence is therefore both significant in its own right and closely related to other forms of equality.

The leaders' perceptions of the actual distribution of influence in America as well as their preferences as to what that distribution ought to be relate to the empirical question "Who governs?" and the normative question "Who should govern?" which lie at the heart of much political analysis. In the United States, there has long been debate on the issue of who actually governs, as opposed to who should govern. The debate centers on the relative power of groups and the relative openness of the government to pressures from different groups. Even the staunchest defenders of the pluralist model of American politics do not claim that contending groups are endowed with equal political resources or that the system has ever been open equally to all groups.

Those who take a fairly benign view of the pluralist struggle see the system as somewhat biased and yet relatively open: groups differ in the amount of political resources they control, but all groups control some, and the disparity between sectors of the society is not severe. More important, they view the system as open to new groups challenging the established order. Entry into the political market is regarded as relatively easy, though successful competition in that market is somewhat more difficult.

Critics of the history of group conflict in America, however, see the system as severely biased. They regard the political struggle among contending groups to be highly unequal. A few groups have an overwhelming resource advantage; others stand only a faint chance of prevailing. In general, the politically advantaged groups are the more affluent, upper-status segments of society. Business, especially big business, is most advantaged in this respect; but established labor groups, technocrats, and others have special access and thereby receive a disproportionate share of the benefits of the political system. In this view of group conflict, there is little opportunity for new groups to penetrate the political market and prosper.

Other observers take an even dimmer view of the American political system. As they see it, the system allows little real competition. The group struggle over political outcomes is a facade for a system dominated by a few potent interests. In the Marxist version of this thesis, the dominant power is corporate capital. In the elitist version, the dominant group is business and perhaps the military. The promise of widespread access that the system appears to offer is merely an illusion to distract those with grievances into the fruitless pursuit of redress.[3]

Usually at issue is the question of who actually governs rather than who ought to govern. Neither the pluralists nor the antipluralists argue that the system ought to be closed to some or even that it ought to be more open to some social groups than to others. They agree that the political system ought to provide equal access and relatively equal influence. The argument is typically over the extent to which this is the case.[4] American leaders similarly differ more on the reality of the case than on what ought to be the case. All agree that influence ought to be roughly equal.[5] They disagree sharply on whether that is indeed the case. The result is that the debate over equality of political influence is empirical rather than normative or, rather, the normative debate derives largely from the empirical one.

The purpose here is not to evaluate the various perspectives on power in America in order to determine which offers the most accurate picture of American life, but rather to approach this issue from the perspective of leaders. Leaders are actors in the American political process, as well as acute observers of it. Their views on the power structure in America give clues to the actual nature of the power distribution. Still, leaders cannot be regarded as objective observers, for they view the world of political influence from particular perspectives. Many of them represent groups embroiled in the political struggle, including business, labor, farmers, civil rights activists, feminists, and political parties, and their views are heavily influenced by their own roles in the contest over political equality. The other groups—intellectuals, the media, and youth—are involved less deeply and may provide a more neutral perspective on the struggle for power.

### Measuring Influence

As with income inequality, both the "is" and the "ought" of political influence are of interest. The leaders were therefore asked about the actual and the ideal influence of various actors in the American political process.[6] As with income, an appropriate measure of perceived and fair influence is also needed, as is a choice of groups whose influence is to be compared. And as with income, political measures simplify one of the most complex concepts in social analysis. They nevertheless provide revealing comparative data.

The leaders were asked to assess the relative influence of a series of target groups by rating each on a seven-point scale ranging from "very influential" to "very little influence" both in terms of how much influence they have and how much they should have (Figure 9.1). The groups were presented together to the leaders in order to measure influence not against some absolute standard but relative to each other. Whereas for comparing the "is" and "ought" of income, occupations were the appropriate units of comparison, for comparing political influence the leadership groups are more appropriate. These represent established as well as challenging groups. Another advantage of using these groups as the objects of influence ratings is that they show how sets of leaders rate the influence of their own group in comparison with the influence of other groups. The target groups exclude youth and include banks and consumer groups along with labor unions, farm organizations, business, media, intellectuals, feminists, blacks, and political parties.[7]

Unlike income, where the earnings of individuals are at issue, political influence involves collectivities: for instance, big business, not individual executives. This necessarily affects the results. Labor unions, for example, are considered at least as influential as big business, whereas a typical executive would certainly be ranked as

**Figure 9.1**

Influence Question

We would like to know how much influence you think various groups *actually have* over American life, and how much influence you think they *should have*. Here is a scale in which "1" represents "very influential" and "7" represents "very little influence."

(Please place your answers below)

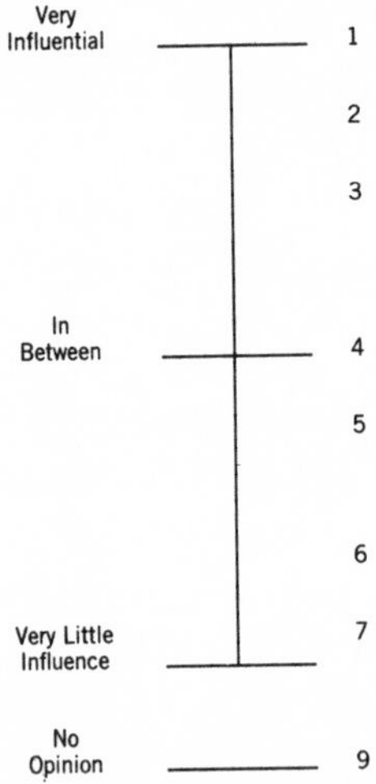

| | | | Actual Influence | Influence They Should Have |
|---|---|---|---|---|
| Very Influential | 1 | Labor Unions | _ _ _ _ | _ _ _ _ |
| | 2 | Farm Organizations | _ _ _ _ | _ _ _ _ |
| | 3 | Business Leaders | _ _ _ _ | _ _ _ _ |
| | | Media | _ _ _ _ | _ _ _ _ |
| In Between | 4 | Intellectuals | _ _ _ _ | _ _ _ _ |
| | 5 | Banks | _ _ _ _ | _ _ _ _ |
| | 6 | Consumer Groups | _ _ _ _ | _ _ _ _ |
| | | Feminist Groups | _ _ _ _ | _ _ _ _ |
| Very Little Influence | 7 | Black Leaders | _ _ _ _ | _ _ _ _ |
| No Opinion | 9 | The Political Parties | _ _ _ _ | _ _ _ _ |

more influential than a typical average factory worker, though not necessarily than an average union leader. The difference in the nature of units in the economic and the political sphere cannot be avoided. We are not interested in either the earnings of collectivities, such as the total income share of executives versus factory workers, or the influence of individuals, such as that of an executive versus an auto worker. Income ends up in the hands of individuals; political influence inheres in collectivities.

To measure the real influence of the groups would involve an elaborate series of case studies of actual decision-making. Even so, the results would still be uncertain, because there is no clear metric for influence. Similarly, the personal views of the different leaders as to the influence that groups have and ought to have are uncertain indices at best. To put a group high on the influence scale does not show how much influence the leaders want that group to have in absolute terms. However, it does show the rating of the group in relation to others—whether it is perceived to have more or less influence than other groups or thought to deserve more or less influence than other groups.

The perceptions of the leaders as to a target group's relative influence can have a twofold effect on its actual influence. On the one hand, reputed influence can become real influence. A group that is believed to be powerless may be ignored and consequently stripped of power. On the other hand, as Samuel Huntington has remarked, "effective power is unnoticed." Given the antipower ideology in America, a group loses much of its power once its influence is widely recognized, just as individuals who become too familiar with their political acquaintances find their influence waning. Both principles operate. Much turns on the visibility of influence. Some groups have reputations for influence but are able to exercise that influence in quiet, less visible ways. This is one source of the power of business in the United States. The public's consensus on the importance of business to the economy as a whole as well as business's established connection with the government give it a privileged position where it can be influential without being overtly so.[8] Other groups have reputations for weakness, yet what little influence they can exert is more overt and noticeable both because they are perceived as powerless and because they are challenging groups without established channels to power. These groups lose both ways: they are weakened because they are thought to be weak, and they are weakened because they are noticed when they act.

Although the accuracy of the leaders' perceptions about the influence distribution in America is all but impossible to judge, their assessments of where they stand in relation to other groups are more easily tested. Their estimates of their own influence can be compared with the perceptions that other groups have of them, including both their allies and their antagonists. Their perceptions also can be compared with the views of more neutral or objective observers. Since the leaders are knowledgeable participants in the political process, a comparison of their perception of their own group's influence with others' perceptions of them locates systematic distortions in their views on influence distribution.

## Perceptions of Influence

American leaders share a similar view of who occupies the top rung of the influence ladder (Figure 9.2). Most groups place business, labor, and the media near the top of the hierarchy. Business and labor

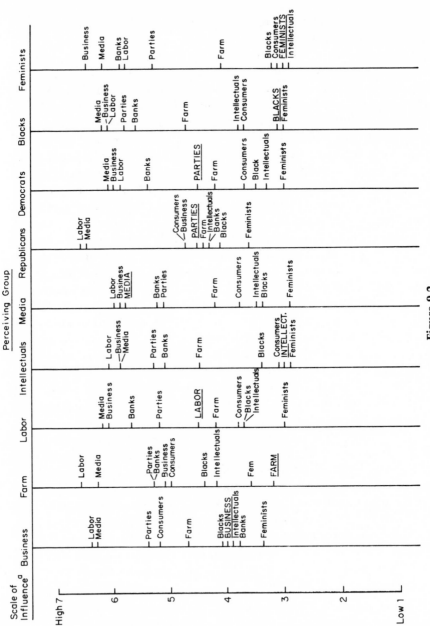

**Figure 9.2**

Perceived Influence of Target Groups

a. Each group's perception of itself is underlined. The placement of the target groups corre-

deviate from this to some extent. Each places itself lower than any other group rates it, in either absolute or relative terms, though business joins with other groups in rating labor high, and labor returns the compliment to business. Of all the groups rated, labor is perceived to be the most influential: five of the nine groups place labor at the top.[9]

There is also consensus on which groups occupy the lowest rungs of the influence distribution. Blacks, intellectuals, and feminists fall near the bottom of the influence ratings of most groups, sometimes joined by consumer groups. Feminists are rated lowest in influence by all groups except two: feminists rank intellectuals slightly below themselves, and farmers put themselves at the very bottom. All groups agree that blacks are more influential than feminists.

The Republicans and Democrats agree on the influence of the political parties, at the midpoint in both cases. But the parties differ on the positions of other groups. The Republicans have a fairly neat view of the world of influence, which is clearly dominated by labor and the media. All other groups cluster together in the middle of the scale, except for the feminists at the bottom. The Democrats see a more gradual differentiation. At the top are the media, business, and labor, followed a bit lower by banks. Parties and the farm sector occupy the middle. Consumers, blacks, and intellectuals are rated nearly as low as feminists, who are ranked at the bottom.

The leaders exhibit a kind of influence denial, tending to underrate their own influence and exaggerate that of the others. Almost every group rates its own influence lower than any other group rates it. The only two exceptions are the feminists, who rate themselves low and are rated even lower by five of the eight groups, and intellectuals, who are rated a bit lower by feminists than by themselves. The media are atypical; although other groups give them a higher rating, they nonetheless see themselves as very influential. In public they adamantly deny such influence, portraying themselves as neutral observers and messengers.[10] But when interviewed confidentially, they display the highest self-rating of any group. On the whole, though, the groups not only see themselves as lacking much political influence but also see other groups as having more of it. They share a particular view of the systemic cause of unequal influence, seeing themselves as the victims not of a system deaf to all groups but of a system that "plays favorites."

The minimization of one's own influence is strongest among business, labor, farmers, blacks, and feminists (Figure 9.3). The self-rating of each group except feminists is well below that given to it by any other group. The disparity is greatest in the case of business and labor. Business puts itself in the lower half of the scale; others see it as far more powerful. The case is similar for labor.

When business and labor evaluate each other's influence, business sees itself as much less influential than labor, and labor sees itself as much less influential than business.[11] Though each group considers its influence lower than others do, business goes further than labor in denying its own influence. The relative ranking that each group gives itself is even more revealing. Labor puts itself below four groups: the media, business, banks, and political parties. This is probably a lower rating than it deserves, powerful though the groups above it are. Business is even more modest, rating itself below six groups: labor, the media, parties, consumer groups, farm groups,

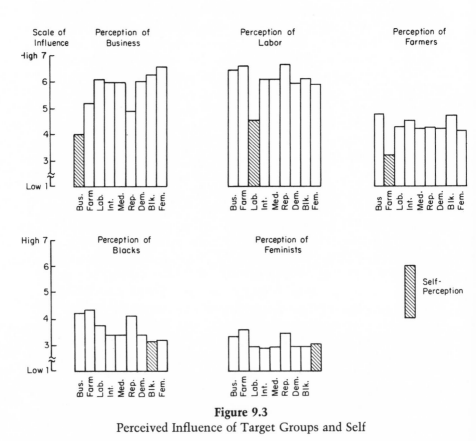

**Figure 9.3**
Perceived Influence of Target Groups and Self

and civil rights groups. Both business and labor hold a dim estimation of their own political strength.

The denial of one's own influence extends to the perceived influence of one's allies. The conservative triad of business, Republicans, and farmers all see business as less influential than does the liberal set of labor, Democrats, feminists, and blacks. The opposite is the case for labor, which the liberal groups see as less powerful than does the conservative set. However, these differences are less extreme in relation to labor, which even the liberal groups see as quite powerful. A similar pattern is found in the assessment of the influence of blacks. The conservative triad, the groups furthest ideologically from the blacks, rate the influence of blacks higher than do those groups more in step with blacks. A similar situation holds for feminists. All groups see the feminists as relatively uninfluential, but business, farmers, and Republicans see them as more influential than do more liberal groups. This ideological pattern does not hold for farmers, who are seen by all groups, except the farmers themselves, as occupying a middle position of influence.

With such wide disparities in influence ratings, it would be valuable to have the opinions of more objective observers. Perhaps the nearest approximation to neutral arbiters of influence in the leadership study are intellectuals and the media leaders. They are in fairly close agreement in their evaluation of political influence.[12]

Yet they too have political views that color their judgments about the influence of groups. When they are divided into those who consider themselves liberals, moderates, and conservatives, the liberals rate those groups at the conservative end of the ideological spectrum as more influential than the conservatives rate themselves, while the conservatives see the groups on the left as being more influential than the liberals see themselves. Although these differences are not great, those intellectuals and media leaders who consider themselves moderate are probably more objective observers. There are enough moderates in each group—60 intellectuals and 96 media leaders— to allow reliable estimates of their positions.

The influence perceptions of these observers differ from the self-perceptions of the groups (Figure 9.4). According to these "neutral" observers, labor is the most influential group, followed closely by business. Farmers occupy a middle position, with blacks and feminists trailing behind. The neutral observers regard labor and business as much more influential than those groups see themselves. Farmers also underrate their own influence. In contrast, the self-

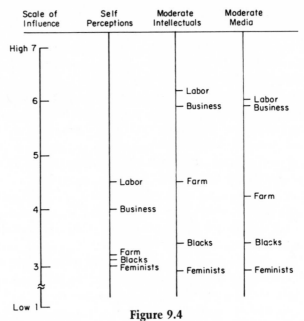

**Figure 9.4**
Perceived Influence of Groups by Self and Neutral Observers

ratings of blacks and feminists are much closer to the ratings of the observers—in fact, slightly higher. Business and labor are not unique in rating their influence low. All groups do so, while rating the influence of others, especially their antagonists, high. Yet business and labor stand out in the extent to which they underrate themselves. Business leaders are especially distinctive in this regard when comparing themselves with consumer groups. They consider such groups to be more influential than business itself, a perception shared with Republicans but rejected by all other groups. Challenging groups, in contrast, have a more realistic view of their own influence.

This discrepancy does not necessarily mean that established groups, such as business, underestimate their own influence. Challenging groups may overestimate the influence of established groups if they feel bitterness or jealousy toward the established groups, harbor an exaggerated impression of how much influence is necessary to become established in the first place, or are simply ill-informed. Even the perceptions of neutral observers are subject to this kind of distortion. Moderate intellectuals and media leaders, though probably the most impartial of the groups, are not necessarily the best-informed about other groups' influence.

Nevertheless, established groups probably underrate their actual influence more than do challenging groups. Despite the lack of a definitive measure of actual influence, labor and business leaders are active and well-connected participants in politics. In fact, compared with the other groups, labor and business leaders know a great number of important public figures and contact them more frequently. This influence is consistent with the privileged position of business in American public life.

Influence denial is a reasonable psychological defense. If groups and individuals regard themselves as less powerful than they really are, or than others see them, and view their opponents as more powerful, they will likely be vigilant in protecting their position. The surprising fact that this reaction is most pronounced among the strongest and best-established groups, like business and labor, may be due to the routinization of influence. Established groups, especially business, have more routine channels of access to government than do challenging groups. Interest groups have two means of gaining influence: an "insider" and an "outsider" strategy. The insider approach involves operating informally yet directly with decisionmakers in legislatures or the executive. This strategy requires frequent personal contact. It is quiet and discreet. The outsider approach involves widening the scope of conflict through, for example, publicity via radio or television, in order to mobilize followers and the public at large.

Interest groups differ in the likelihood that they will seek to achieve their goals through insider tactics, such as talking with a member of Congress, or through outsider tactics, such as taking to the airwaves (Figure 9.5). Established groups, such as labor, farm, and especially business, are more likely to adopt an insider than an outsider strategy, while challenging groups, such as blacks and feminists, are about equally likely to use either approach. In general, a group that has a choice between the two strategies usually chooses the insider approach. The direct inside influence of a personal acquaintance has all the advantages over the outsider campaign that a phone call has over a letter. Despite uncertainty over whether the established position of groups in America is the cause or the result of their political connections, these groups clearly enjoy closer ties to government, which facilitate an insider strategy.

This may be a partial key to the discrepancy between actual and perceived influence. The disparity may reflect the less visible, insider way in which influence is exercised by established groups. The very fact of their establishment makes them less aware of their own

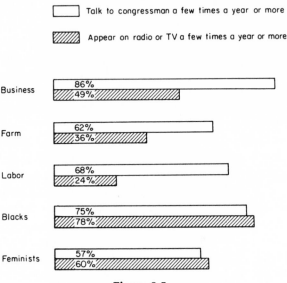

**Figure 9.5**

Use of Insider and Outsider Strategies by Groups

influence. As influence becomes routinized, it ceases to be perceived as influence at all. This may explain business's view of itself as weaker than most other groups. Business, more than any other contending group, probably has the largest number of routine channels into the government. Since business and business organizations far outnumber other organizations, including labor unions, business influence is dispersed, seemingly disorganized, and hence less noticed by those exerting it. A similar, though less pronounced, routinization probably explains the underestimates by farm and labor organizations of their own influence. In contrast, emerging groups such as the feminists have no routine modes of influence, no set of relationships in which influence is exercised without being recognized as such. Thus, whatever influence they have, or do not have, is overt and easily recognizable.

The difference between routine insider influence and more conspicuous outsider influence probably heightens the impact of failure on insiders in contrast to outsiders. Successful influence in an insider setting is often not noticed, for this is simply the way things work. Failure for an insider, however, stands out. The outsider is more aware of the contest of wills that politics entails. Success and failure are equally noticeable.

Although the routine exercise of influence may make its users less aware of their own influence, it does not make that influence invisible to sophisticated observers. Other groups, for example, rate business and labor quite high. Thus, influence denial, and the resulting difference of perception across groups, may be due to the underestimation of one's own influence among the established groups.

Another possible explanation for influence denial could be the antipower ethic of American political culture. The leaders of the various groups might underestimate their own influence because they believe, and they expect others to believe, that the exercise of political influence is somehow disreputable. This explanation, however, is not plausible, because leaders admit to wanting significantly more influence than they perceive themselves to have.

**Ideals of Influence**

American leaders' perceptions of the influence hierarchy can be explained only with difficulty. These perceptions are complicated by partisan leanings, membership in established or challenging groups, and psychological factors such as influence denial. Yet when asked to rank the target groups according to how much influence they ought to have, the leaders advance views that are somewhat less equivocal (Figure 9.6). For the top position on this ideal influence hierarchy, each set of leaders elects the same group: itself. The sole exceptions to this rule are feminists and intellectuals, who would place themselves a close second behind consumer groups. The leaders would be expected to put themselves at or near the pinnacle of the hierarchy, since one does not become a top representative of a group unless one believes that the group has something important to say. Still, the uniformity is striking. Beyond that, most groups believe that feminists ought to be least influential—except the feminists themselves. And most groups would place the civil rights groups near the bottom, with the major exception of blacks themselves. Feminists, however, would like blacks to be quite influential. The blacks do not reciprocate.

In their placement of consumer groups, the leaders follow two clear patterns. Most would place consumer groups either first or second in the influence hierarchy, along with their own groups. The more conservative groups—business, farmers, and Republicans— who are allied on all the other issues, rank consumer groups much lower. Indeed, all conservative groups would put consumer groups

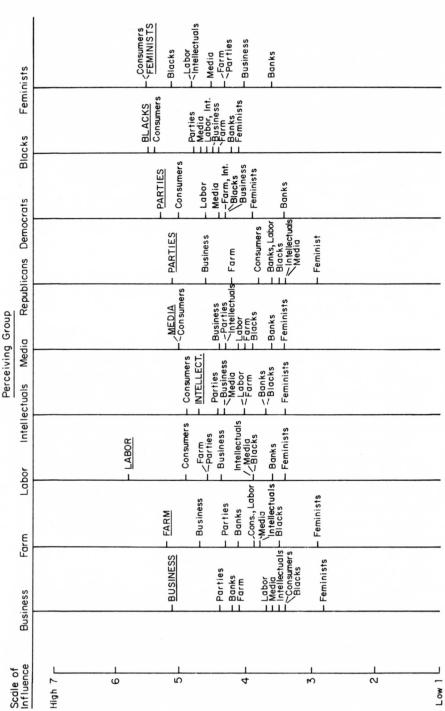

**Figure 9.6**

lower than each of themselves. Because consumer groups lean to the left on most issues, they consistently fare better among the more liberal groups. More to the point, consumer advocates are wont to complain about product quality and prices, a tendency that does not endear them to the conservative groups. Business and farmers are the ones who make the products and set the prices that consumer groups complain about, and Republicans are the ones who care especially about business and farm votes.

Consumer groups purport to be "the voice of the public," and there is something very American about the suggestion that the general public ought to have considerable influence in the way things are run. It is illuminating, therefore, that most of the groups, except the conservatives, would place themselves close to—either slightly behind or ahead of—consumer groups in influence. Perhaps the groups see themselves too as spokesmen for the public.This may be one reason that each group feels deserving of top influence: its leaders regard themselves as representatives of the public will.

This suspicion is corroborated by the placement of political parties in the influence hierarchy. With the striking exception of feminists, all the groups rank the parties as one of the top three groups in desired influence. It is probably no coincidence that the groups which consistently do best among all the leaders are consumer groups, parties—the two voices of the public—and what might be called the "self." These groups constitute the top three groups in over half of the desired influence rankings, and at least two of them are in the top trio for every group but one. One of the main forces underlying this pattern of ideal influence is apparently the feeling that public opinion ought to carry more weight than any other voice, except perhaps for the voice of each particular leader. This suggests that the leaders see their own voices either as more important than the public's or, more likely, as closest to the heart of public opinion— even closer than consumer groups and parties. Significantly, this pattern holds up across liberals and conservatives alike.

Feminists are the notable exception. While eight groups consistently would put parties among the top three groups, feminists would put parties eighth, or third from the bottom, ahead of only business and banks. Here feminists diverge sharply from blacks, who follow the general liberal pattern of ranking parties only behind themselves and consumer groups. Because gender discrimination has not yet become as much a partisan issue as racial discrimination has, feminists stand to gain little from a system where party leaders have a great deal of influence. At the time of the survey, neither party had seriously committed itself to gender equality. Blacks, in contrast, probably recognized that they had a powerful ally in Democratic leaders and were therefore willing to accept the mixed blessing of highly influential party leaders as a whole. In 1980 the two parties began to diverge in their stances toward gender equality, and accordingly, feminists began to assume a more active role in the Democratic party.

This interpretation is supported by the Democratic and Republican parties' desired ranking of the groups. Not surprisingly, Republicans put blacks and feminists very low on the influence ladder. Democrats, on the contrary, rank blacks high, well ahead of feminists, whom they rank second from the bottom, ahead only of banks.

The Democrats' low rating for feminists is especially significant because it makes feminists the only group ranked very low by both parties. The two parties are generally split on the desired influence of other groups, with the result that almost everybody else is fairly high on one or another of the parties' proposed hierarchies. But this is not true for feminists:

| Target group | *Highest rank received from either party* (1–10) |
|---|---|
| Parties | 1 |
| Business | 2 |
| Farm | 3 |
| Labor | 3 |
| Media | 4 |
| Blacks | 5 |
| Intellectuals | 6 |
| Feminists | 9 |

The feminists stand out in the preferred influence rankings: they alone wish to give the political parties little influence, and the two parties are no more generous in return.

Each group would prefer an influence distribution that is more nearly equal than the one it perceives to exist; the ranges of influence are larger on the actual than on the ideal scale. This effect can be measured more precisely by the means and standard deviations of the group ratings of actual and ideal influence (Table 9.1). The standard deviations of the actual ratings are substantially larger than those

**Table 9.1**

Comparison of Perceived and Fair Distributions of Influence

| Group | Mean influence ratings of all target groups | | Standard deviation of influence ratings of all target groups | |
|---|---|---|---|---|
| | Perceived | Fair | Perceived | Fair |
| Business | 4.7 | 3.7 | 1.2 | .7 |
| Farm | 5.2 | 3.8 | 1.0 | .5 |
| Labor | 4.7 | 4.3 | 1.3 | .9 |
| Intellectuals | 4.6 | 4.1 | 1.5 | .5 |
| Media | 4.7 | 4.2 | 1.3 | .6 |
| Republicans | 5.0 | 3.6 | 1.2 | .5 |
| Democrats | 4.8 | 4.3 | 1.3 | .5 |
| Blacks | 4.8 | 4.7 | 1.5 | .5 |
| Feminists | 4.8 | 4.7 | 1.6 | .7 |
| Youth | 4.6 | 4.3 | 1.5 | .5 |

of the ideal ratings, indicating that the leaders would like to see a narrower spread in influence than now exists. In addition, the means for the ideal are consistently smaller than for the actual and are consistently closer to the center of the seven-point scale of influence. Thus, all of the groups would prefer a more equal distribution of influence, slightly lower and closer to the center of the scale, although they differ over the proper order of groups within that hierarchy.

The leaders' ratings of their own actual and desired influence give a clearer picture of their views (Figure 9.7). Arrows indicate the direction and amount of desired change. Each group, with the exception of the media, would raise its own influence. The groups that see themselves as lowest on the influence scale—farmers, intellectuals, blacks, and feminists—would raise themselves the most.

The media are the only group that sees its own influence as too high. They apparently consider their substantial political clout to be inconsistent with their professional role of observer and messenger. They are perhaps the only group that truly subscribes to the antipower ethic. In public, they deny having political sway, because they consider it inappropriate to their job. In private, they acknowledge the magnitude of their influence and suggest that it be curbed.

Influence would be far more equal if groups could change the influence hierarchy according to their own desires. The ideal level of influence is roughly the same for all groups, while there is wide variation among the actual levels of influence. If each group could choose its own position, influence would be more equally distributed than in the situation as each group believes it now exists.

The views on perceived and desired influence of the contending groups—business, farmers, labor, blacks, and feminists—show a contrasting pattern (Figure 9.8). Each group would readjust the influence distribution by moving itself up to the top and demoting any group perceived to have a lot of influence. For business and farmers, this would entail reducing the influence of all the other contending groups, including each other's influence. Labor's main interest is to raise itself and lower business. Business and labor are the mirror images of each other: each sees the other as currently the most influential, and each would reverse their relative positions. Labor, unlike business and farmers, would not reduce the influence of all contending groups. Indeed, aside from its change of position with business, labor would slightly increase the influence of the other groups.

Blacks and feminists would reduce the influence of both business and labor. Even though blacks and labor are members of the Democratic coalition and are attitudinally quite distant from business, blacks feel that both business and labor are too powerful and deserve nearly equal reductions in power. Labor in turn thinks black groups are slightly more powerful than itself. Labor leaders would change the position of blacks only a little but would move themselves well ahead of blacks. These influence ratings show once again that though blacks and labor are coalition partners, they differ substantially on the issue of race.

Blacks and feminists view each other as having similar influence, and each group would raise both itself and the other. But feminists would raise blacks substantially more than blacks would raise feminists. In the feminists' hierarchy, blacks would be endowed with only slightly less influence than they themselves. Blacks, on the contrary, want an influence hierarchy in which they are well ahead of feminists.

The views of the remaining groups show similar contrasts (Figure 9.9). The Republicans would leave business and farmers where they are and would lower the other groups to have less influence than business and farmers. This reshuffling involves a substantial reduc-

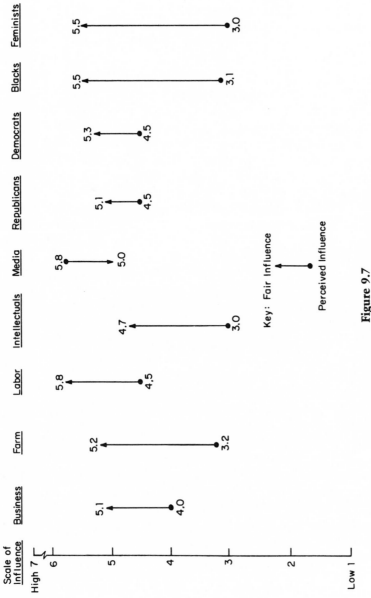

**Figure 9.7**

Perceived and Fair Influence of Self

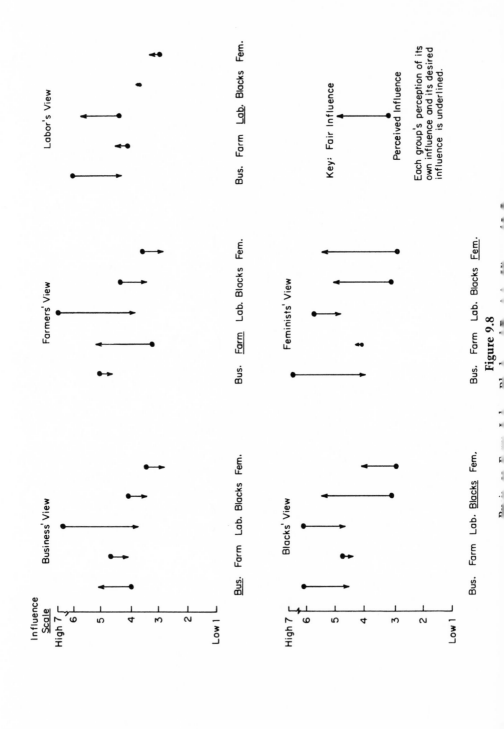

**Figure 9.8**

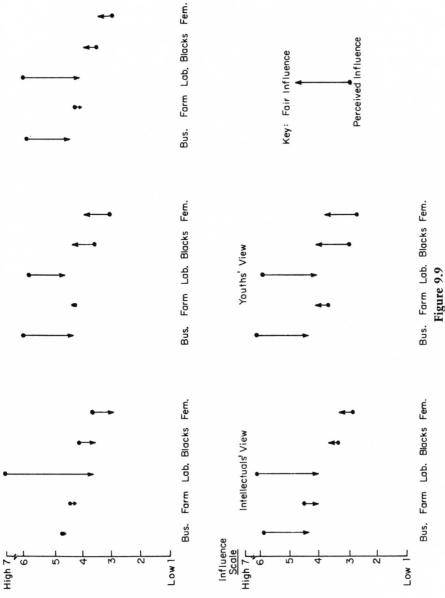

**Figure 9.9**

Party, Media, Intellectual, and Youth Views of Influence

tion in the influence of labor. Republicans and Democrats differ in their treatment of their most powerful coalition partner. Republicans would not raise business's influence—a well-advised stance for a partner in a coalition—nor would they diminish it. Democrats have a more uneasy relationship with their partner, labor. Democrats see both labor and business as quite powerful and would reduce them substantially. Labor and the Democrats are similarly far apart at times on certain equality issues, as compared with the cheek-to-cheek positioning of business and the Republicans. Democrats feel more of a threat from big labor than Republicans feel from business.

Democrats would increase the influence of blacks and feminists so that the contest between the established business and labor groups and the challenging black and feminist groups would be much more equal. In this respect, the Democrats resemble the media, intellectuals, and youth. Each of these groups would equalize the contest by reducing the influence of business and labor and increasing the influence of blacks and feminists.

Almost all of the desired changes in influence among groups would have an equalizing effect: groups seen as powerful would have less power, and groups seen as weak would receive more. The result would be a distribution that is more equitable, though by no means completely equitable. Each group places itself at the top of the ideal world, sometimes by a substantial amount in comparison with its antagonist groups, although the amount is never as large as a group's perceived influence disadvantage vis-à-vis the antagonist groups. The consensus among leaders that cuts should be made in the influence of the groups perceived to be most influential—labor, business, and the media—is shared by the public at large. Big business, labor unions, and newspaper editors, along with politicians, rank highest, according to the public, among groups with too much power.[13]

However, this consensus on the equalization of political influence is coupled with disagreement as to how one goes about achieving such equalization. Groups have different perspectives on the present distribution of influence. From the point of view of business, the changes it wants would make the influence structure more equitable. But from the point of view of labor, these same changes would make the influence structure less equitable. The changes that business sees as providing redress for an imbalance by raising business and lowering labor would be viewed by labor, which considers itself much less influential than business already, as increasing the imbalance between labor and its antagonist.

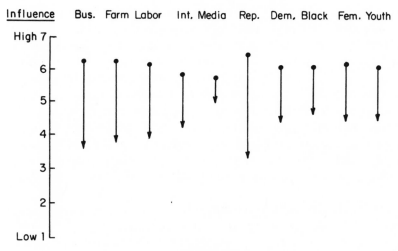

**Figure 9.10**
Views of Media Influence by Group

The neutral observers—politically moderate media leaders and intellectuals—would view the changes that either labor or business desires as providing a much less balanced influence system. If business had its way as to how things should change and if the media are correct as to how things are, the resulting system would be dominated by business; if labor had its way, labor would dominate. Thus, the basic ideal of equal influence would not be realized if any individual group were allowed to institute its own plan for equalization. At least in the abstract, there is a generally accepted norm that no group should dominate the political process, but the working out of this norm in practice is affected by two factors. One factor is the wide divergence in perceptions of the reality of influence, and of how influence is actually distributed. The other is the natural tendency of groups to entrench their own influence by fending off others. These two factors lead each contending group to prefer an influence distribution that ensconces itself safely at the top. Despite the accepted ideal of political equality, each group's antagonists would view the result as a highly unequal influence distribution.[14]

The media are central to American political life. All groups recognize the influence of the press (Figure 9.10). In addition all would reduce its influence, including the press itself. Established groups— labor, business, and farmers—suggest a bigger cut in media influence than do challenging groups, and Republicans want a larger cut than do Democrats. Newer challenging groups may be less opposed to the media because the media are perceived by them to be more biased against the conservative and established groups in society. Or the media may be equally unbiased against challenging and established groups, but their uniformly impartial coverage may operate more to the disadvantage of the establishment. If power recognized is power weakened, established groups have an edge over challenging groups in that their influence is somewhat routine and unobtrusive. Consequently, even if the media were perfectly balanced in their coverage, established groups might still be more likely to disapprove of their probing eye, for they have the most to lose from greater publicity.

Yet another possibility is that different opinions toward media influence are the result of neither differential biases nor differential effects of media coverage but simply of the different needs of various groups. Even if the press were more biased against challenging groups and more harmful to them, challenging groups might still support the influential role of the media, for they have nowhere else to go. Challenging groups tend to rely more heavily on outsider strategies for political pressure and change, and such strategies are virtually impossible without the media. Thus, even if the media presented the demands and priorities of challenging groups in a manner that those groups saw as imperfect, unflattering, or even unfair, the groups might still find themselves faced with no choice but to use the media as best they could. The more established groups might share the attitude that the media are unfair and not very helpful, but they have the alternative of avoiding the public spotlight and pursuing their goals through less conspicuous channels. For challenging groups, the only alternative to the media may be to go altogether unheard and unrecognized.

### Political Allies

Most groups think they have less influence than others think they have, and they want more. In politics, however, a group is concerned about not only its own power but also the power of its friends and enemies. The more influence its opponents have, the less the group has. Thus, groups are apt to favor reducing the influence of those who disagree with them. The situation is less clear, however, when it comes to potential allies who share a group's point of view. If those who agree with the group are more influential, they benefit the group by their ability to promote its cause. But the price of a powerful ally is that the group may sacrifice some of its influence within its own coalition. Democratic leaders, for example, want to reduce the influence of labor leaders, despite the Democratic party's reliance on support from labor, whose strength enhances the party's power in many struggles with the Republicans.

Friends have a common political understanding and share similar attitudes. In this sense, business and the Republican party are friends. The helpfulness of one group in assisting another group to achieve its own goals is one measure of an ally. Those who hinder a group from achieving its goals are enemies.

For each leadership group, the relationship of the perceived influence of the target groups to their perceived helpfulness indicates how they currently rate the power of their friends and opponents (Figure 9.11).[15] The leadership group's perception of its own influence also shows how it compares its influence with that of its friends and enemies. The data on perceived influence in relation to helpfulness reveal that most groups feel relatively vulnerable. They see both themselves and their friends, if they have any, as relatively weak. Their opponents, in turn, appear more powerful. This pattern is found most clearly among business, labor, and feminists: each group feels it has one or two weak allies and a number of powerful opponents. Farmers have the same perception, although they believe their only ally, banks, is fairly influential. Blacks have a very different view. They are the only group that thinks its opponents are outnumbered by its supporters, two of which, labor and the media, it perceives to be quite influential. Like all the other groups, however, blacks also feel they have extremely influential opponents—in their case, business and banks.

All the groups except blacks not only perceive more enemies than friends but also think that their enemies are a greater hindrance than their friends are a help. Most groups have some very hindering opponents, but no group thinks it has a very helpful friend. The group considered most helpful is blacks, as regarded by the feminists, but even they are only halfway helpful. Thus, the groups think their enemies are not only more numerous but also more hindering than their friends are helpful—a twofold vulnerability.

In both absolute and relative terms, there is a large difference between the rankings that feminists and blacks assign each other.

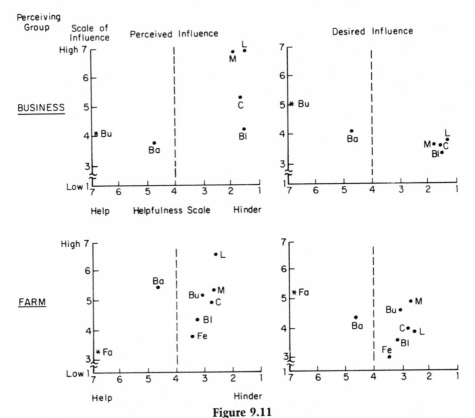

**Figure 9.11**

Helpfulness and Influence of Groups[a]

a. For each leadership group there is a pair of graphs. The left graph shows how that group perceives the influence of several target groups (their positions on the vertical axis) and how it perceives the helpfulness of these groups (their positions on the horizontal axis). The dotted line roughly divides friends from opponents: those to the left of the dotted line were placed by the perceiving group on the helpful side of the "help/hinder" scale, those to the right were put on the hindering side of the scale. Also included is the leadership group's perception of its own influence. The right-hand graphs show the same pattern for desired influence. Every leadership group in the study was not asked about each target group, so the views of only five groups are shown in this figure.

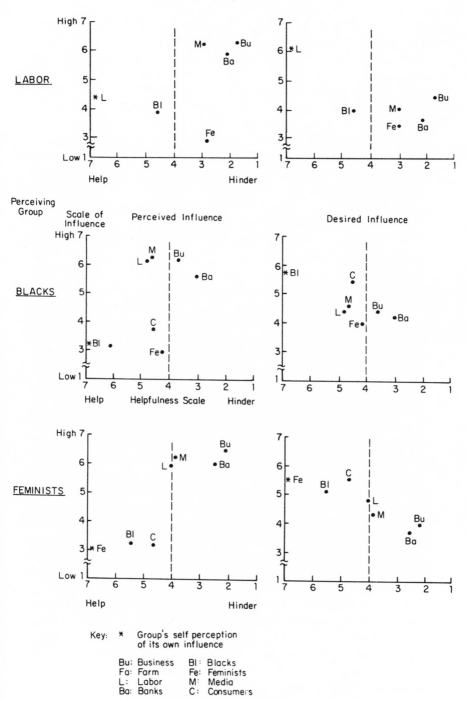

**Figure 9.11** (continued)

Feminists see blacks as their strongest ally, giving blacks the highest score received by anyone on the helpfulness scale. However, blacks put feminists near the middle of the scale, below the median rank. In terms of attitudes on policy issues and changes in the influence hierarchy, feminists are more supportive of blacks than vice versa, partly because they see in blacks more helpful allies than blacks see in feminists.

Finally, the media fare poorly. All the groups except blacks think that the media are less of a help than a hindrance. Blacks see the media as mildly helpful, but even they subscribe to the universal view that the media have too much influence.

To deal with their self-perceived weakness, groups have two possible strategies: to increase their own influence, or to increase their own influence as well as that of their friends. The patterns of desired influence in the table reveal that in general the groups would prefer to go it alone by wielding more influence than both those perceived as hindering and those perceived as supportive. Business and labor think that they each have one ally—the banks and blacks respectively—which is even less influential than they are themselves, and a number of opponents, which are quite influential. Given the chance to change the structure of influence, both groups would raise themselves and lower their opponents. They would also leave their uninfluential friends behind, staying about where they are now. As a result, business or labor would be powerful, with everyone else—whether hindrance or help—much less influential. Farmers would make similar alterations, raising their own influence, cutting the influence of opponent groups, and even cutting the influence of the one group on their side, the bankers.

Blacks would also put themselves in the highest position by raising themselves and undercutting most other groups, including the two powerful groups on their side, labor and the media. But they show more inclination to share influence, for they would raise the place of consumer groups to a level close to their own. Feminists, however, show the greatest tendency to share influence with their allies. They perceive that they are relatively low in influence, along with blacks and consumer groups. In their ideal world, they would be more influential than their opponents, whose influence they want to decrease, but they would also significantly increase the influence of blacks and consumer groups, creating an influential coalition among the three groups. Feminists are more generous with influence than is any other group.

## Source of Attitudes

The views of American leaders on the proper distribution of political influence, like their views on income distribution, are related to their general attitudes on equality and to their personal characteristics. However, the particular factors that predict attitudes toward the structure of influence differ from those that predict attitudes on income. Group membership, equality attitudes, demographic characteristics, and party affiliation all have different effects on the desired change in the influence of the target groups (Table 9.2). Demographic characteristics, such as family income, education, and age, have little effect on the groups' evaluations of influence. Group membership is a more potent predictor of views toward the structure of influence. Individuals take a bloc view of the conflict over influence; the conflict is among groups. Leaders, as representatives of these groups, have distinct positions based on their affiliation. Party affiliation affects a person's view of the influence of unions and of the parties themselves, since those groups are tied closely to partisanship, but otherwise it has little effect.

General ideological positions on equality, as measured by the six equality scales, are related to the views on influence of some groups but not of others. The groups' evaluations of the influence of the media, parties, and farm groups are largely independent of their general positions on equality. If the evaluations were specifically of the Democratic or Republican party rather than simply of "parties," however, they would probably have been more ideologically grounded. The lack of ideological evaluation of the farm groups is not surprising, since the relationship of the farm sector to general issues of equality is equivocal at best. But one might have expected more ideological basis for the evaluations of the influence exerted by the media, since the newer challenging groups are less opposed to media influence than the more established groups. Nevertheless, the evaluation of the media's influence is unrelated to an individual's position on the equality scales.

In contrast, the evaluation of the influence wielded by other target groups is related to the leadership group's position on the New Deal scale. This is especially true in relation to attitudes toward the influence of big business. Attitudes toward banks and consumer groups are also closely related to positions on the New Deal. There are statistically significant coefficients for unions and intellectuals as well, but these are not as large as those for other groups. The

**Table 9.2**

Effect of Social Background, Party, and Equality Attitudes on Desired Influence[a]

| Social background, party, and equality attitudes | Target group | | | | | | | | | |
|---|---|---|---|---|---|---|---|---|---|---|
| | Business | | Banks | | Farm | | Unions | | Media | |
| | Beta | F ratio | Beta | F ratio | Beta | F ratio | Beta | F ratio | Beta | F ratio |
| Family income | -.07 | (6.7) | -.02 | (.6) | .07 | (8.5) | -.01 | (.2) | -.04 | (2.2) |
| Age | -.07 | (5.7) | -.00 | (.0) | .08 | (7.2) | -.03 | (1.6) | -.04 | (1.9) |
| Education | .04 | (1.8) | .04 | (2.8) | .03 | (1.6) | .04 | (3.6) | .04 | (1.7) |
| Party | .09 | (7.9) | .06 | (3.9) | .03 | (.7) | -.15 | (29.0) | -.09 | (6.3) |
| New Deal attitudes | .41 | (83.8) | .29 | (48.2) | -.05 | (1.3) | -.16 | (16.4) | -.08 | (2.9) |
| Gender attitudes | .07 | (4.0) | .06 | (3.7) | .01 | (.0) | -.03 | (1.5) | -.04 | (1.3) |
| Redistribution attitudes | .07 | (4.2) | .04 | (1.8) | .01 | (.2) | -.11 | (16.7) | .01 | (.0) |
| Quota attitudes | -.05 | (1.5) | -.05 | (2.1) | -.05 | (2.4) | -.00 | (.0) | -.08 | (4.4) |
| Causes of inequality attitudes | .04 | (1.4) | .08 | (6.1) | .06 | (3.7) | -.01 | (.1) | -.03 | (.6) |
| Race attitudes | -.06 | (2.5) | -.07 | (4.4) | -.02 | (.4) | -.15 | (22.2) | -.07 | (3.6) |
| r | .53 | | .35 | | .24 | | .49 | | .35 | |
| r² | .28 | | .13 | | .06 | | .24 | | .13 | |

**Table 9.2** *(continued)*

| Social background, party, and equality attitudes | Intellectuals | | Parties | | Target group Consumers | | Blacks | | Feminists | |
|---|---|---|---|---|---|---|---|---|---|---|
| | Beta | F ratio | Beta | F ratio | Beta | F ratio | Beta | F ratio | Beta | F ratio |
| Family income | -.00 | (.0) | -.04 | (2.7) | .05 | (6.8) | .04 | (5.7) | .01 | (.1) |
| Age | -.00 | (.0) | -.04 | (1.8) | .02 | (1.4) | .01 | (.4) | -.03 | (1.5) |
| Education | -.09 | (14.3) | -.02 | (.6) | -.03 | (2.5) | .05 | (7.1) | .03 | (2.2) |
| Party | -.05 | (3.5) | -.23 | (50.6) | -.06 | (6.8) | .01 | (.2) | -.03 | (1.4) |
| New Deal attitudes | -.16 | (17.0) | .08 | (3.8) | -.24 | (58.2) | -.04 | (1.9) | -.15 | (15.8) |
| Gender attitudes | -.13 | (22.2) | -.01 | (.2) | -.09 | (15.8) | -.11 | (23.3) | -.44 | (255.2) |
| Redistribution attitudes | .03 | (1.0) | .01 | (.1) | -.00 | (.0) | -.05 | (4.2) | -.07 | (7.1) |
| Quota attitudes | -.07 | (5.1) | .00 | (.0) | -.06 | (4.7) | -.29 | (128.3) | -.15 | (24.7) |
| Causes of inequality attitudes | -.02 | (.7) | .01 | (.2) | -.03 | (1.1) | -.16 | (45.5) | -.02 | (.6) |
| Race attitudes | -.08 | (6.1) | -.15 | (18.6) | -.01 | (.2) | -.27 | (110.9) | -.04 | (1.8) |
| r | .52 | | .24 | | .66 | | .71 | | .64 | |
| r² | .27 | | .06 | | .43 | | .51 | | .42 | |

a. Desired influence ratings were regressed on social background, party, equality attitudes, and group membership. The coefficients for group membership are not reported.

b. Attitudes on the six equality issues are measured by factor scores.

reason that position on the New Deal scale is not as closely related to attitudes on union influence as on business influence is probably that opposition to the influence of unions is quite strong among Democrats, who are liberal on the New Deal, as well as among groups more conservative on that issue. In contrast, there is little opposition to business power among Republicans. Thus there is a more consistent left-right split in views of business influence than in views of labor influence.

Beyond this, the redistribution factor, so closely related to attitudes on income distribution, has little effect on attitudes toward the distribution of influence. However, some of the factors that were unrelated to income issues are closely related to evaluations of the political influence of particular groups. The two clearest cases are attitudes toward the influence of blacks and feminists. Attitudes toward the influence of blacks are closely related to one's position on racial equality and quotas. Similarly, attitudes toward the influence of feminist groups are strongly related to one's position on equality of the sexes. Those who hold liberal attitudes on racial equality are likely to favor more influence for blacks, and those who hold liberal attitudes on matters of gender equality are likely to back the influence of feminist groups.

AMERICAN LEADERS take an egalitarian view of political influence. Their attitude reflects adherence to a general norm of political equality. Where they perceive wide disparities in influence, they would reduce or eliminate them. This attitude is consistent with an antipower ethic. However, the commitment to this norm of equality is tempered by an unwillingness to accept a position of less influence than other groups have. The groups do not apply the antipower ethic to their own positions. Each group, except the media, would raise its own political influence and would endorse an influence hierarchy with itself on the top—a view that is hardly egalitarian or antipower. Yet an egalitarian, antipower ethic may still be embedded in these views, for the influence hierarchy that each group proposes is decidedly more equal than that which it perceives to exist. Still, because each group sees the hierarchy from its own vantage point, creating fundamental uncertainty about each group's influence, and because each group wants to be on top, the general egalitarian or antipower ethic loses much of its meaning when translated into the specific influence hierarchy that each group prefers. Each group adopts a position that might appear fair from its own perspective but unfair from the perspective of others.

The commitment to equality of political influence is qualified in another way. It appears to be a commitment to equality, not across individuals, but across blocs. This means equal political influence for each group no matter what its size. The size of a group would be crucial if the standard of influence were based on an individual majoritarian principle. In fact, there is little if any relationship between the size of a group and the influence that others wish it to have. If there were, labor would outrank business, and consumers would outrank them both. The groups' views on equality are collectivist or corporatist. Groups are not saying "one person, one vote." Rather, they are saying "one interest (or one sector, or one collective actor), one vote."

The amount of influence that a group ought to have also appears unrelated to the group's resources. Business and labor both command substantial resources, as other groups recognize in their views of actual influence. But when it comes to the ideal of influence, groups would substantially reduce business and labor influence. They apparently recognize the fundamental group nature of political conflict. If there is to be equal attention to all positions, it is achieved not by giving each person an equal voice but by giving each major interest sector equal influence.

The perceived extent of a group's influence is crucial to the group's actual influence. Influence may be more or less visible, more or less easily recognized. It is weakened when it becomes recognized, at least in the American context, where anti-influence attitudes predominate for groups other than one's own. To say that a group has a great deal of political influence is to suggest that a problem exists in need of correction. But on the other side of the coin, the reputation for having influence or, even more so, the reputation for having no influence may be self-fulfilling. The influential must be heeded; the powerless can be ignored.

In fact, both forces may be at work at the same time. Reputation for power may indeed enhance power. But the visible exercise of power may generate resentment or resistance. In some cases, both forces work to enhance a group's influence. If the group has a general reputation for influence but exercises that influence quietly, it may be able to gain the respect of decision-makers and other political actors to enhance its position, while shielding itself from much of the resistance that overt influence engenders. In the United States, this dual advantage accrues mostly to business leaders. They are insiders who are more likely to have a professional staff "working" the government and to enjoy easy social relations both with congressional representatives in the constituencies and with bureaucrats in state and national government. This easy, routine access makes the exercise of influence less obtrusive. Other groups, such as unions, farm organizations, or other lobbies, have similar access, but probably to a lesser degree. Furthermore, business benefits from its special role in the national economy. Government policy favoring business is seen not as a response to the special interests of business but as a policy that serves the economy generally.

Labor is a group whose reputation for influence is high but whose use of it is more overt and noticed, so the group's reputation counts against it. Furthermore, labor is not accorded the special position of business as the mainstay of the economy. Union activity is seen to represent more segmented interests. The result is that the influence of labor is resisted more than that of business. Most groups consider labor more powerful than business. Perhaps more important, this perception is found among the neutral observers, moderate intellectuals and media leaders. Even labor's own party, the Democrats, perceives labor to be equal to business in influence.

Just as groups see labor as more powerful than business, they want to cut its political influence more. On average, groups would reduce labor's influence by 33 percent, business's by 23 percent. The differential treatment of labor and business by their allied political parties is even more marked. Labor's ally, the Democrats, would cut the influence of labor substantially, almost as much as it would cut that of business. The Republicans would reduce labor's influence even more substantially than would the Democrats, but they would not cut the influence of their own ally, business. The neutral observers are the best exemplars of this asymmetrical treatment. They perceive a hierarchy of influence in which labor is above business, but they would prefer a hierarchy in which business is more influential than labor. Business's influence is, apparently, more legitimate than labor's.[16]

When it comes to perceptions and values about influence, blacks and, even more so, feminists lose both ways. Their weakness is apparent both to themselves and to others. In addition, they must exercise more overt influence because their access to established channels is limited and they lack the special legitimacy of business. Just as established groups such as business get the double benefit of a reputation for considerable influence and the unobtrusive exercise of that influence, the challenging groups have the double disadvantage of a reputation for little influence and the need to be obtrusive in attempting to exercise what little influence they have.

Neither the antipower ethic, which contributes to the groups' desire to reduce each other's influence, nor the routinization of influence, which contributes to the advantages of established groups and the disadvantages of challenging groups, can wholly explain why established groups seriously underrate their own influence compared with the assessment of others. It is not that business is blissfully unaware of its own influence while other groups are perceptually accurate. The source of influence denial lies elsewhere. Political conflict, unlike economic rivalry, is subject to a strong normative ideal of equality, is waged over resources that are not easily gauged, and has a constant-sum quality which fosters feelings of insecurity about relative rank. In combination, these factors lead all groups to rate their own influence low and inadequate. When business engages in the universal practice of rating its influence low, it misses the true mark, which is accurately perceived by others; when the challenging groups similarly disparage their own influence, they are close to the accurate assessment of others.

# 10

## Economics and Politics

Much of political analysis explores the relationship between political influence and economic well-being. The classic works of political sociology are about political and economic stratification. Students of political economy examine the impact of political arrangements on economic allocations, and vice versa. Students of political participation are concerned with the ways in which economic resources are translated into political influence, and vice versa. Students of interest groups worry about bias in favor of the affluent, as do students of campaign reform. And on and on.

The much-probed links between politics and economics lie at the heart of equality. Contrary to the Marxist prophecy, equality in one domain is no guarantee of equality in the other. One can have money yet not influence, or influence yet not money. In general, however, affluence and influence go hand in hand. And the relationship is causal: wealth can be the key to obtaining influence, just as influence can open the door to wealth. As a result, the hierarchy in one domain is likely to match that in the other.

### Differences Between Income and Influence

In both the economic domain of income and the political domain of influence there is a struggle for advantage. In most cases, influence is the instrumental goal; income the terminal goal. The affluent use income to gain influence in order to protect or improve their economic position. However, influence itself might also be the terminal goal. For instance, Irving Kristol has argued that the real goal of the redistributionists is to place not money in the hands of the poor but power in the hands of the liberals: "No proposals for the redistribution of large fortunes will get liberal support unless that money goes into the public treasury, where liberals will have much to say about how it should be spent. That is the 'dirty little secret'—the hidden agenda—behind the current chatter about the need for 're-distribution.' The talk is about equality, the substance is about power."[1]

Influence and income have much in common. Each is highly desirable; people want more, not less. And each is desirable because it is a stepping-stone to other valued commodities. Income can buy consumer goods, leisure, and autonomy. It can also buy political influence. Political influence, in turn, can be converted into many other goods, including higher income. As evidence of the premium placed on income and influence, all the leadership groups in the study, with rare exceptions, want to see their own income and influence enhanced.

Yet the contest over economic equality takes a different form from that over political equality because equality means something different in each case. The differences involve the extent to which equality in each domain represents a constant-sum game, is measurable, and is favored by social norms. A constant-sum game is one in which a gain for one contestant means a loss for others. Constant-sum games are often called zero-sum. A variable-sum game is a contest in which all can gain or at least one person's gain is not necessarily another's loss; here the competition can be more benign. In part the distinction between a constant-sum and a variable-sum contest depends upon the availability of the desired goods—in this case, income or influence. If the amount is limited, the contest is usually constant-sum. If the amount of goods is growing or capable of growing, as in an expanding economy or, perhaps, an expanding political system, the contest may be variable-sum. The nature of the contest also depends upon how the contestants evaluate their own positions. Those who constantly compare their own lot with that of their opponents see the contest as constant-sum. Their opponents gain, they lose—even if in an absolute sense they have not changed. If one's absolute position is what counts, then—given a growing pie to divide—all can gain at once.

Neither the contest over income nor that over influence is purely constant-sum or purely variable-sum. For political influence, the contest is constant-sum vis-à-vis one's adversaries, those who oppose one's goals or favor alternative goals. A gain in influence by those who take an alternative view represents a loss in one's own influence. One's absolute position depends solely upon how one stacks up against one's opponents. Yet in relation to one's allies the contest is variable-sum. When their influence increases, so does one's own, at least indirectly. Thus, much depends on whose influence is being compared with whose.

In an expanding polity the influence of all groups could grow at once. If government programs were steadily expanding and each societal group carved out a special area of concern of little interest to other groups, each contestant could increase its influence within its own area without detracting from the others.[2] However, given a limited governmental budget, a crowded political agenda, and the fact that in times of economic constraint government programs favoring one group limit the resources available for others, an expanding political pie is impossible. Benign conflict, where each group can dominate its area of interest without threatening other groups, would therefore be unlikely. In times of economic contraction, the contest for political influence across groups tends to be sharpest. Similarly, James Tobin has referred to the constant-sum nature of the vote market: "The aggregate supply of votes is intrinsically inelastic. Allowing a free market in votes could not augment the power of the electorate as a whole; it would serve only to redistribute it differently."[3]

The contest over income differs from that over influence. An expanding polity, in which all groups gain, is simply a pipe dream. Yet an expanding economy, in which the income of all groups can increase together, is eminently feasible. Furthermore, in the realm of income some inequality is needed to provide incentives for economic progress, although the proper amount is a matter of debate. When the rich get richer, the poor do not necessarily get poorer; they may actually gain. Therefore, the contest need not be virulent. Unlike influence, however, there is less to be gained from an improvement in the income of others who share one's point of view. The income is theirs, not one's own.[4]

Under certain circumstances, the contest over income may approximate a constant-sum game. In a stagnant economy, if one group gains, others lose. Thus, at least in the short run, income conflict may intensify. Furthermore, even if income can improve in an absolute sense for all at the same time, income may be subjectively closer to a constant-sum contest. The deciding factor here is one's satisfaction with one's income, which appears to be based on one's relative position. The proportion of the population satisfied with its income has stayed about the same, even as real per-capita income has risen. Since this satisfaction depends on one's rank in the income hierarchy, another's gain is one's own loss.[5]

Hence, with respect to the contests over income and over influence, it is impossible to classify one as strictly constant-sum and the other as strictly variable-sum. Both are to some extent constant-sum. The pie is not necessarily expanding, and in any case, people compare slices. Nevertheless, conflicts over influence are more likely to take on the character of a constant-sum contest than are conflicts over income. One group may gain income without taking it directly from another; thus groups are not likely to see themselves in direct competition for the same earnings. But where there is political conflict over government policies, each group is in a constant-sum contest with others who want to steer the government in a different direction.

Another difference between influence and income is that income is much easier to measure than is influence. Again the distinction is not absolute. What ought to count as income is ambiguous, and much income can be hidden or obscured. Nevertheless, individuals or groups are fairly easily compared in terms of their monetary income, either in absolute dollars or in their share of total income. Although precise measurement of a group's income may be difficult, it is usually possible to make a rough approximation and determine who is better off than whom. But for influence there is no clear metric, no government statistical service to collect data, and no Internal Revenue Service to compel precise recording or reporting. The problem is even more severe when the influence is not of individuals but of groups or segments of society. The major debate over the power structure in America concerns the amount of influence actually held by various actors. For want of an accurate measure, the debate may never end.

A final difference between income and influence inheres in their relation to social norms. The norm of equality is more powerful in relation to political influence than to wealth. American ideals have never promoted economic equality in the same way that they have insisted on political equality. Political influence in America, unlike money, has always been seen as a right, as a corollary of human dignity. Conversely, Americans condemn disparities of political power more than disparities of income or wealth. American leaders, including the more radically egalitarian among them, do not advocate anything resembling complete equality of income. Each group overwhelmingly subscribes to the view that rewards should be based roughly on effort and talent; income should not be equal. Full economic equality would presumably harm society by removing incentives for work and investment. This ethic of free enterprise and individualism does not apply to political influence. Disparities in influence, though recognized and probably deemed inevitable, are widely deplored as unjust. Nor is inequality in political influence regarded as an incentive to good citizenship in the way that income inequality is defended as an incentive to hard work.[6] There are people who think that appropriate influence should sometimes reflect varying levels of skill or interest in specific areas: for example, blacks should be given more weight on civil rights matters, poor people on food stamp policy, or foreign policy experts on national security issues. For political influence in general, however, inequality is deemed inappropriate. Americans hold norms that at once legitimize inequality in economic matters and encourage greater equality in political affairs.[7]

Public attitudes on equality are reflected in public policy. Inequality of income has neither been legislated out of existence nor ruled unjust by the courts. For example, in *San Antonio School Board v. Rodriguez* the issue was whether public education based on local taxes was constitutional if it resulted in better-financed schools in richer communities. The Supreme Court ruled that education, health care, and income are important social objectives but are not "fundamental" liberties like the right to vote.[8] The Court did not invoke strict judicial scrutiny. In contrast, equality in political influence has been zealously guarded by the Court and subjected to congressional limitation. Court decisions on such matters as reapportionment, as well as congressional legislation such as the Voting Rights Act and the Campaign Finance Act, show a commitment to equality in rights of political participation. Campaign finance legislation is a clear expression of the belief that disparities deemed legitimate in the economic sphere are illegitimate if carried over to the political sphere. Hence there is a ceiling on the amount that individuals can contribute to a campaign.

However, the commitment to political equality is more apparent in the abstract than in the specific influence hierarchies that leadership groups consider fair. The ideal of equal influence is hard to reconcile with the desire of most of the leadership groups to increase their own influence beyond that of all other groups. Apparently a protective instinct in each of the groups manifests itself in this desire to gain the upper hand. The result is a much more qualified commitment to political equality than the general norm would imply. Americans wish for equality but—to paraphrase George Orwell—would like to be a bit more equal than others. That position is understandable in light of the constant-sum characteristics of the struggle for political position. In politics, unlike economics, each group's relative position is crucial. No group considers itself well-off until it has reached the top.

These three major differences between income and influence suggest that there are differences in the nature of the conflict over equality in the political and economic domains. The constant-sum nature of the conflict over political influence makes relative position crucial, leading individuals and groups to want to reduce the sway of those groups they see as influential, particularly groups taking different policy positions. The mere fact of other groups' power causes their own weakness. The situation is less clear-cut with respect to income. Much depends on the state of the economy and on individual perceptions. A constricted economy or a sense of comparative deprivation may make income a relative good, like influence. As a result, individuals would want to cut the income of those perceived to have the most. Yet one can also consider one's income in absolute terms. Another's gain may not be seen as a loss for oneself; indeed, it might even be a benefit to the economy and indirectly to one's own income.

The precision with which income and influence can be measured also affects the conflict in both domains of equality. The issue of who wields the most influence is more subjective, and thus more controversial, than is the question of who earns the most. Thus, controversy over perceptions plays a more significant role in connection with influence than with income.

Finally, the dispute over income equality involves values about how much equality there ought to be rather than perceptions of actual income. The apple of discord over income is the proper size of the gap between those at the top and those at the bottom. In the realm of influence, on the other hand, there is more agreement on the norms—consensus on the ideal of political equality coupled with a self-protective view of who should be most influential—but greater conflict over the question of who in fact is the most influential.

The three characteristics of political influence—general agreement on the ideal of equality of influence, uncertainty as to who has the most influence, and the constant-sum nature of this influence—give the conflict over it a particular cast. A group that is perceived to be more influential than other groups is also perceived to be illegitimately so, because it violates the general ideal of influence equality. It also poses a threat to other groups. Given the constant-sum nature of influence, one group's strength is another's weakness. Added to this is the uncertainty as to who is in fact influential. Each group sees the world differently. Typically, each group sees its antagonists as influential and itself and its allies as weak. The result is a common agreement that influence ought to be equally distributed, coupled with a sharp disagreement as to what changes in the influence hierarchy have to take place to achieve this common goal.

While there is little consensus on the distribution of either income or influence, the disagreement in one domain concerns the ideal, and in the other domain it concerns both reality and the nature of the ideal. With respect to income, groups are in agreement on what the actual situation is, but they disagree on how wide an income gap is proper between the top and the bottom of the hierarchy. In relation to influence, they agree that the distribution should be equal, as long as it is skewed in their favor, but disagree on the actual distribution. Thus, both norms and perceptions of influence are in dispute—perhaps the latter even more than the former. In addition, jockeying for position is more intense in the political domain than in the economic, since influence hinges on rank. As for income, the gap among groups or occupations is considered more important than the ranking; hence, conflict is far more benign.

**Perceptions Versus Values**

These hypothesized differences between income and influence can be tested with the questions on what is real and ideal in each domain. For income, pairs of occupations, each including a better- and worse-paid calling, are compared in terms of how wide each leader believes the income gap to be between the two and how wide each believes it should be. For political influence, pairs of interest groups, each containing a more and a less influential group, are also compared in terms of the real and ideal gaps. This gives four types of ratios: "is" and "ought" ratios for income; "is" and "ought" ratios for influence.[9] The measure of consensus is the standard deviation of the group mean ratios across the groups. The larger the standard deviation, the greater the disagreement among groups on that score.

The results of the comparisons among ratios clearly support the hypothesis that the variation across the leadership groups in ideal income is greater than the variation in perceived actual income, while the variation on actual influence is at least as great as the variation on ideal influence (Table 10.1). With respect to income, there is more consensus across groups on the real than on the ideal. The standard deviations of the ideal income ratios are substantially larger than are those for perceived income. Groups agree with each other more on the actual income distribution than on the ideal. For influence, this pattern is reversed. There are higher standard deviations for the perceived ratios than for the ideal, indicating more consensus on how influence ought to be distributed than on how it now is.[10] These data are also consistent with the fact that political influence is less precisely measurable than is income. The actual distribution of influence is the subject of more political debate than is the current distribution of income.[11]

Because income is more measurable, the groups disagree less on the facts of its distribution than they do in the case of political influence. One consequence of uncertainty about the facts of influ-

**Table 10.1**
Disagreement among Groups on Perceived and Fair Income
and Influence Ratios[a]

| Ratios | Standard deviation | |
| --- | --- | --- |
| | Perceived group ratios | Fair group ratios |
| Executive/auto worker income | 1.8 | 2.7 |
| Executive/elevator operator income | 2.8 | 5.2 |
| Business/labor influence | .29 | .16 |
| Business/feminist influence | .23 | .19 |
| Business/black influence | .30 | .18 |

a. The higher the figure, the greater the variation across groups; e.g., there is less variation in what groups perceive as the executive/auto worker income gap than in what groups desire that gap to be. In this table and those following, logged income is used.

ence is that these facts become part of the political debate. One's perceptions, like one's attitudes, are therefore determined less by reality than by one's social position and ideology. The views of American leaders on the proper distribution of income or influence depend at least in part on the particular leadership group to which they belong and on their general ideology on matters of equality. This has already been demonstrated. What is special about influence in contrast to income is that the same factors which determine views on ideal influence also determine views on actual influence, these factors being social position and ideology. In contrast, these variables have little or no effect on perceptions of real income, though they do affect ideal income.

The estimated effects of group membership, demographic characteristics, party affiliation, and self-described ideology on each "is" and "ought" ratio show that income contrasts sharply with influence (Table 10.2). In relation to income, ideology and group membership explain the ideal ratios much better than they explain the actual ratios. For the desired income ratios, they explain about a third of the variance. For the ratios based on perceptions of actual income, ideology and group membership explain only 6 percent of the variance. Clearly, perception of the actual income gap between the top earners and those lower on the scale is not tied to group membership or ideology.

Influence stands in stark relief. Ideology and group membership

**Table 10.2**

Effect of Social Background, Party, and Ideology on Perceived and Fair Income and Influence Ratios

| Ratios | Overall variance explained[a] | |
| --- | --- | --- |
| | Perceived ratios | Fair ratios |
| Executive/auto worker income | .06 | .32 |
| Executive/elevator operator income | .06 | .37 |
| Business/labor influence | .38 | .33 |
| Business/feminist influence | .32 | .37 |
| Business/black influence | .37 | .33 |

a. Total $r^2$ for regression equation with group, social background, party, and ideology as explanatory variables.

explain the real about as well as they explain the ideal. Indeed, for two of the three influence ratios, the background factors explain more variance in perceptions than in values. In other words, group membership as well as other characteristics, including ideology, have at least as much effect on perceptions of the actual influence hierarchy as on views of an ideal hierarchy.

Ideology has an impact on real and ideal income and influence over and above the effect of the other factors (Table 10.3). Its impact is similar on both ideal income and ideal influence. It has a weaker effect on real income and influence. But while the impact of ideology on income perceptions is essentially zero, its impact on influence perceptions is substantially larger. Perceptions of influence are clearly part of the ideological debate among the leadership groups.

The difficulty of measuring political influence undermines the effort to establish a common baseline for comparing the influence of different groups. Thus, in the realm of politics far more than in economics one's perception of fact is colored by one's values. Where leaders stand on the question of how much influence various groups have depends on where they sit. The group one belongs to and one's general attitudes on equality affect how much income equality one thinks there ought to be, not how much there is in fact. The clash among groups is over what should be. As for influence, group membership and ideology affect both what one would like to see and what one actually sees, producing a clash among groups over what should be and what is. The duality of the dispute over influence

**Table 10.3**

Effect of Ideology on Perceived and Fair Income and Influence Ratios

| Ratios | Added variance explained by ideology[a] | |
| --- | --- | --- |
| | Perceived ratios | Fair ratios |
| Executive/auto worker income | .01 | .12 |
| Executive/elevator operator income | .01 | .16 |
| Business/labor influence | .07 | .10 |
| Business/feminist influence | .04 | .13 |
| Business/black influence | .07 | .13 |

a. Increase of $r^2$ when ideology is added to regression equation with social background, party, and group membership.

intensifies the conflict, for even two groups which agree on where they should be placed relative to each other would probably disagree on what must be done to achieve that placement. Agreement on standards would not end the dispute.

## Degree of Inequality

In one respect, American leaders look at the income and influence hierarchies in a similar manner: they would decrease the inequality they see in each domain. The groups differ in how much they would reduce inequality, but all believe that a fair distribution in each domain would leave less distance between the occupants of the top and bottom positions on the hierarchy. This similarity is revealed by using standard deviation statistics to compare how much existing variation each of the leadership groups currently perceives in the income and influence hierarchies, across occupations or target groups, with how much variation in income and influence each group thinks would be appropriate (Table 10.4). The larger the figures, the more differentiated is the group's view of the current or ideal distribution. The standard deviations for the perception of income or influence are consistently larger than are the standard deviations of the ideal income or influence.

**Table 10.4**

Variation among Groups in Views of Perceived and Fair Income and Influence

| Group | Standard deviation of income | | Standard deviation of influence | |
|---|---|---|---|---|
| | Perceived | Fair | Perceived | Fair |
| Business | 65.6 | 56.4 | 1.05 | .64 |
| Farm | 53.6 | 29.2 | 1.07 | .63 |
| Labor | 71.6 | 31.8 | 1.11 | .73 |
| Intellectuals | 66.7 | 31.4 | 1.33 | .47 |
| Media | 63.9 | 33.2 | 1.14 | .53 |
| Republicans | 60.2 | 39.2 | 1.00 | .65 |
| Democrats | 63.6 | 31.7 | 1.20 | .53 |
| Blacks | 57.2 | 33.7 | 1.29 | .44 |
| Feminists | 65.1 | 22.5 | 1.47 | .63 |
| Youth | 66.8 | 27.7 | 1.38 | .43 |

On the income side, the standard deviations are in most cases twice as large for the perceived income distribution as for the ideal distribution. Even business, which alone shows a less pronounced distinction on income, desires less variation in the incomes of various occupations than it perceives to exist. The situation is similar in relation to influence. The standard deviations of perceived influence are in many cases twice as large as the deviations of ideal influence. Among the more established groups, this distinction between the differentiation of influence a group perceives and the differentiation it would prefer is less sharp but still substantial. Simply put, each group would prefer to see less differentiation in income and in influence than it perceives to exist.

## Ranking of Hierarchies

The similarity between groups in their treatment of the economic and political hierarchies masks more fundamental differences between their views of each domain. These are consistent with the more constant-sum nature of the political hierarchy. In relation to income, the leaders would reduce the size of the gap between those at the top and those at the bottom but would preserve the overall ranking of the occupations. In relation to influence, the ranking would change (Table 10.5). Each group believes that business executives receive the highest incomes. Although all groups would reduce the dollar amount of that income, each group believes that executives still ought to be the highest paid. In contrast, no group wants the group it perceives as the most influential to remain at the top of the influence hierarchy, and most groups would give themselves the greatest influence. Although each group wants to narrow the gap between the top and bottom of the income hierarchy, it leaves the hierarchy intact. Each group with little exception wants to replace those at the top of the influence scale with itself.

This distinction between income and influence also emerges in the groups' perceptions of their own income and influence relative to business executives, as shown by each group's perceived and ideal incomes for itself, namely the answers to the question of what "someone at your level in your own occupation" earns and ought to earn (Figure 10.1). As before, an arrow begins at the income a group reports for itself and points to the income the group thinks it ought to earn. Each group believes that it ought to earn more than it does earn, but not much more. To obtain some perspective on the

**Table 10.5**

Groups That Have and Should Have Most Income and Influence

| Group | Most income | | Most influence | |
|---|---|---|---|---|
| | Perceived | Fair | Perceived | Fair |
| Business | Executive | Executive | Labor | Business |
| Farm | Executive | Executive | Labor | Farm |
| Labor | Executive | Executive | Media | Labor |
| Intellectuals | Executive | Executive | Labor | Consumers |
| Media | Executive | Executive | Labor | Media |
| Republicans | Executive | Executive | Labor | Parties |
| Democrats | Executive | Executive | Media | Parties |
| Blacks | Executive | Executive | Business/Media | Blacks |
| Feminists | Executive | Executive | Business | Consumers |

modesty of these desires, arrows also indicate the leaders' views toward the income of the top occupation, executives.[12] The arrows run from the amount that each leadership group thinks a top executive earns to the income they think executives deserve. In each case, the increase in income that a group thinks it deserves and the substantially larger decrease that it wants for executives would fail to close the large gap between the earnings of the two groups.

The same format indicates where each group thinks it stands on the influence hierarchy and where it would like to stand (Figure 10.2). Arrows indicate the position each group perceives to be held by the target group it considers most influential—in each case either labor, business, or the media—and the position it thinks the most influential group ought to hold. The scales of income and influence in the two instances are of course different, and comparisons across them must be made with caution. But comparison of relative positions on each of the scales—the relationship among one's own perceived and ideal positions and the ideal position for the top earning occupation and the most influential group—tells much about the difference in the leaders' attitudes toward the overall shape of the two hierarchies.

Every group except the media wants to raise its influence. Groups want more of a gain in influence than in income relative to other groups. Each group perceives itself to be less influential than the top group and wants to gain enough influence to exceed the top group.

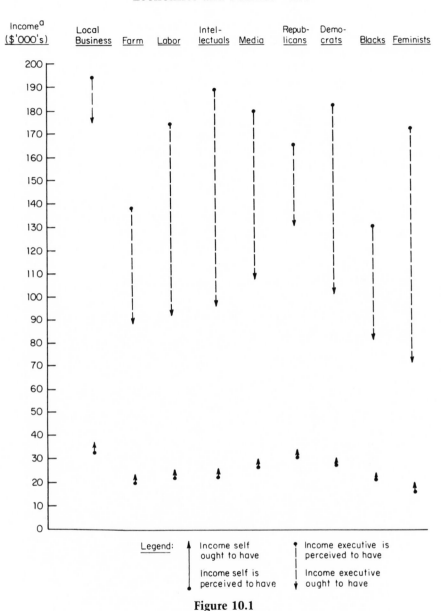

**Figure 10.1**
Perceived and Fair Income of Self and Executive
a. The income for each individual leader was logged, means for the leaders
were computed, and then anti-logs of the means were taken to convert back
to the original scale in dollars.

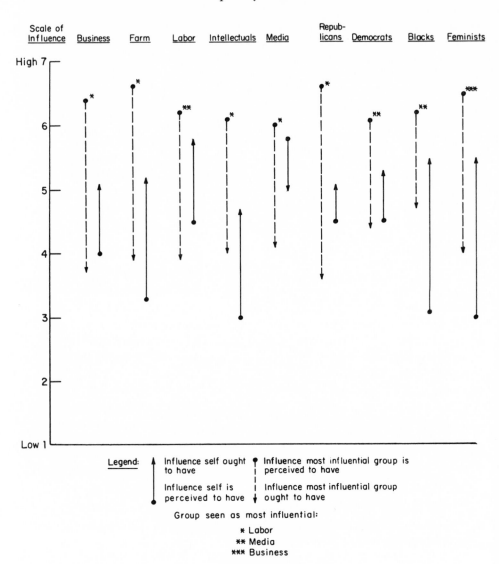

**Figure 10.2**
Perceived and Fair Influence of Self and Most Influential Group

This contrast illustrates again the difference in views on income and influence. The desire for more income in no way conflicts with the universal belief that business ought to have the highest income rank. However, when each group considers changes in the influence hierarchy, it would rearrange matters substantially. The difference between income and influence is consistent with the difference between economic and political equality in the extent to which each approximates a constant-sum game. That each group wants to perch itself at or near the top of the influence hierarchy is what one would expect in a constant-sum conflict. It is not enough for a group merely to acquire more influence than it currently has, as is the case for income; the group must have more influence than any other.

**Redistribution**

The similarities and differences between the two domains of equality lead one to expect that groups want to reduce the income and influence of those perceived to be at the top of each hierarchy. The higher a group's rank in the hierarchy, the greater the reduction desired. But since the norms of equality are not as strong in relation to income, the equalizing effect should be less in that domain than in the domain of influence.

The relationship can be plotted between the average income that the leaders perceive an occupation to earn and the average change they would like to see in that income, and the same relationship can be shown for influence (Figure 10.3). Each point on the graphs represents an occupation (for income) or a target group (for influence). For both domains, there is a clear linear relationship between the perceptions of the position that a group has and the amount of change desired in that position. The higher the perceived income or influence, the greater the proportion by which American leaders would reduce it.

Although these averages across all the leaders can be misleading, a similar tendency appears within each of the groups (Table 10.6). For each group, the correlation between the perceived level of income or influence and the percentage change desired is strongly negative, indicating that each group favors the greatest reductions in influence and income for those who have the most. Business is less likely to cut the highest incomes, but its correlation is negative as well. The negative relationship remains strong even after taking into consideration other factors. Across the entire spectrum of Amer-

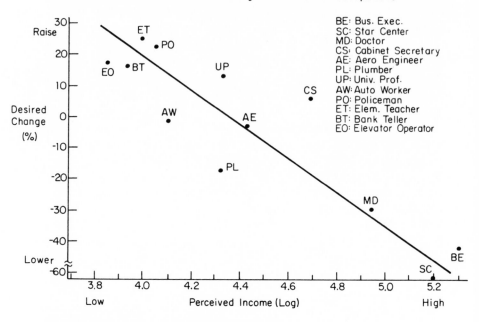

A. Perceived Income and Desired Change in Income for Occupations

BE: Bus. Exec.
SC: Star Center
MD: Doctor
CS: Cabinet Secretary
AE: Aero Engineer
PL: Plumber
UP: Univ. Prof.
AW: Auto Worker
PO: Policeman
ET: Elem. Teacher
BT: Bank Teller
EO: Elevator Operator

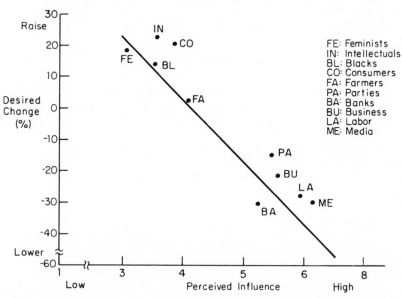

B. Perceived Influence and Desired Change in Influence for Target Groups

FE: Feminists
IN: Intellectuals
BL: Blacks
CO: Consumers
FA: Farmers
PA: Parties
BA: Banks
BU: Business
LA: Labor
ME: Media

**Figure 10.3**
Perceived and Desired Change in Income and Influence

**Table 10.6**
Perceived Position and Desired Change in Income and Influence

| Group | Correlation of perceived income with desired change in income[a] | Correlation of perceived influence with desired change in influence[b] |
|---|---|---|
| Business | − .42 | − .71 |
| Farm | − .76 | − .76 |
| Labor | − .92 | − .69 |
| Intellectuals | − .80 | − .90 |
| Media | − .80 | − .80 |
| Republicans | − .70 | − .67 |
| Democrats | − .80 | − .87 |
| Blacks | − .86 | − .93 |
| Feminists | − .88 | − .97 |
| Youth | − .92 | − .92 |

a. Correlation between the (mean) income that members of a group believe each occupation has and the change in income desired for each occupation.

b. Correlation between the (mean) influence that members of a group believe each target group has and the change in influence desired for each target group.

ican life, regardless of deep ideological divisions, all groups share the sense that those who possess the greatest political influence should suffer the greatest reductions in influence. This is the case for income as well. Even after taking into account the differences in preferences due to group membership, demographics, party allegiance, and ideology, the groups still favor larger income reductions for those who earn the most.

These data show little difference between income and influence. In each domain, the more resources a group is seen to have, the larger the proportional cut that the leaders want to make. However, since the leaders do not want to change the income hierarchy, although they do want substantially to restructure the influence hierarchy, it seems likely not only that they would take proportionately more from those well endowed in either influence or income but that they would do so even more in the case of influence. This is seen in the relationship between how much influence or income a group is perceived to have and how much it ought to have (Figure 10.4). In the case of income, this relationship is positive. The more an occupation is thought to earn, the more the groups feel it ought to earn. This contrasts with the finding that the more an occupation is seen to earn, the more the groups feel it ought to be cut. The two patterns, however, are not inconsistent. For example, although the leaders would reduce executive income by 32 percent—more than for any other occupation but the professional athlete, whose income is cut by 50 percent—they would keep executives at the top of the income hierarchy by a substantial margin. The desired income changes would reduce the distance between the incomes of different occupations but would roughly preserve the present order of groups within the income hierarchy. However, the influence that target groups are perceived to have bears no such relation to the influence that they ought to have. The drastic reductions in the influence of those at the top would result in the leveling of the influence hierarchy.

The contrast between the views that leaders take of the income hierarchy and the influence hierarchy is analogous to the difference between a progressive and a confiscatory tax. The desired income changes would operate like a progressive tax on income. Those perceived to earn the most would lose proportionately more earnings than those perceived to earn less. The opposite would be true for those thought to earn the least, who would be given an income boost. But this progressive redistribution would not upset the income hierarchy. It would leave the top earners with substantially higher earnings than those below them. With respect to influence, the desired changes are comparable to a confiscatory tax on the most influential groups and a countervailing negative tax on a groups that are lowest in influence. The resulting difference between the economic and political domains is striking. In the economic domain, there would be marginal changes in the status quo but the income hierarchy would remain. In the influence domain, something very close to equality of result would be achieved, in which each group had a similar degree of influence.

The differing views toward income and influence are shared by all of the groups (Table 10.7). Within each group the perceived and ideal income of the various occupations are strongly correlated. That is, under the desired reforms of each group, the occupations earning the most would wind up with the most, even if they took a substantial cut. In the domain of influence, the real and ideal are uncorrelated. The only significant positive correlation occurs among the media, and that is not very strong.

There is a strong negative correlation for feminists between perceived and fair influence. They would impose more than a confiscatory tax. They would levy a penalty tax on influentials and give

A. Perceived Income and Fair Income for Occupations

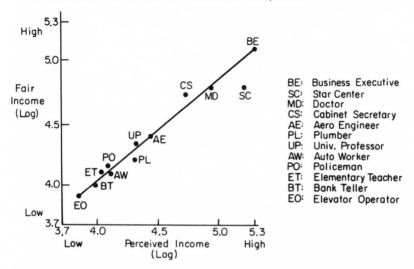

BE: Business Executive
SC: Star Center
MD: Doctor
CS: Cabinet Secretary
AE: Aero Engineer
PL: Plumber
UP: Univ. Professor
AW: Auto Worker
PO: Policeman
ET: Elementary Teacher
BT: Bank Teller
EO: Elevator Operator

B. Perceived Influence and Fair Influence for Target Groups

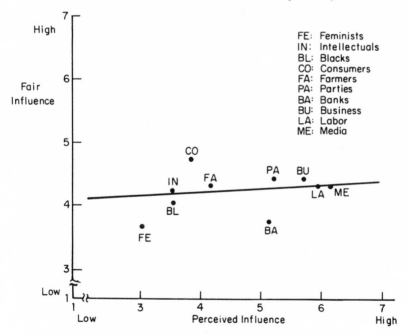

FE: Feminists
IN: Intellectuals
BL: Blacks
CO: Consumers
FA: Farmers
PA: Parties
BA: Banks
BU: Business
LA: Labor
ME: Media

**Figure 10.4**
Perceived and Fair Income and Influence

**Table 10.7**
Perceived and Fair Income and Influence

| Group | Correlation of perceived income with fair income[a] | Correlation of perceived influence with fair influence[b] |
|---|---|---|
| Business | .92 | .03 |
| Farm | .93 | −.07 |
| Labor | .97 | .07 |
| Intellectuals | .93 | .03 |
| Media | .93 | .34 |
| Republicans | .90 | .00 |
| Democrats | .95 | −.04 |
| Blacks | .98 | −.28 |
| Feminists | .91 | −.76 |
| Youth | .95 | −.14 |

a. Correlation between the (mean) income that members of a group believe each occupation has and the (mean) income they believe it ought to have.

b. Correlation between the (mean) influence that members of a group believe a target group has and the (mean) influence they believe it ought to have.

compensatory relief to those low in influence. Feminists would not merely flatten the influence hierarchy but turn it upside down. In part, this is because feminists see themselves as the lowest group in terms of influence and would place themselves close to the top. Other groups also generally rate themselves low and would increase their own influence, but not as much as the feminists. The only group that comes close to the feminists on both these counts is the blacks. In fact, blacks would raise themselves higher in relative terms for they would put themselves first, while feminists would put themselves second to consumer groups. Nevertheless, the correlation of perceived and desired influence is considerably different for feminists and blacks. Although blacks would amend the influence hierarchy more than most other groups, and their proposed changes are generally in line with those suggested by feminists, they advocate less extensive revisions than feminists do. The feminists would essentially turn the influence ladder on its head, slashing the influence of business, banks, media, labor, and parties while substantially elevating the influence of blacks, consumers, intellectuals, and themselves. Blacks display less ideological fervor in their amendments, proposing milder cuts for currently influential groups, especially political parties, and only modest gains for some less influential groups, especially feminists.

The feminist reversal of the influence hierarchy illustrates the way in which a generally egalitarian view may be supplanted by a less egalitarian view in terms of the specifics of the influence hierarchy. Feminists are perhaps the most egalitarian in the study, not only in their views of gender equality but in their views on all equality issues. They are quite generous in their egalitarianism, giving more support to equality for blacks than blacks give to equality for women, and they are more willing to share influence with other liberal groups than are other groups to share influence with them. Yet they move themselves from the bottom almost to the top of the influence hierarchy. Even in this reversal, however, they are relatively egalitarian compared with other groups. They do not place themselves at the top; they bestow that honor on consumer groups. Furthermore, the strong reversal that feminists desire derives more from the low position they perceive themselves to hold than from the high position to which they aspire.

In sum, attitudes toward influence more than attitudes toward income approximate a constant-sum contest. Relative position is crucial in relation to influence. Groups want to flatten the hierarchy or even reverse it and put themselves on top. In relation to income, groups tend to favor some adjustment but would not change the basic proportions and rankings of the overall hierarchy.

### Allies and Opponents

Both allies and opponents have a role in a group's attitudes toward income and influence equality. Influence resembles a constant-sum game because a gain in the influence of a group's opponent is a loss for that group. Influence is determined by a group's position relative to those with opposing views. As a result, groups want to see less influence in the hands of those groups that oppose their position and more in the hands of groups that support them.[13]

There is less difference between attitudes toward the income of friends and opponents. The income earned by others, whether they concur with one's group on political matters or not, is for their benefit and usually does not help one's own group or its cause. Yet the income that others earn does not necessarily injure a group either, unless it is taken away from that group. Even a group with a constant-sum view of income, evaluating its income position in purely relative terms, may not care much whether friend or foe gets additional income, although it may care whether the additional income goes to those previously earning more or less than itself. An income loss for a group's political opponents and an income gain for its political allies might aid its cause by increasing the resources available to its side, but that connection is indirect. A change in the influence of the group's allies or opponents has a much more direct impact on its own position.

In general, then, groups would be expected to take a markedly different view of the relative position of allies and opponents in relation to influence than in relation to income: decrease the influence but not necessarily the income of opponents relative to that of friends. This hypothesis can be tested by means of the leaders' evaluation of the helpfulness of various groups in attaining the leaders' goals as shown on a help/hinder scale. For two of these target groups, business and labor, the leaders' views as to the groups' helpfulness are compared with their preferences as to the two groups' influence and income (Table 10.8). The income and the influence domains are not precisely comparable, for influence concerns groups, namely business and labor, which are the collective actors in the political process, while income concerns individuals, namely top executives representing the business community and auto workers

**Table 10.8**
Helpfulness, Income, and Influence of Business and Labor

| Correlation of perceived helpfulness with fair income and influence | Beta[a] | F ratio |
| --- | --- | --- |
| Helpfulness of business and fair influence for business | .24 | 71.3 |
| Helpfulness of business and fair income for executives | .15 | 27.0 |
| Helpfulness of labor and fair influence for labor | .27 | 152.9 |
| Helpfulness of labor and fair income for auto worker | .03 | 1.8 |

a. Partial betas with group membership in the equation.

representing organized labor. Nevertheless, the comparison is meaningful since income is mostly a private asset while political influence belongs primarily to groups.[14] For both business and labor, perceived helpfulness, as measured by their scores on the help/hinder scale, is related much more closely to desired influence than to desired income. For business, the relationships between helpfulness and both influence and income are positive and statistically significant, but the relationship with influence is substantially larger. For labor, helpfulness is related to influence but not to income at all.

These findings are consistent with the difference in the contest over income and influence. A group wants more influence for its friends and less for its opponents.[15] However, with respect to income, it neither rewards friends nor punishes enemies, whose earnings have no effect on its own earnings. Or if the earnings have an effect, in the sense of arousing envy and a sense of loss from another's gain, this effect is not differentiated by the group's perception of the supportiveness of the other group. This distinction between income and influence suggests that one group's behavior toward other groups is shaped largely by self-interest. In the domain of political influence, a group rewards friends and punishes enemies, because it stands to gain. In the domain of income, where rewarding its friends or punishing its antagonists would be of no clear benefit, a group is less apt to engage in such behavior.

## Conflicting Perspectives

The differences between attitudes toward income and influence reflect the greater precision with which income can be measured compared with influence and the stronger social norms in the political domain. There is greater perceptual consensus than ideological consensus on income, and more ideological agreement than perceptual agreement on influence. Values about income are part of a larger ideological debate among social groups, while both facts and values about influence are part of that larger debate. Leaders' attitudes also reflect the constant-sum nature of the conflict over political influence, as shown by the more radical changes that they want in the influence hierarchy compared with the income hierarchy. For example, all groups would put themselves at or close to the top of the influence hierarchy by raising themselves and lowering those perceived to have the most influence. The general egalitarian norms associated with political influence presume a leveling of the influence hierarchy. But the constant-sum nature of the contest over influence leads each group to move beyond leveling the hierarchy to enhancing its own relative position.

These findings explain how hierarchy is maintained in both the political and economic domains. A working consensus in favor of equality is difficult to achieve in both income and influence, but for a different reason in each domain. In relation to income, the reason for the lack of egalitarian consensus is ideological. American leaders agree that nothing approaching full income equality should exist in the United States. Even the most egalitarian leaders consider a substantial income gap between top and bottom earners appropriate. They disagree, however, on how large the gap ought to be. They agree on a norm of inequality and disagree on how much.

There is less ideological disagreement on influence. Most groups believe in influence equality as an abstraction. They are concerned, however, about their own relative positions. This concern is sharpened by their perceptual disagreement; each group thinks that it is deprived of influence and its adversaries are advantaged. As a result, the general consensus has little equalizing potential. If any contending group were in a position to do so, it might try to equalize the distribution of influence. But if it did so according to its own perceptions of reality, it would only make the situation more unequal from the perspective of other groups. Business would reduce the influence of labor, making things more equal from its perspective and much less from labor's. Labor would return the favor.

Different perceptions of influence, coupled with the urge to self-protection associated with a constant-sum struggle, intensify the conflict over influence. Consider organized labor's view of its own and business's current influence and what it would deem fair, and business's corresponding view of labor (Figure 10.5A). Labor believes it has less influence than business, and it would reverse that situation. It would move itself up 1.3 points on the influence scale (from 4.5 to 5.8) and move business down 1.7 points. The result from labor's perspective is a self-protective position 1.4 points higher than business. The resulting gap is nearly identical, in both size and location, to the one that labor currently perceives to exist, but with the positions of the two groups reversed. Business would doubtless view such a change with little enthusiasm. But such a change would look especially unfavorable to business if applied to the world as business currently sees it. Labor goes up 1.3 points and business goes down 1.7 points, as labor wants, but the starting point is business's

A. Labor's Preference for Changing the Influence Hierarchy from the Perspective of Labor and Business

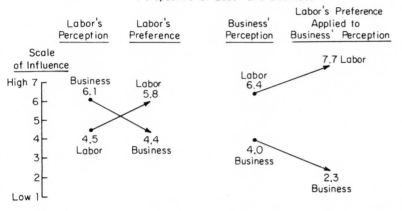

B. Business' Preference for Changing the Influence Hierarchy from the Perspective of Business and Labor

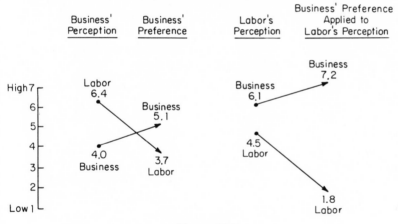

**Figure 10.5**
Desired Change in Influence by Business and Labor

perception that labor is already far ahead. The result is that business would be at the very bottom of the influence scale, and labor almost at the top.

Labor would lower business influence and raise its own. From labor's perspective, it has turned the hierarchy upside down—a change consistent with the constant-sum nature of influence. But from business's perspective, labor has gone even farther. Business perceives labor's proposals as a reduction in influence for a sector (itself) already well below the level it should occupy and an increase for another group (labor) already the most influential in society. Surely business would not be alone in considering this degree of inequality illegitimate. A similar scenario can be produced for labor's perspective on business's proposed changes in the influence hierarchy (Figure 10.5B).

THE CONFLICT over influence may be more intense than the conflict over income, despite the seemingly greater normative consensus on influence. American leaders dispute the proper size of the income gap but they agree that the hierarchy of income groups should stay the same. A narrowing of the gap may be threatening to those at the top, but the threat is minimized by the consensus that those at the top should remain there. For influence, groups want a complete reversal of position. To turn a hierarchy upside down is more threatening than merely to constrict its range.[16]

The conflict associated with changing the influence hierarchy is even more severe because the antagonists have such different perceptions of where they and where their adversaries are. Each group, viewing the preferences of the other in terms of its own perceptions of influence, sees itself as starting from a deprived position and winding up even more deprived. It also sees its opponent, already at the top of the influence hierarchy, as demanding more influence. Such a conflict calls into question the legitimacy of the demands of the other group. The groups generally agree as to a fair distribution of influence: it is a relatively equal distribution in which no group dominates the others. But groups do not agree on what changes would produce a fair influence distribution in the particular case of the contemporary United States.[17]

In some respects Americans "talk the same language" on equality. They conceptualize equality issues in the same way, using the same underlying attitude structure, even if they do not agree substantively. On the question of income distribution they agree on where things stand—who earns the most, who the least. In addition, Americans agree more or less on what a fair income hierarchy would look like and on which group should occupy each position, although they disagree on how far apart the top and bottom incomes should be. Still, though they disagree on the proper size of the income gap, they are all debating the same configuration.

In the realm of politics, on the other hand, Americans are debating about a reality they do not share in common. Americans disagree fundamentally on who should occupy the top and bottom of the influence hierarchy. Ironically, then, although equality may be more of a normative ideal in politics than in economics, incongruent perceptions and the constant-sum nature of politics make the attainment of equality as unlikely in political as in economic affairs.

# 11

## Equality in Perspective

In the United States, equality is a recurring theme. It has flared into a fervent moral issue at crucial stages of American history: the Revolutionary and Jacksonian periods, the Civil War, the populist and progressive eras, the New Deal, and the 1960s and 1980s. In each era, the legitimacy of American society is challenged by some set of people unhappy with the degree of equality. New claims are laid, new understandings are reached, and new policies for political or economic equality are instituted. But the equality issue endures outside these moments of fervor. Ideologies in favor of extending equality are arrayed against others that would limit its scope; advocates of social justice confront defenders of liberty. In the moments of egalitarian ascendancy, libertarians are on the defensive. In the moments of retrenchment, egalitarians cling to previous gains. And in either period the enemy is likely to be the "special interests" that have too much power. In egalitarian times, these are the moneyed interests. In times of retrenchment, these are labor or big government and its beneficiaries.

The periods of fervor in American politics—the moments of creedal passion, in Samuel Huntington's words[1]—have usually been outbursts of egalitarianism. In part, the passion springs from the self-interest of those who would benefit from a more equal distribution of goods or political influence. But the passion also springs from ideology and values, including deep religious justifications for equality. The passion accompanying the discovery or rediscovery that ideals do not match reality is particularly intense when the ideal is as deeply felt as is equality. Yet there can be passion on the inegalitarian side as well. The self-interested passion to protect an established position may be even more powerful than the passion to redress inequity, though its expression may be more muted. Devotion to inequality may also be based on ideals, such as liberty, individualism, and the free market, which are no less ancient and venerable. Like the ideals of equality, these alternative ideals serve as yardsticks for measuring whether society has moved away from its true principles.

Historically, each of the political upheavals that spawned egalitarian reform also provoked antiegalitarian backlash. The spirit of reform during Reconstruction dissipated in the face of spent political struggles, sluggish social institutions, and outright mendacity. Society's entrepreneurial energy was channeled into economic activity, and the courts failed to endorse many of the reformers' grandest visions. The egalitarian thrust of the Populists around the turn of the century inspired an antiegalitarian counterthrust over the next two decades.

The Reagan presidency, beginning in 1981, ushered in the latest spell of antiegalitarian fervor. Intellectuals—new and old conservatives alike—criticized the egalitarian thrust of previous decades. The Reagan administration tried to turn back the tide, with some success. The administration approached its task, in the tradition of American politics, by seeking to reduce the disparity between ideal and reality. The Reagan ideal, however, was found not in the egalitarian symbols of the Declaration of Independence but in the individualistic symbols of the marketplace. The biggest affront to American ideals was not the inequality produced by discrimination or uncontrolled economic fluctuations. Rather, it was the artificial equality imposed by institutions that interfered with the free market. American ideals would become closer to reality with the elimination of regulations, high taxes, and the nonmarket provision of social services. As Reagan put it, "the central political error of our time [is] the view that government and bureaucracy [are] the primary vehicle for social change."[2] The administration's arguments followed the well-trodden path of American political discourse against the power of special interests, in this case government, bureaucrats, and their clients for special programs. The purpose of the Reagan program, as one sympathetic observer put it, was to restore "incentives in our economy to produce income and wealth and raise the absolute level of income on average . . . and this in turn depends in no small measure on our ability to achieve a degree of control over the exploding growth of transfer payment programs."[3]

The program was accompanied by a rise in inequality. Although the extent of the growing inequality and whether it derived partly from changing labor markets brought by changing technology are open to debate, the policies of the administration, stressing tax advantages for the relatively affluent and reductions in poverty programs, clearly widened the income gap between rich and poor.[4] In the ensuing controversy over the administration's approach, opponents of it argued that it was depriving individuals of the basic level of government support necessary for a decent life. But these opponents did not call for major income redistribution. They merely wanted the basic social protections of the welfare state to be maintained. Indeed, the Reagan administration upheld such a social safety net; it disagreed only on how much safety the net should provide.

Thus, the equality debate goes on. Concern with that debate and with the concomitant beliefs about equality might seem irrelevant to people who hold that beliefs and values have little to do with the real conditions of equality or inequality. Indeed, the two dominant philosophies of resource distribution—free-market theory on the right, Marxism on the left—consider self-interest rather than ideology to be the driving force behind individual and collective behavior. They minimize the role of values and ideas, subordinating them to individual or class interests. A central theme of this study, however, is that values and the conflict over values play an important part in determining the nature and extent of equality. Ideas, after all, have consequences.

In recent years, there has been a steady accumulation of evidence that values are autonomous. One of the most compelling and counterintuitive discoveries of social science research over the last 30 years is that the influence of self-interest on most political thought and action is tenuous. Values do not merely rationalize action in accordance with self-interest. Often they arise quite independently of an individual's life experiences and in turn play an independent role in molding political behavior. Such behavior reflects people's group attachments and antipathies, and concern for larger purposes that transcend their own immediate situation. Thus, politics often resembles more closely the world of religion than the world of economics.

The evidence for this resemblance comes from a wide range of life experiences. Analysis has revealed that it is illogical for rational, self-interested individuals to volunteer for large-scale group endeavor. Yet the ubiquity of collective action in the United States suggests that people in fact pursue goals that transcend their self-interest. Attitudes toward the war in Vietnam were found to be linked much less closely to an individual's own experience with the war—such as personal or family involvement in military service—than to general views on foreign policy. Attitudes on busing to achieve integration were also found to be strikingly disconnected from individuals' own experiences with busing in their communities. What counted was their beliefs and values about busing. Similarly, business people's attitudes on foreign and defense policy were found to depend on their general liberal or conservative outlook rather than on how closely their business was related to defense.

The most consistent evidence for this disjunction between life experiences and politics is found in the economic sphere. Personal economic distress is only weakly related to political action. Being unemployed, for example, appears to have less impact on an individual's political values and behavior than does the individual's attitude toward unemployment. Perceptions of the unemployment rate or beliefs about unemployment policies affect individuals' votes more than do their actual experiences in the job market. Not that unemployment has no effect on attitudes or behavior; it is traumatic, affecting what people do and how they view their lives. But the effects tend to be encapsulated within the personal sphere; values and beliefs about public affairs occupy a separate realm. The findings in relation to unemployment are repeated for other economic matters. For example, people's own financial troubles affect their voting choices much less than do their views on the state of the national economy. Pocketbook politics takes a back seat to macroeconomic politics. This undoubtedly reflects the commanding importance of individualism in American values: people believe that they alone are responsible for their financial successes and that they, not the government, should shoulder the blame for their hardships. In short, self-interest based on personal economic circumstances is not as closely tied to political values and political behavior as might have been expected. Ideas and perceptions about public life are more potent.

These findings about the autonomy of ideas in the public are fully consistent with the findings about the attitudes of American leaders. Indeed, among leaders, ideas would be expected to have special potency, for leaders are better educated, more involved in political matters, and more articulate about them. And their values about political matters by no means reflect narrow self-interest. One learns little about the equality attitudes of the leadership groups from their demographic characteristics; one learns a lot from their leadership positions. Nowhere is this clearer than in the comparison of the views held by leaders of the two political parties. Their views on matters of equality are widely divergent, whereas their social and economic positions, and by implication their objective interests, are by no means as distinct. The group with the most consistently pro-equality stance, the feminists, is solidly middle-class and socially little different from other much more conservative groups.

The values of individual leaders on equality matters are best predicted by the social group they lead. But the different leadership groups are by no means homogeneous in their attitudes. This variation is not a function of the leaders' social characteristics. Income, for instance, which one would expect to be a powerful predictor of attitudes toward economic redistribution, has nothing to do with leaders' attitudes on the subject. What shapes the leaders' attitudes is their general values on equality. In contrast, views on the question of how wide an income gap between themselves and others would be fair depends much more on the leaders' own income than on their general ideology.

These facts are crucial to an understanding of the equality issue. Few issues so strongly affect the interests of so many people. To talk of more or less equality is to talk of policies that deprive some and advantage others: you win, I lose. To be sure, the clash over equality issues reflects the self-interest of the participants. Those in the leadership study who hold conservative ideologies about equality are likely to enjoy established and privileged positions, which they want to protect. Those who would supplant the existing distribution with a more equal one generally come from those segments of society most likely to benefit. But the clash over equality entails much more. It is also a clash over ideas, over the nature of a just society. And much as cynics may doubt it, the idea of what is just does not merely reflect what is self-serving.

Equality values, whether formed by self-interest or founded on a sense of justice, are complex. This complexity has many roots. Chief among them are the tensions between competing ideals of equality (opportunity versus result), competing units of comparison (individual versus group equality), competing standards of judgment (reality versus ideal), and competing domains (politics versus economics). Furthermore, there is no single norm of equality. As the leadership study shows, different values may be applied, often by the same individual, in different domains. Michael Walzer has argued that the various spheres of equality should be separated to prevent any one from influencing or "contaminating" any other.[5] This separation finds support both among American leaders and, more generally, in American ideology about equality. Economic inequality is accepted and justified because it is believed to originate in the differences of talent and effort among individuals. Economic inequality falls into disrepute only when it intrudes too noticeably in other spheres, especially the sphere of politics. There are no laws setting a top limit on income, and leadership groups as well as the public at large oppose such laws. But there are laws limiting the extent to which individuals can use their financial resources in political campaigns. And such laws receive widespread approval. But while the isolation of one realm of equality from another may be a sound ideal for a just society, this separation is far from perfect in reality. Indeed, most of the real-world conflicts about equality and many of the difficulties in achieving equality in any single domain arise from the difficulty of keeping the domains of equality separate.

The various equality domains are linked in intricate ways. Imagine a Rubik's cube, each many-celled face representing a different aspect of equality. When the cube is manipulated so that the desired outcome, such as a certain pattern of colors, is achieved on one face, the other faces are thrown into disarray. Each adjustment on one face necessitates an adjustment on some other face of the cube—in some other domain of equality. Only the most adroit and complicated strategies have a chance of achieving acceptable outcomes in more than one domain at once.

So it goes in the real mechanism of the American economy and polity. One gear turns another; changes in the distribution of wealth inevitably affect the allocations of political power, and vice versa. Achieve one form of equality and another may be lost. Equalize income between two groups, blacks and whites, for instance, and the result may be greater inequality within the groups. Increase equality between men and women and risk decreasing it between blacks and whites. The domains of equality are connected by diverse and often obscure linkages; because of these linkages, American beliefs have far-ranging and unforeseen effects, which could lead to a rethinking of the beliefs themselves.

Given the complexity of the domains of equality and the inter-relationships imposed upon them by the real world, American attitudes about equality are of necessity multidimensional. There are no egalitarians or antiegalitarians in any straightforward sense, for there is no single continuum along which to place their beliefs. The leadership study isolated six issues upon which Americans might be more liberal or more conservative, each determined by a set of values considerably more complex than any simple "American ideology" might suggest. There is not one equality issue, but many; not one set of beliefs about equality, but many.

The overlap of equality issues accounts for their salience on the American political agenda. Their complexity makes the United States at once the most and the least equal of modern democracies. Because no single aspect of the equality question dominates, the question is never fully resolved in favor of one extreme or the other. If this were not the case—if, for example, racial equality had clear priority over economic equality—American society would have a simpler normative structure and clearer issue choices. With one dominant issue, the conflict over equality would be more intense, but its conclusion would be swifter and surer.

In reality, however, the conflict is not nearly so linear, and thus it is not easily concluded. The resolution of one aspect of equality runs up against the continuing dispute over another. None of the issues of equality can be settled before settling them all, and to settle them all is unlikely, given the many contradictions in the concept of equality. Race issues crisscross economic considerations, and both overlap perspectives of gender and region. Therefore, American society can emerge neither clearly egalitarian nor clearly inegalitarian.

The complexity of equality is such that egalitarian forces within each domain are countered by inegalitarian reactions, and the intertwining of the domains creates further countervailing pressures. Three areas of struggle for equal treatment and equal position illustrate the different barriers that both channel that struggle and keep it alive: the conflict over economic equality, over political equality, and among groups—especially racial and gender groups. In the political domain, Americans cannot decide who has power; in the economic domain they cannot decide who should have wealth. The groups face a reckoning of a different sort: they must decide whether they want to be equal as members of a group or as individuals.

## Economic Equality

Nearly all issues of equality have an economic component. If income were equal across individuals, it would also be equal between blacks and whites, men and women. Furthermore, the main threat to political equality, the inequality of individual resources, would be eliminated. Income equality might be the key to equality in general, but it is unlikely to be achieved. Americans of every political stripe accept the premises of the capitalist system. They agree that rewards should be based on success in the competitive market; the distribution of wealth should be based on skill and effort. This belief system judges the competitive market to be highly egalitarian, and capitalism's compatibility with equality partly explains its attraction in America. The market is deemed egalitarian because it judges everyone in the same way—by how well they compete—with no reference to characteristics such as race or gender. Champions of the market as an indispensable adjunct to democracy argue rightly that it rejects the structured hierarchies of closed systems like feudalism. In practice, however, the market system, even in its own terms, is less than egalitarian. Opportunities are far from equal. Those who win at first are at a distinct advantage in further play. But the underlying premise that rewards can be widely disparate yet fair is generally accepted.

The findings of the leadership study are that some groups want more income equality, but almost none wants complete equality. Equality of results has few proponents among American leaders. Nor does any group want the government to put a ceiling on income. The most telling indication of this consensus against radical equalization occurs in attitudes toward income distribution. For example, even the group with the most egalitarian view of income considers a ratio of more than eight to one between the incomes of a top executive and an unskilled worker to be legitimate. Public opinion surveys similarly reveal little support for radical redistribution. These views are consistent with the income distribution that actually prevails. The United States is a far remove from the level of equality that has been achieved in many other industrialized democracies. Furthermore, income distribution in the United States has been remarkably stable for a long time. The consensus against redistribution hampers any radical movement toward greater equality.

Even though most leaders and citizens accept and even favor fairly

**Table 11.1**
Commitment to Income Equality by Liberal Groups in the United States

| Commitment | Those who call themselves "far left" or "very liberal" among | | | |
|---|---|---|---|---|
| | Democrats | Union | Blacks | Feminists |
| Favor equality of results (%) | 20 | 14 | 9 | 10 |
| Favor equal pay (%) | 26 | 23 | 23 | 25 |
| Favor top limit on income (%) | 45 | 32 | 22 | 37 |
| Fair income ratio of executive/elevator operator | 12.0 | 9.8 | 12.2 | 8.2 |
| Proportion of group far left and liberal (%) | 23 | 22 | 32 | 46 |

wide income disparities, the United States might be pushed toward greater equality if a small and articulate vanguard of leaders held more radically redistributionist views. But there is no such group. Even among feminist, black, union, and Democratic party leaders—the leaders most critical of the current distribution in the United States—radical views are few. Such views are strikingly absent even among the members of these groups who consider themselves to be "far left" or "very liberal." About one-fourth of Democrats and union leaders, one-third of blacks, and close to one-half of feminists so label themselves. Their stance on income equality, as shown by their views on redistribution, are hardly radical (Table 11.1). In no case do as many as a quarter endorse strong redistribution on the issues of equality of opportunity versus result or of differential versus equal pay. There is more support for a top limit on income, a policy that still would not preclude wide income differentiation, but in no group does a majority support this position. Most revealing are the desired income ratios between the top and bottom earning categories. All are substantial. None are sharply different from the responses expected from the more conservative groups.

This evidence might seem to reveal little about what makes American leaders distinctive. Strict income equality is perhaps such an extreme proposition that one would expect little support for it anywhere, at least in any country that upholds personal freedom and individual development. Furthermore, if income gaps are needed to drive economic productivity, as many sociologists and most economists argue, one would be surprised to find informed opinion anywhere favoring radical redistribution. However, opposition like that found in the United States to income equality is not universal, even in democracies. Consider Sweden, which is a democratic system with a working economy.[6] Comparison of the views of two sets of American leaders with those of their Swedish counterparts—Democratic party leaders in the United States with Social-Democratic party leaders in Sweden, and union leaders in the United States with leaders of the largest Swedish labor federation—reveals striking differences (Table 11.2). The Swedes do not endorse full equality of result, but equal pay is supported by over half of the party and union leaders. And the acceptance of a top limit on pay is fairly wide in Sweden. More revealing, the proper income gap between top and bottom earners—between top executives and dishwashers in Sweden and top executives and elevator operators in the United States—differs sharply. The ratio between top and bottom earnings considered to be fair is a little over two to one in Sweden, compared with ratios of more than eleven to one in the United States. The Swedish

**Table 11.2**
Commitment to Income Equality in Sweden and the United States

| Commitment | Social Democrats (Sweden) | Democrats (U.S.) | Blue-collar union (Sweden) | Union (U.S.) |
|---|---|---|---|---|
| Favor equality of results (%) | 21 | 9 | 14 | 4 |
| Favor equal pay (%) | 58 | 12 | 68 | 11 |
| Favor top limit on income (%) | 44 | 17 | 51 | 13 |
| Fair income ratio of executive/ dishwasher in Sweden and executive/ elevator operator in U.S. | 2.4 | 15.2 | 2.2 | 11.3 |

leaders do not want full equality, but their views depart startlingly from those of their American counterparts.

This comparison may be somewhat misleading, since the groups in each country are not equivalent. The Democratic party represents a broader coalition than the Swedish Social Democrats. Furthermore, unions in the United States include blue- and white-collar workers, while the Swedish union is blue-collar. Swedish leaders thus represent a more radical segment of their society than American leaders of theirs. The gulf between American and Swedish attitudes is highlighted dramatically by the views of conservative Swedish leaders. Even the least egalitarian leaders in Sweden, those of big business, are considerably more egalitarian not only than their business counterparts in the United States but also than the most radical American groups. When asked about the proper earnings ratio between a top and bottom earner, Swedish big business leaders suggest a ratio of 4.7 to 1. The parallel business group in the United States endorses a ratio of 26 to 1. More striking is the fact that Swedish business leaders are sharply more egalitarian than any group in the United States, including left-liberal groups. Few American leaders take as egalitarian a position on the proper gap between top and bottom incomes as does the average Swedish business leader. In sum, American leaders stand out in their lack of support for radical redistribution.

Attitudes and preferences, though abstract in themselves, have practical implications. The acceptance in principle of wide income differentials affects actual differentials through both private and public policies. Earnings for various occupations are set in the private sector. These earnings reflect market forces, union bargaining power, and the like. But some earnings, particularly the executive earnings at the top, which set a boundary for the income gaps, reflect norms as to what is appropriate.

The broad consensus against radical redistribution also affects actual earnings through its effect on public policy. It is not that there is no controversy over public policies relating to equality, but the consensus sets the boundaries of that controversy. The controversy exists despite Americans' ideological acceptance of the market system, because the market is imperfectly egalitarian, even in its own terms. All may begin at the same place with equal opportunity, but those who succeed in the first round will parlay that success into second-round advantages for themselves or their children. This is where politics enters the picture. Those who are successful in the market can then use their new wealth to protect their gains. Success is converted into privilege through laws that favor the accumulation of wealth, such as tax programs that are generous in their treatment of capital gains or inheritances.

The market, moreover, has never been fully open and free. Despite Americans' individualistic ideology, competition has often been limited through discrimination. Blacks and women are the most obvious examples, but other groups have suffered as well. The group that is denied an equal start in the race labors under a severe handicap.

The market's failure to live up to its own ideals fuels policy controversy. The agreement among leaders on the market norm of equality of opportunity carries with it a good deal of disagreement over the extent to which the United States lives up to that norm and, in turn, the extent to which the government should interfere with the workings of the market. The policy controversy, however, remains within bounds set by the broad value consensus. The American public largely accepts a government-supported floor under income, but only so long as the floor consists of a government guarantee of a job so one can earn that minimum. American leaders, even the most egalitarian ones, similarly opt for measures to increase equality that are consistent with the norm of opportunity.

That actual policy proposals for increasing income equality, even somewhat radical proposals, tend to fall within the domain of equality of opportunity is illustrated by the controversy over "comparable worth" compensation. In what many consider a radical proposal, feminists and some unions insist that equal pay for equal work be replaced by equal pay for work in different jobs of comparable worth. The purpose of the proposal, which has received some support in the courts, is to eliminate the pay bias remaining from the days of sex-segregated jobs whereby "women's work" receives less pay than jobs of comparable skill and responsibility that are reserved for men. This proposal may be radical, but it harmonizes with the ethic of opportunity. The goal is not to reduce the income gap between the top and bottom of the earnings hierarchy. Rather, the goal is the typically American one of reconciling earnings with skill and effort—a goal fully consistent with the American dream of equal opportunity.[7] In sum, a turn toward a more radical economic egalitarianism in the United States is unlikely, because it would go against widely held values.

## Political Equality

The obstacles to political equality are different from, but no less significant than, those constraining economic equality. One obstacle is the mutual reinforcement of economic and political inequality; money is converted into political influence. A more equal polity may elude Americans without a more equal distribution of economic resources. But the impetus for economic leveling may be hard to find. There is little desire for radical redistribution even among the more radical groups and even less among groups whose affluence gives them more political clout. Economic equality is hard to achieve, both because few want it and because those who want it least have the most say. This in turn affects the political system, as economic inequality becomes political inequality, which makes the antiredistributionists more politically potent—thereby closing the circle.

In politics the norm at least is more egalitarian. Traditionally, Americans object more to differing levels of political influence than to differing levels of affluence. Violations of a one-person, one-vote rule or gross variations across individuals in campagn contributions are offensive. Americans have tried to limit these inequities by law. If they cannot and do not want to equalize income as a means of equalizing political influence, perhaps the solution is to insulate politics from economic inequalities—to keep politics, in Walzer's terminology, in its proper "sphere of justice." This is, in a sense, the logic behind laws eliminating the poll tax or limiting each citizen, rich or poor, to one vote. As the Supreme Court put it in declaring the poll tax unconstitutional, a state "violates the Equal Protection Clause of the Fourteenth Amendment whenever it makes the affluence of the voter or the payment of any fee an electoral standard. Voter qualification has no relation to wealth nor to paying or not paying this or any other tax."[8]

Equalization of political influence by severing its connection to economic resources may be a more promising approach than attempting to establish political equality on a base of economic equality. This insulation might in turn bring about greater economic equality. If the polity were equal—if no bias were built into the system in favor of the affluent—more extensive governmental intervention aimed at economic equality might then follow. Even if it did not, this fact would reflect more certainly the preferences of the American public as expressed through an equal political process than the preferences of the better-off as expressed through the workings of a skewed political process.

Such insulation, however, is probably impossible. Given the wide disparity of economic resources, they cannot easily be prevented from leaking into the political realm. A transfer of economic resources into politics can take place directly or indirectly. Direct transfer is hard to control; indirect is even harder.

Consider the direct use of economic resources in politics:

Income/wealth → Political influence

This takes place when an individual spends money on election campaigns or in other ways directly employs economic resources to influence political outcomes. Controlling such use of money is daunting. In the first place, appropriate legislation is hard to pass, and once passed, it is often ineffective. The Campaign Finance Act, for instance, was slow in coming and mixed in result. In the second place, controls on the use of money in politics may run up against the First Amendment. Witness the Supreme Court's decision allowing individuals to spend freely on their own to support candidates.[9] If it is legitimate to have a disparity in income or wealth, it is legitimate to use that wealth politically.

Although direct controls over spending may be hard to achieve, they are much easier than controlling the indirect effect of unequal resources. The wealthy are more likely to be highly educated, to be informed about political matters, to feel that they can influence politics, and to be acquainted with people in politics or in the media. They have, in short, more resources and stronger motivation than do the less affluent. The effect is indirect:

Income/wealth→Education/skills/motivation→Political influence

The assets found among politically influential citizens, including money, education, political involvement, information, a sense of competence, and connections, are linked: wealth buys education, which fosters motivation that leads to acquiring information, and so on. Public policies could help to equalize matters by bestowing some of these assets upon the less affluent. Such policies might include free public higher education, campaigns to increase citizen motivation and awareness, open public hearings, ombudspersons, and poverty lawyers. These policies might help motivate some people who would otherwise be inactive and might instill political activism in those at lower levels of motivation and resources. It is unlikely, though, that they would fully redress the imbalance. Stronger policies would be needed to limit the use of the resources and the motivation of advantaged citizens. But such policies might be impossible to reconcile with democratic rights.

All this saps the practical effect of the norm of equality in politics. In the economic sphere equality is seen as opportunity, and the result is stratification in wealth and income. Equality in the political sphere, in turn, cannot defend itself from the effects of economic inequality. As long as wide disparities in economic position are legitimate and individuals are free to participate in politics, the translation of economic advantage into political advantage will be hard to limit.

A further obstacle to insulating politics from economic inequality is the unevenness of perceptions. In the absence of a metric for determining who has most political influence, the exact degree of inequality in the political system remains unclear. In the few cases where inequality is noticeable and measurable, there may be attempts to eliminate it. As Robert Dahl has pointed out, Americans would be outraged if asked to accept a three-tier system of voting as in pre-World War I Prussia, where the value of the vote varied sharply across social strata.[10] Similarly, gross disparities in campaign contributions, because they are observable, are subject to egalitarian attention. After these inequities had become especially blatant around the time of Watergate, attempts were made to reduce them. However, political activity and influence assume a myriad of forms, some more visible than others. Differences in political influence are easily obscured and, therefore, likely to be overlooked.

This means that political equality is elusive even if all agree that it is desirable. Each group would find the others' definition of an equitable distribution to be quite unfair. For instance, labor and business might agree that America should move closer to the goal of equal political influence, but they would march off in opposite directions. Furthermore, the inconsistent perceptions across groups are not fully symmetrical. They tend to be biased against the disadvantaged. The more established groups, especially business, rely on less overt forms of political activity which they may not even consider to be political. Though more politically active, they tend to be less visible in their activity than the disadvantaged groups. They are thus more likely than other groups to underestimate their own influence. Less advantaged groups, lacking routine inside channels, engage in more conspicuous activity. Thus, whatever influence they have is fully acknowledged and perhaps overestimated. Business, for example, considers consumer groups to be more influential than business.

Even if each individual and group could be audited and its share of "Gross National Political Influence" measured, and even if all Americans agreed that influence shares should be equal, there would still be debate on the issue of which units should be equal. It makes a difference whether all individuals, or all significant social groups, are to have equal influence. Even if each individual could be given an equal amount of political influence—such as one person, one vote, if only voting counts; or one person, one unit of participation, if there is some more general metric of influence—each individual might not be guaranteed to feel equally influential. Members of minority groups, who are in the minority on most issues, would feel disenfranchised. One person, one vote is not a comforting principle for black Americans, who would be politically disadvantaged for all time if the issues they care about pitted one race against the other. They might want special guarantees, such as a veto over legislation that is damaging to them, or other provisions recognizing a special status. At that point, one person, one vote ceases to be the generally accepted equality principle. It is replaced by some form of group-based equality.

But this kind of equality raises other difficulties. Equality among groups is all but impossible to put into operation. There would be no easy agreement on which groups to make equal, whether classes, races, ethnic groups, or sexes. And equality among groups would receive the opposite criticism from equality among individuals: members of large groups would be deprived of political influence. Like citizens of large states in matters of senatorial voting, their individual votes would count less.

The political road to equality contains deep potholes. The spill-over effects of economic inequality, as well as the differences in perception, counteract the pressure that the general consensus on equality would otherwise exert. This is unfortunate from the point of view of social harmony. Political inequality creates especially sharp resentments. For one thing, it does violence to deeply held norms. For another, because political conflict is constant-sum, or is perceived to be so, inequality in politics is particularly damaging to the actor who feels disadvantaged, and all actors see themselves as disadvantaged. Self-perceived disadvantage raises the political stakes. It makes political equality harder to achieve; groups and individuals are unwilling to yield influence to others, for that would mean worsening their own position. Thus the constant-sum nature of political influence makes both political equality harder to achieve and political inequality more damaging to social harmony.

## Group Equality: The Divided Voices

Neither the economic nor the political route to equality is promising. But there is another route. The drive for equality in America has been more intense when more narrowly directed toward specific groups. Here there is a passion for equality unlike the ambivalence associated with the drive for economic equality. The strength of campaigns for equality by particular groups and the weakness of more general movements for income equality are not unrelated. Equality in America has by definition always involved equality among individuals in the opportunities open to them. Furthermore, class conflict based on economic position has never been as pronounced as conflict based on other social characteristics, such as race or ethnicity. This suggests that Americans think in terms of both individuals and groups. Indeed, the two modes of thought about equality are not contradictory. The serious group-based conflicts in the United States, whether on grounds of race, ethnicity, religion, region, or more recently gender, have crosscut economic differences. In this way, they have diminished the importance of class as an organizing principle of social conflict. Thus, economic equality is relegated more to individual than to class competition.

One paradox is that despite the American individualistic ethic, effective egalitarian movements are likely to be based on group distinctions. Theodore White has described the strategy of blacks in the 1984 election as one designed to "transform the traditional credo of American politics, 'equality,' into the credo of 'group equality'... what blacks want most is public acceptance of equality, not only on the basis of individual merit, but the group results and group shares." The rising forces include not only blacks but women, homosexuals, and groups emerging from the new waves of immigration and ethnic pride.[11] These forces, though especially potent in 1984, are certainly not new. They represent the latest version of the group-based claims to equality that have always been a counterpoint to the dominant individualistic theme.

The race for the Presidency in 1984 provided a stage for lively debate over group equality. White, a veteran campaign chronicler, anticipated that as the campaign drama unfolded, its underlying plot would be the "testing ... of the meaning of the word 'equality,' " with blacks and women playing leading roles.[12] With the first serious black candidate seeking a party's Presidential nomination and the first woman running on a major party's Presidential ticket, 1984 was a watershed in group political gains. Significantly, the announcement of the selection of the first woman Vice Presidential candidate was couched in language that put it squarely within the American equality ethic. Opponents criticized the selection of Geraldine Ferraro, implying that it was not based on merit, even charging that it was a case of affirmative action.[13] The Democrats claimed that the motives were egalitarian, but individual not group-based, reflecting the norm of equal opportunity rather than equal result. At the announcement ceremony Ferraro said, "American history is about doors being opened, doors of opportunity, for everyone no matter who you are as long as you're willing to earn it." Vice President Mondale praised his running mate as a person who "earned her way here today. Our message is that America is for everyone who works hard and contributes to our blessed country."[14] Other equality issues formed subplots of the campaign, including the Democratic attack against Reagan's generosity to the rich and unfairness to the poor, and the counterattack which portrayed Walter Mondale as the captive of special interest groups.

If the drive for equality continues, it may come from an alliance of disadvantaged minorities rather than from a broad majority of the less affluent. An alliance of equality-oriented minorities, each with its own agenda, seems more workable than an equality-oriented coalition including the less affluent 51 percent of the population. The less affluent coalition would be so diverse in other ways, and indeed in income, that it would lack sufficient cohesiveness and motivation to be effective.

But the prospects for an alliance of disadvantaged groups, each with its own grievance somehow related to equality, are mixed. The three challenging groups in the leadership study—blacks, feminists, and labor—each representing different equality constituencies, could together form a general equality coalition; indeed they already function as such on many issues. The concerns that bind them together tend to be economic. The three groups are close in their support of New Deal policies. They cluster together in favor of a more egalitarian distribution of income across occupations. When economic controversies arise, such as those over the Reagan administration's proposed tax changes or cuts in social welfare programs, these groups can be expected to line up together.

As an equality coalition, however, these groups have weaknesses.

For one thing, each has its own set of priorities. Economic issues hold them together, but on core issues, the alliance disintegrates. Blacks rate racial equality just below jobs in importance, much higher than do the other groups. Labor puts racial equality quite far down on its list, below crime reduction, national defense, and other issues. Feminists rank racial equality higher than does labor but closer to the middle than to the top of the list. As for gender equality, blacks and union leaders rank it near the bottom of their priorities. In sum, an equality coalition might be held together by economic concerns, but because the equality issues that animate blacks and feminists differ, they are not effective political adhesives.[15]

Relations among the three challenging groups are uneasy largely because the different themes of equality tend to clash. Racial equality may conflict with gender equality when choosing goals for a jobs program or an affirmative action campaign. Gender or racial equality may conflict with economic equality if the basis for special social programs is gender or race rather than poverty. Poor white males, for example, may wind up worse off while somewhat more affluent women or blacks take advantage of the programs. And labor leaders' desire to help their own clientele may conflict with gender, racial, and even economic equality insofar as unionized workers are disproportionately white, male, and well-paid. The permutations of conflict are almost endless. In the 1984 primary election campaign, Jesse Jackson echoed a frequently heard criticism of the women's movement when he chided black women for supporting a movement that speaks for the narrow interests of "upper middle-class white females."[16] Here class, gender, and race are all intertwined. The promise of an effective merger of the challenging groups begins to erode when these conflicts appear.

One organization that is in a strategic position to assemble an equality coalition is the Democratic party. The several egalitarian interest groups are all overwhelmingly committed to the Democratic party. Moreover, the major parties are hardly identical on the issue of equality. Even if they offer no coherent ideologies opposed to one another, differences on equality appear at all party levels— among organizational leaders, elected officials, partisan identifiers, and voters. The differences are confirmed in opinion surveys, official platforms, and congressional voting. And they cut across the equality domains of race, gender, and economic well-being.

In this sense, equality appears on the public agenda as a thoroughly partisan issue. There are substantial differences between the two parties. Economic inequality would be significantly diminished in the United States if the nation had an income gap of the magnitude desired by Democratic rather than Republican leaders. Nevertheless, Democratic leaders, even those who describe themselves as most liberal, do not opt for extreme egalitarian distributions, nor do they favor such radical measures as hiring quotas. They are not ready to spearhead an equality coalition.

In addition, the divisions within the Democratic party confuse its stand on equality. If economic equality were the only equality issue on the agenda, the position of the Democratic leaders would be as simple as that of the Republican leaders. Democratic leaders stand on the liberal side of the fence of economic issues, quite close to their most potent allies, labor leaders. Black and feminist leaders fall somewhat further to the left of these issues, and the Democratic public somewhat further to the right. The gaps among the groups are moderately wide, which may cause problems for party leaders trying to balance the positions of their black and feminist allies and their mass support groups. But the problem is eased by the fact that the mass of Democratic supporters, though nearer the center than the Democratic leaders, are still much closer to the leaders of their own party than they are to the Republican leaders. If both Democratic and Republican leaders presented policy positions consistent with their own views, Democratic voters would, on that basis at least, be drawn to the Democratic party.

The Democratic position is complicated by the fact that the positions of the groups allied to it are quite inconsistent one with another across the other equality issues. In particular, labor divides from blacks and feminists on race issues, while both blacks and labor divide from feminists on gender issues. This makes it difficult for Democratic leaders to take positions that satisfy their disparate allies. Furthermore, on these two concerns, the majority of Democratic supporters are in fact closer to the Republican leaders than to the Democrats.

In all three equality domains, then, the positions of Democratic leaders are quite distinct from those of Republican leaders. In this sense the parties do offer alternatives to the public. But the range of these alternatives is restricted, particularly in the economic realm. Furthermore, an equality coalition in the Democratic party would be a most uneasy one, with the allied groups pursuing divergent equality agendas.

AT FIRST BLUSH, the American ideology toward equality appears straightforward. It does not take a Tocqueville or a Myrdal to ascertain that the nation is fundamentally concerned with equality. Americans approve of equality and actively seek it through the powers of the state and the actions of individuals. It is the *form* of equality that arouses debate. For a nation so taken with equality, there is a striking degree of contention over the goal. Americans can agree on equality only by disagreeing on what it means.

Different facets of equality have vied for political attention throughout American history. There has been calm, and there has been conflict; there have been advances and retreats. The historical struggle over equality traces a pattern that seems to have no end. There are boundaries to the extremes of equality and inequality precisely because there are few boundaries that define and constrain the American social structure. That structure is porous: classes meld, hierarchies shift, the economy permeates the polity and vice versa. When one form of equality is advanced or rebuffed, there are reactions in equality's other domains; new claims are forwarded, and new defenses thrown up, as the balance is struck once again.

The future will doubtless bring more conflict but little more equality. There is no relentless march to the perfectly egalitarian society, for there can be no such society. As Samuel Huntington has observed, to have faith in all forms of equality is incoherent. Yet Americans do not have an ideology that assigns clear priority to one value over any other. At every historical juncture where equality was an issue, its proponents failed to do all that they had set out to do. By the same token, the swell of conservatism embodied in the Reagan administration will find its limits too. Swings in the equality of social conditions are restrained not just by institutional obstacles but by fundamental conflicts of values that are a traditional element of American politics. Faith in the individualistic work ethic and belief in the legitimacy of unequal wealth retard progression to the egalitarian left. As for contemporary conservatism, the indelible tenet of political equality firmly restrains the right. A swing to the right does not eliminate America's commitment to the disadvantaged. In seeking equal opportunity over equal result, Americans forego a ceiling, not a floor. Americans may amend the uneven distribution of affluence and influence, but they will not abolish it. Intense conflict within narrow confines will remain the hallmark of the American politics of equality.

Appendixes A-E

Notes

Index

# Appendixes
*G. Donald Ferree, Jr.*

## A. Sampling Opinion

The persons who completed the questionnaire did not, nor were they intended to, represent the universe of "American leaders," for the purpose of the study was not to conduct a public opinion poll of undifferentiated leaders. Rather, it was to examine the consensus and dissensus among groups of American leaders. Thus, the statistically most efficient way of proceeding was to sample each group. The first task was to define groups whose attitudes we wished to explore and to devise the actual strategies that would identify specific individuals from those groups.

We wanted to sample from a broad range of groups while keeping the number of groups small enough to permit both reliable point estimates of their characteristics and examination of major cleavages within the groups. We thus decided on nine groups, each with an initial size of 600. Allowing for response rates of 50–80%, this would produce samples of around 300–400 for each group.

Groups were selected from several sectors of American society. Within each sector, we looked to the main organization and selected leaders of those organizations. One sector, described as "established," comprised economic groups with an established legitimate voice in modern industrial society. These groups were represented by business, labor, and farmers. A second set of groups, designated as "challenging," sought change in an egalitarian direction. The challenging sector was represented by leaders of feminist organizations and black organizations. A third broad sector, characterized as "intervening," was neither inherently supportive nor fundamentally challenging of the economic status quo but mediated the positions of other groups. This sector was represented by the two major political parties, the media, and intellectuals. The fourth group was "future" leaders, represented by undergraduates at leading colleges.

Anticipating a distinction between cosmopolitans and locals, we drew comparable local and national samples. For efficiency and comparability, we drew local leaders in various leadership categories from the same set of localities. To obtain a sample of localities from which to draw local leaders, we used the *Rand McNally Commercial Atlas of the United States* (1975). This volume provided a list of 425 "metro-areas," each defined as a "major market," which together contained some 75% of the total U.S. population. The first stage of the locality sampling was to select metro-areas randomly with a likelihood proportional to population. In order to ensure that the likelihood of sampling any particular area was independent of whether or not another particular area had been sampled, the areas were randomly ordered. Then the total population of all the areas was divided by 150, the desired number of localities, to derive a skip interval of 1,030,049. Some cities with populations greater than the skip interval could be selected more than once. Multiple selected metro-areas were broken up into their component parts for a second level of selection. At the end of this process, 146 of the 150 localities had been assigned. The remaining four were assigned to metro-areas in a third random wave. The final results identified 150 localities in 137 distinct cities from 40 states and the District of Columbia and included 91 of the Rand McNally metro-areas.

## The Groups

For each of the groups the sampling was done in a variety of ways. Business leaders were divided on the basis of two criteria: national versus local, and banking and finance versus other. Each of the resulting four categories had a target sample size of 150. At the national level the president or chairman of the board of a sample of the *Fortune* 500 largest corporations and 200 largest banks was taken. At the local level, the chief executive officer of the local Chamber of Commerce as well as the chief executive officer of the largest local bank not already sampled at the national level were chosen.

Farmers were also divided on two criteria. The first was the distinction between membership associations of individual farmers and commodity associations. The former involved three groups: the American Farm Bureau Federation, the National Farmers' Organization, and the Farmers' Union. The second distinction, which was not entirely orthogonal to the first, was along national-local lines. Specifically, the national sample originally consisted of some 240 persons drawn from the national officers of the three larger federations and national commodity organizations. Fewer than 300 persons were chosen because of the small number of significant commodity organizations and the desire not to sample the entire universe. The local sample was drawn equally from each of the three membership organizations, looking to the counties in which the 150 sample localities lay. Substitutions were made for such obviously inappropriate places as Kings County—Brooklyn—in New York State. Since both the Farmers' Union and the National Farmers' Organization are more geographically restricted than is the Farm Bureau, a subsidiary sample of approximately 10 localities was drawn in each case to fill out the local sample to a potential of 100 for each of the organizations.

Labor was also divided into a local and national component. The national sample was drawn from the national officers of international unions with memberships above 25,000. The local sample was drawn on the basis of a rotation scheme among these same unions within the 150 localities. Beginning at a random point in the list of unions, we looked for the next two unions which had locals in the sampled locality. The presidents of the locals were the designated respondents. This procedure amounted to selecting locals proportional to the likelihood of the national union being represented in a locality, and it empirically provided a good mix on different unions in different locations.

There was a further complication in the sampling of the labor group. The study began as a collaborative effort between the center for International Affairs at Harvard University and the Washington *Post*. Soon after the first mailings were sent out, that newspaper became involved in a bitter strike with its pressmen. We ran into a good deal of resistance to the survey among labor leaders and had to suspend that part of the sample. The following year, in January 1977, another sampling of labor leaders was done, and a slightly modified questionnaire was mailed with a revised cover letter. Fortunately, the response rate for this second attempt at labor was comparable to that ultimately achieved for the other groups. Although it would have been better to gather data from all the groups simultaneously, this two-wave approach was preferable to losing one important group altogether.

Intellectuals, the first group in the intervening sector, were not sampled along the national-local distinction. A four-point division of arts, humanities, social sciences, and natural sciences was used. A *Who's Who* type of directory in each of these fields served as the basis for a random sample of 150 persons in each field, for a total of 600 persons in all.

The media, the second intervening group, were doubly stratified. Along with the national-local split, electronic journalism, primarily television, was distinguished from print journalism, primarily newspapers. Thus, four separate subsamples represented the national-local and electronic-print cross-classification. The national samples were selected randomly from lists of the congressional radio or television and press galleries. The local samples consisted of the news director of the largest television station and the managing editor of the newspaper with the largest circulation serving each locality.

Political parties, the last intervening group, were divided along national-local lines and between Republicans and Democrats. At the national level, three persons from the national committee of each party for each state were sampled, or 150 people for each of the two political parties. The local samples consisted of county or city chairperson of each party in each locality.

Blacks were divided into a local and national component. The local sample consisted of local officials of the National Association for the Advancement of Colored People and the Urban League for the localities where those organizations had local chapters. In addition, the local sample included the highest-ranking black elected official in each locality. The national sample consisted of the entire Congressional Black Caucus as well as a random sample of higher black elected officials who were not in the local sample, drawn from the list of such officials invited to the National Black Political Convention by the Joint Center for Urban Affairs in 1975.

Although organizations of feminists were plentiful, the feminist movement had something of an antiorganizational bias and tended to emphasize local networks. For that reason, the feminist sample was locally based. It consisted of local leaders of the National Organization for Women, Federally Employed Women, Coalition of Labor Union Women, Women's Equity Action League, National Women's Political Caucus, and state commissions of the status of women. These organizations covered a broad range of activities, and all had a sufficient number of local chapters to make the locality sample practicable.

The final group was college youth. To maximize the chance of getting future leaders, students were selected at leading universities across the country. The sample consisted of 60 seniors at each school— 30 men and 30 women—chosen at random from student lists at Berkeley, Chicago, Duke, Harvard, Indiana, Princeton, Rice, Stanford, Wisconsin, and Yale.

## Data Collection

The survey instrument was a mail questionnaire which covered four pages and contained approximately 200 individual items. The vast bulk of questions were common to all groups, but several group-specific items dealt with issues relevant to a particular group as well as with one group's perceptions of the others. The instrument was mailed to all 5400 original potential respondents except for labor on February 27, 1976. The questionnaires contained nothing that would identify any specific respondent. There were two follow-up mailings at intervals of about four weeks. The first follow-up was sent on March 21; the final one was sent on April 18.

Early indications were that the national business group had a relatively high noncompliance rate. Since such persons are an over-sampled population, a special effort seemed warranted. During the second week of May 1976, the national business sample was telephoned and asked once again to complete the survey. This effort proved successful, and the final response rate for national business was high.

## Response Rate

The overall response rate, calculated by dividing the number of completed, usable questionnaires received by the total list size, minus those persons who could not have completed the questionnaire, was 56% (Table A.1). This figure is high for the kind of research involved. It is also a conservative estimate, since the only correction to the original potential sample size was for persons known not to be able to complete the questionnaire because their addresses were inaccurate or they were deceased. The single highest response rate, 67%, was for feminists. Most groups hovered in the low or middle 50's, with no group below 52%. In particular, the fact that labor wound

**Table A.1**
Rates of Return for Mail Questionnaire

| Group | Potential no.[a] | No. usable questionnaires | Percentage returned[b] |
|---|---|---|---|
| National business | 281 | 145 | 52 |
| Local business | 291 | 167 | 57 |
| National labor | 265 | 141 | 52 |
| Local labor | 240 | 125 | 52 |
| National farm | 222 | 114 | 52 |
| Local farm | 284 | 152 | 54 |
| Intellectuals[c] | 519 | 296 | 57 |
| National media | 282 | 163 | 57 |
| Local media | 296 | 155 | 52 |
| National parties | 286 | 149 | 52 |
| Local parties | 287 | 158 | 55 |
| National blacks[d] | 178 | 92 | 52 |
| Local blacks | 333 | 174 | 52 |
| Feminists | 551 | 367 | 67 |
| Youth | 576 | 364 | 63 |

a. The number of persons originally drawn for each group, less deductions for bad addresses, illnesses, defective questionnaires, and the like, thus the maximum number who could have completed the questionnaire.

b. A conservative estimate of the true response rate, since some persons in the first column might not have been able to respond, e.g. someone who had died but whose family, rather than returning the questionnaire, simply discarded it.

c. Bad addresses and defective questionnaires were concentrated here.

d. Redefined after drawing, but before mailing, to eliminate elected officials below the level of alderman, lest the level of office held be lower for the national sample.

up with a more or less typical rate indicates that the second-year effort was worthwhile. The response rate for feminists likely reflected the fact that they were a relatively undersurveyed population, in contrast, say, with national business leaders. Indeed, a number of comments received from feminist respondents indicated appreciation for the interest shown in them as a group and for the topics on the questionnaire.

While the response rates were acceptable, the question remains as to whether or not the sample was representative. There were no clearly defined populations with known characteristics to compare with the achieved samples. Still, there are two reasons for confidence that the achieved samples did not differ appreciably from the theoretical populations from which they were drawn. First, the groups had roughly similar response rates. Any process that determined who responded and who did not was likely to be roughly similar across the groups. Since the groups differed significantly on background variables as well as on attitudes, the process that determined who responded was probably not associated with attitudes to equality. Second, the patterns of the timing of responses were broadly similar across the groups, indicating little systematic difference in willingness to respond (Table A.2).

Response rates can say little directly about the characteristics of nonrespondents. However, it is possible to make inferences about those characteristics from characteristics of the achieved sample.[1] In general, nonrespondents are more likely to be similar to those who respond later and with more prodding than to those who respond earlier. Thus, if early respondents did not differ systematically from late respondents, one could assume that respondents were similar to nonrespondents. This, in turn, assumes that whatever determines nonresponse is not a simple dichotomous switch but a more variable barrier that may be overcome by various factors.

To compare early and late respondents to the questionnaires, note was made of the postmark and date of receipt of each questionnaire.

### Table A.2
Pattern of Timing of Return
(% of each group falling in each wave)

| Group | Wave I | Wave II | Wave III |
|-------|--------|---------|----------|
| Business | 52 | 17 | 31 |
| Labor | 52 | 21 | 28 |
| Farm | 53 | 24 | 23 |
| Intellectuals | 66 | 21 | 13 |
| Media | 61 | 19 | 20 |
| Republicans | 63 | 20 | 17 |
| Democrats | 60 | 20 | 20 |
| Blacks | 47 | 23 | 30 |
| Feminists | 60 | 22 | 18 |
| Youth | 57 | 24 | 20 |

This made it possible to classify respondents into one of the three waves, according to the number of appeals to which they had been exposed. If there was a response bias, it would be reflected in differences among the waves. Note was then made of any statistically significant differences among the waves in responses to a variety of attitudinal and background questions. Two hundred cross-tabulations were run with 20 variables, against wave for each of the groups. Chi-square was used as a test of significant departure from independence because it would be sensitive to *any* such departure. Of the 200 tables, 14 produced a chi-square with a significance level less than .05, close to what one would expect by chance. There was a slight tendency for late respondents to be less well educated, but the difference was found only in three groups. All in all, there appeared to be no systematic bias.

**The Public at Large**

In addition to the survey of leaders' attitudes on equality, a nationwide random telephone survey was conducted in May 1976, to tap mass attitudes. The survey contained a subset of the items dealing with equality, reformatted for telephone use. The survey was conducted using random digit dialing plus a random technique within the household. The final achieved sample consisted of 1521 respondents.

# B. Factor Analysis

A number of statistical techniques have been devised to perform dimensional analysis. These provide numerical summaries of the dimensions along which attitudes are organized. They also allow estimates of the power of the "explanation" of individual attitudes. In order to use the individual items as indicators of more general issue positions, however, it is necessary to distill the individual attitudes down to the underlying factors. This requires being able to estimate the factor scores for each subject, or the values on the hypothesized underlying variables that would account for the patterns among the observed variables.[1]

The answers given by individuals to the items on the questionnaire presumably reflect three basic components. The first is the underlying dimension tapped by the individual question. The second is the specific characteristic of the individual issue, beyond the general attitudes. The third component is the set of special circumstances that, above and beyond the first two components, determines the specific answer given to this question at this time by this respondent. Methodologists usually call this component "error," although "nonsystematic factors" is perhaps more accurate. For the purposes of the study, the first component was of interest. Thus, the first step was to define the variables that seemed a priori to tap what appeared to be the basic dimensions of equality.

Factor analysis provides several sorts of crucial information. The technique starts with the correlations between individual items. It then assumes that these relationships result from the fact that the observed variables are themselves linked to unobserved variables. For example, if two items are correlated .25 with one another, this could be owing to the fact that each is correlated .5 with a third common factor. From all the items, a first factor is then extracted that explains as much of the observed structure as possible; a second factor, unrelated to the first, is extracted that explains as much of the remaining structure as possible; and so on.

For each factor, there are three kinds of information. The first piece of information is the eigenvalue, which indicates how much total variance is explained by the factor. Since all the variables are equally weighted and each is standardized to have a variance of 1.0, the sum of the eigenvalues is the same as the number of variables in the factor analysis. Thus, the eigenvalues tell how much of the variance in the original items can be summarized by each extracted factor.

The second piece of information is the loading of each variable on each factor. The loading is equivalent to a standardized regression coefficient (predicting each variable from the factors) and expresses how many standard deviations higher or lower on the original variable a case is expected to be if it is one standard deviation higher or lower than another case on the extracted factor.

The third sort of information is the communality of variables. This is the proportion of variance in the original variable that is accounted for or explained by all the factors together. The amount left over is either the unique variance in that variable which is unrelated to the factors under consideration, a sort of special factor, or an error of one sort or another. Communality is a measure of the size of the first component in relation to the total variance in a variable.

Interest in the first component of variance dictated the choice of factor analytic methods. Metric factor analysis may be broadly separated into methods that seek to derive exact linear combinations of original variables, which rely on both the first kind of variance and the second item-specific type, and methods that are based only on the variance which variables have in common. Mathematically, the first set of methods involve use of the original correlation matrix among variables with 1.0's on the main diagonal. The second set begins by substituting communality estimates on the main diagonal, estimating factors, reestimating communalities from that structure, substituting those estimates on the diagonal, reestimating factor structure, and so on, until the estimates "converge."[2] The second set, the one used in the study, is often called "classical" factor analysis; the first set is often termed "principle component" or "principle axis" factor analysis.

The factor analysis was run on 22 items from the questionnaire, each of which was selected to deal with equality on the basis of substantive content and preliminary analysis:

"If a company has to lay off part of its labor force, the first workers to be laid off should be women whose husbands have jobs." (Four points, agree/disagree format.)

"If blacks are not getting fair treatment in jobs, the government should see to it that they do." (Four points, agree/disagree format.)

"White people have a right to refuse to sell their homes to blacks." (Four points, agree/disagree format.)

"There should be a law limiting the amount of money any individual is allowed to earn in a year." (Four points, agree/disagree format.)

"Racial integration of the public elementary schools should be achieved even if it requires busing." (Four points, agree/disagree format.)

"Women are usually less reliable workers than men." (Four points, agree/disagree format.)

"The Equal Rights Amendment, which aims at eliminating distinctions in the treatment of men and women, should be ratified." (Four points, agree/disagree format.)

"All except the old and the handicapped should have to take care of themselves without social welfare benefits." (Four points, agree/disagree format.)

"The government should work to reduce substantially the income gap between rich and poor." (Four points, agree/disagree format.)

"The government in Washington should see to it that everyone has a job" vs. "It is not the role of government to see to it that everyone has a job." (Seven points, with label "in between" position.)

"If women tried harder, they could get jobs equal to their ability" vs. "Discrimination makes it almost impossible for most women to get jobs equal to their ability." (Seven points, with labeled "in between" position.)

"The main cause of poverty is that the American system doesn't give all people an equal chance" vs. "Those who are poor almost always have only themselves to blame." (Seven points, with labeled "in between" position.)

"Quotas in school admissions and job hiring should be used to insure black representation" vs. "School admission and job hiring should be based strictly on merit." (Seven points, with labeled "in between" position.)

"If blacks would try harder, they could be just as well off as whites" vs. "Social conditions make it almost impossible for most blacks to overcome poverty even if they try." (Seven points, with labeled "in between" position.)

"Under a fair economic system, all people would earn about the same" vs. "Under a fair economic system, people with more ability would earn higher salaries." (Seven points, with labeled "in between" position.)

"Quotas in job hiring should be used to increase the number of women in good jobs" vs. "Job hiring should be based strictly on merit." (Seven points, with labeled "in between" position.)

"The private enterprise system is generally a fair system for working people" vs. "Under private enterprise, working people do not get a fair share of what they produce." (Seven points, with labeled "in between" position.)

"Administration of justice in the U.S. mainly favors the rich" vs. "Administration of justice in the U.S. benefits most Americans equally." (Seven points, with labeled "in between" position.)

"Taxing those with high incomes to help the poor is only fair" vs. "Taxing those with high incomes to help the poor only punishes the people who have worked hardest." (Seven points, with labeled "in between" position.)

"Racial integration is not going fast enough" vs. "Racial integration is going too fast." (Seven points, middle labeled "racial integration is going just about right.")

"In general, women will be better off if they stay home and raise families" vs. "In general, women will be better off if they have careers and jobs just as men do." (Seven points, with labeled "in between" position.)

"Here are two ways to deal with inequality; which do you prefer? 'Equality of opportunity: giving each person an equal chance for a good education and to develop his or her ability' vs. 'Equality of results: giving each person a relatively equal income regardless of his or her education and ability.' " (Seven points, with labeled "in between" position.)

From a substantive point of view, these items clearly share a common domain. The eigenvalues strongly suggest that a good portion of the variance in the individual items can be accounted for by a small number of factors (40% of the total variance among individuals in their answers to the 22 items can be explained by one common factor, 49% by two common factors, and 54% by three).

Once we had determined the list of variables which would be used to establish the factors—which in turn were intended to summarize the variables—other decisions about the analysis still had to be made. The first decision concerned the number of factors deemed sufficient to explain the set of variables. Mathematically, all the interrelationships of 22 items can be perfectly explained by no more than 22 factors. The question is how many fewer than the theoretical maximum will suffice.

There are two classic aids in this decision. The first aid, usually referred to as "Kaiser's criterion," holds that any factor worth retaining ought to explain at least as much variance as a single indicator, which is mathematically expressed as an eigenvalue of at least one. The second aid, often referred to as the "scree test" with reference to the debris left behind by glaciers, is based on the presence of "discontinuities," or sharp differences in the amount of variance accounted for by factors. It is thus intended to avoid a situation where, for instance, any case for including the fifth factor applies almost as well to the sixth factor; in other words, it looks for clear dividing lines. A case could be made, based on either of these classical criteria, for either a four- or a six-factor solution.

Because the underlying variables are not directly observed but represent combinations of observed variables, a variety of specific solutions can equally well account for the structure among the original items. Rotation is the mathematical process of transforming one of these solutions into another. The factor analysis sought the solution that was substantively most meaningful. Thus, for example, a factor on which all the variables "load" is not likely to be of as much use as a factor on which some variables load high and others load very low. Factors coming closer to the latter criterion are of more use in differentiating separate domains of variables.

A further question to be resolved concerned the use of an "orthogonal" rotated solution, in which the factors are forced to be unrelated to one another, as opposed to an "oblique" solution, in which they are permitted to be correlated among themselves. They are mathematically equivalent in the amount of variance in the original items of which they account. Oblique rotation may yield factors that correspond more to actual "underlying dimensions," which are unlikely to be completely independent. Since one of the purposes of the factor analysis was to isolate dimensions of equality and use them substantively in further analysis, the choice was oblique rotation.[3]

The factor solution used in the remainder of the work was a six-factor oblique rotation. This was by no means the only defensible solution, but it met the standards of methodological sufficiency and was substantively cleaner. The final rotated solution gave factors that made a good deal of substantive sense. The factors could readily be substantively identified. Few variables loaded strongly on more than one factor. Those cases in which a variable loaded on more than one factor were substantively interpretable and interesting.

# C. Testing for Group-Specific Structure

In addition to focusing on the structure of leadership opinion on equality issues, the study focused on whether groups organize their views on equality the same way. This question does not refer merely to consensus or dissensus, although exploring the structure of the equality issue also makes possible more authoritative statements on this subject. Rather, the question refers to the extent to which different groups view equality in the same terms. Are attitudes markedly more structured for some groups than for others? Are the dimensions the same for all groups? Do feminists, for example, judge all equality-related issues in terms of feminism? Do labor and business use the same yardsticks in taking their positions? Is it more meaningful to speak of the overall dimensions of equality, along with groups may well take different positions, or to speak of the dimensions used by the media, intellectuals, the parties, and the like?

This concern affects the extent to which the summary measures represented by the factor scores have real utility for data reduction purposes. Should each group have a "unique structure," then the summary measures could not be used meaningfully to summarize the equality attitudes of any one group. The concern translates into two related questions: how well does the overall solution fit each group, and is there any major group-specific structure beyond the overall structure applied to all groups?

To answer these questions, the factor scores representing the positions of each person on the underlying dimensions are used to derive for each case the score he or she would have had on each of the 22 variables that went into the factor analysis if the structure applied to all groups and if there were no other influences on the 22 items. For each of the 22 variables separately, each of the six factor scores for each case is multiplied by its loading, which represents the standardized regression coefficient predicting the original item for the factor. The result predicts, on a standardized scale, the attitude each individual would have on each item if the entire attitude structure were explained by the six factors. These predicted scores are subtracted from the standardized observed scores to yield standardized residuals. For each case, this residual indicates whether the individual is higher or lower than one would expect based on his or her position on the factors. These residuals can be used in a variety of ways to see what, if any, group-specific structure remains once the overall structure is taken out.

Normally, residuals are taken to connote individual error. Here they are rather different, representing either nonsystematic variation, namely more or less classical "error," or group-specific structure not already part of the common solution. If the latter, then the common solution is inadequate.

Group-specific structure would show up in one of two ways: either as a pattern among the residuals within a group or as a large mean deviation, indicating that group members were substantially more or less liberal than the overall factor scores would suggest. The second type of group structure would represent less a specific within-group structure than a systematic tendency for a group to vary from the common structure. Both possibilities were explored.

The standardized residuals for all of the respondents in each of the ten groups taken together form a pattern (Table C.1). Because the loadings are taken as standardized regression coefficients, all the variables are measured on a standardized metric with a mean of zero and a standard deviation of one. The mean residual items provide a confirmation that the predicted scores are neither systematically high nor low. The standard deviation refers to the amount of deviation "left over" among individuals after the overall structure has been fit. For example, the standard deviation of the difference between the standardized score on the first variable, REDIST (attitude toward income redistribution), and the predicted score on that variable is only .55, compared to an original of 1.00. This number is analogous to a "standard error of estimate" in a regression equation.

**Table C.1**
Residual Analysis for All Leaders

| Issue | Mean residual items | Standard deviation | Proportion explained by factors |
|---|---|---|---|
| REDIST | 0.00 | 0.55 | 0.700 |
| GOVTJOB | 0.00 | 0.55 | 0.703 |
| POOREQL | 0.00 | 0.55 | 0.694 |
| CAPFAIR | 0.00 | 0.60 | 0.645 |
| RICHLAWS | 0.00 | 0.74 | 0.455 |
| FAIRTAX | 0.00 | 0.61 | 0.633 |
| FEMLAZY | 0.00 | 0.88 | 0.229 |
| LAYOFF | 0.00 | 0.67 | 0.547 |
| ERA | 0.01 | 0.71 | 0.489 |
| FEMEQUAL | −0.01 | 0.63 | 0.604 |
| FEMROLE | 0.00 | 0.68 | 0.540 |
| LIMINC | −0.01 | 0.77 | 0.408 |
| EQUALPAY | 0.00 | 0.61 | 0.622 |
| EQUALITY | 0.00 | 0.62 | 0.616 |
| BUSING | −0.01 | 0.64 | 0.594 |
| SPEEDINT | 0.01 | 0.58 | 0.662 |
| FEMQUOTA | −0.01 | 0.42 | 0.827 |
| BLKQUOTA | 0.00 | 0.28 | 0.923 |
| BLKEQUAL | 0.00 | 0.41 | 0.831 |
| BLKJOB | 0.00 | 0.73 | 0.474 |
| ETHPUR | 0.00 | 0.67 | 0.547 |
| WELFARE | 0.00 | 0.72 | 0.476 |

It can be converted into a variance by squaring in order to calculate how much variation there is in the unexplained portion of each variable. This, in turn, yields the ratio of the explained variance to the total variance in the original item. The statistic is analogous to *R*-square. It is also related closely to the "communality estimate" from the factor analysis, although it is not identical with it because the estimated factor scores are not perfectly correlated with the hypothetical underlying scores. The proportion explained in the last column confirm that the overall factor structure does indeed explain a good deal of the variation in the original items. It is a reassurance that the computed factor scores do summarize much of the information in the original variables.

This analysis is repeated for each of the groups separately; that is, for each group and for each variable, calculation is made of the amount by which, on average, the predicted score is high or low and the amount of deviation among group members left over after the overall structure is fit. It is assumed not only that the overall structure fits in the sense of the factor scores being meaningful, but also that the predictive patterns of those underlying dimensions are precisely the same in each of the groups. This stringent assumption has one peculiar consequence. Normally, the amount of variation explained must be positive. Either knowing the value of one variable for one case tells nothing about the value of another variable for that case, in which case a coefficient of explanation is 0.0, or one can be predicted from the other. This is why $R$-square, for example, must range between 0.0 and 1.0: one cannot do worse than zero explanation, and one cannot explain more variation than there is. The factor analysis, however, is different, for when the overall structure is forced to fit exactly, the lower limit is no longer zero. It is possible, specifically, for members of a group to be more similar on an item than would be predicted by their factor scores.

Substantively, this makes sense. There are presumably factors that account for equality attitudes in general. Individuals can be placed on scales representing their views on these underlying attitudes. For most people, the underlying attitudes (factors) account for positions on specific issues. For some groups, however, something may operate to make their members more similar than would be expected. If so, the standard deviation of the residual will be larger than the standard deviation of the original variable. In this sense, explanation could be negative.

Of the amount explained for each group/item pair, there are few instances of negative explanation (Table C.2). Of the 220 instances (22 variables across 10 groups) only three cases of negative fit appear. Republicans have a marginally negative explanation for the question of whether or not there should be an upper limit on income. On the original scale, Republicans were very similar to one another on this variable (standard deviation of .46). Taking their factor scores and the overall loadings for predictors, the standard deviation of prediction is even greater (.47), though still small. A similar case is observed for black leaders on whether or not the government should intervene to guarantee fair treatment for blacks on the job, which shows an unexplained variance larger than the original. Feminists show the same pattern for attitudes to the ERA. All of these cases

**Table C.2**

Proportion Explained by Common Structure

(variance of predicted scores compared to original items)[a]

| Issue | Group | | | | | | | | | |
|---|---|---|---|---|---|---|---|---|---|---|
| | Bus. | Far. | Int. | Med. | Rep. | Dem. | Blk. | Fem. | You. | Lab. |
| REDIST | .42 | .69 | .67 | .61 | .59 | .60 | .43 | .60 | .70 | .59 |
| GOVTJOB | .44 | .66 | .61 | .61 | .61 | .57 | .48 | .64 | .57 | .59 |
| POOREQL | .33 | .62 | .62 | .62 | .46 | .61 | .46 | .59 | .70 | .54 |
| CAPFAIR | .38 | .52 | .60 | .54 | .46 | .59 | .31 | .58 | .70 | .49 |
| RICHLAWS | .28 | .35 | .28 | .32 | .32 | .38 | .30 | .42 | .29 | .14 |
| FAIRTAX | .43 | .54 | .68 | .51 | .52 | .43 | .42 | .62 | .65 | .47 |
| FEMLAZY | .20 | .12 | .22 | .14 | .27 | .23 | .25 | .04 | .22 | .21 |
| LAYOFF | .39 | .51 | .55 | .45 | .45 | .52 | .51 | .39 | .53 | .57 |
| ERA | .30 | .26 | .42 | .45 | .48 | .42 | .27 | a | .42 | .43 |
| FEMEQUAL | .47 | .49 | .56 | .54 | .52 | .56 | .48 | .48 | .55 | .61 |
| FEMROLE | .41 | .46 | .51 | .46 | .55 | .46 | .41 | .37 | .50 | .47 |
| LIMINC | .12 | .37 | .41 | .19 | a | .47 | .32 | .43 | .52 | .29 |
| EQUALPAY | .43 | .51 | .62 | .48 | .57 | .69 | .41 | .56 | .70 | .57 |
| EQUALITY | .58 | .51 | .59 | .53 | .54 | .64 | .51 | .65 | .69 | .58 |
| BUSING | .31 | .35 | .56 | .49 | .38 | .43 | .22 | .40 | .48 | .55 |
| SPEEDINT | .47 | .44 | .64 | .55 | .48 | .62 | .40 | .56 | .56 | .60 |
| FEMQUOTA | .75 | 68 | .83 | .78 | .70 | .82 | .65 | .80 | .81 | .75 |
| BLKQUOTA | .89 | .85 | .92 | .90 | .86 | .92 | .82 | .92 | .92 | .90 |
| BLKEQUAL | .76 | .79 | .84 | .80 | .76 | .80 | .75 | .80 | .84 | .82 |
| BLKJOB | .27 | .44 | .44 | .39 | .34 | .38 | a | .37 | .39 | .43 |
| ETHPUR | .34 | .43 | .50 | .44 | .42 | .42 | .38 | .39 | .44 | .55 |
| WELFARE | .36 | .36 | .45 | .42 | .36 | .42 | .35 | .43 | .43 | .46 |
| Total | .40 | .48 | .56 | .51 | .48 | .55 | .43 | .56 | .58 | .53 |

a. Denotes those instances in which variance predicted on the basis of the factor scores was *larger* than the actual variance in the original variables. For example, feminists were more similar to one another on ERA than would be predicted based on the factors.

make substantive sense, reflecting attitudes with a group-specific content. The fact that this occurs only in three cases out of a possible 220 confirms the overall fit.

The total explained for each group is simply the sum of the amount explained for each of the 22 variables. A comparable figure for the overall samples is .60. These data show a substantial amount of explanation for each of the groups separately. Among business leaders, the least is explained, but still a full 40% of the original variation within the group is explained by the common structure. The next lowest explanation is for blacks (43%), followed by farmers (48%) and Republicans (48%). The degree of explanation is highest among youth (58%), feminists (56%), and intellectuals (56%). The relatively modest amount of intergroup variation should not obscure the fact that the common structure, even by this most conservative measure, fits each group to a good extent.

The existence of common structure is also seen in the absence of any substantial group-specific deviation from the predicted scores based on the original structure (Table C.3). In fewer than one in four of the 220 instances, the original items are .1 or more points sys-

**Table C.3**
Summary of Mean Residuals Within Groups
(only those more than .1 away from 0)

| | Group | | | | | | | | | |
|---|---|---|---|---|---|---|---|---|---|---|
| Issue | Bus. | Far. | Int. | Med. | Rep. | Dem. | Blk. | Fem. | You. | Lab. |
| REDIST | | | | | | | | | | |
| GOVTJOB | | | | | .12 | −.23 | | | | −.25 |
| POOREQL | | | | | | | −.15 | | | |
| CAPFAIR | −.14 | | | | | −.16 | | | | |
| RICHLAWS | .41 | −.13 | | −.21 | .35 | .12 | | | | −.26 |
| FAIRTAX | | | | | | −.12 | | | | |
| | | | | | | | .17 | | | |
| FEMLAZY | | | | | .19 | −.11 | | | | −.14 |
| LAYOFF | .10 | −.29 | | | | −.24 | | .16 | | .26 |
| ERA | | .14 | −.11 | | .10 | −.12 | | −.11 | | |
| FEMEQUAL | | | | | | −.14 | | .22 | | |
| FEMROLE | | | | | | | | | .20 | −.20 |
| LIMINC | | | −.22 | .11 | | .10 | .21 | | −.10 | .15 |
| EQUALPAY | | | | .11 | | | | | −.13 | |
| EQUALITY | | | | | | .10 | | | | |
| BUSING | | | | | | | −.26 | | | |
| SPEEDINT | | .11 | | | | .15 | −.14 | | | .23 |
| FEMQUOTA | | | | | | | | −.11 | | |
| BLKQUOTA | | | | | | | | | | |
| BLKEQUAL | | | | | | | | | | |
| BLKJOB | | | | | | −.11 | | | | .11 |
| ETHPUR | −.10 | | | | | | | | | |
| WELFARE | | −.17 | | .16 | | | −.14 | | | .16 |

tematically higher or lower than predicted from the factor scores and original structure. The standard deviation of four-point scales is typically no larger than about 1.0. Residuals of .1 standard deviation thus are no more than about one-tenth the distance between strongly agree and agree, or between any other two adjacent points on the four-point scale. In the seven-point scales, which typically have standard deviations no larger than about 2.0, a standardized residual of .1 corresponds to about one-fifth of the distance from strongest agreement with one alternative to the next weaker agreement with that same alternative, or one-fifteenth of the way from complete agreement with either alternative to the neutral position.

Thus, the 53 instances, among 220 possible cases, represent a modest systematic deviation from the general prediction. Of these 53, only 16 are deviations of .2 or more, and only two—RICHLAWS for business and Republicans—are over .3 standard deviations in magnitude. The deviations thus are in general very modest, if they appear at all.

Beyond analysis of the residuals themselves, a further step in investigating how well the overall solution fits the individual groups was to investigate how much within-group structure might exist "on top" of the overall structure. To test this, a second-order factor analysis was performed on the 22x22 correlation matrix of residuals for each group, involving 10 separate factor analyses. If the common structure perfectly and completely accounted for all variation in each group, all correlations would be precisely 0.0, and there would be no common within-group factors at all. If there were a group-specific dimension or dimensions beyond the common ones, this would show up with one or more factors in the second-order analysis. Thus, the procedure followed in looking for evidence of structure was similar to that used for finding the overall structure within the groups (Table C.4).

The eigenvalues of the first four factors after initial extraction, and before substitution of communality estimates on the main diagonal, are analogous to the eigenvalues chosen as the basis for the number of factors for the overall solution. They are scaled assuming that all variables have equal variance and that the total variance is 22.0 (1.0 times the number of variables). Since much of the original variance has already been accounted for by the overall solution, however, this scaling might make second-order factors look more meaningful than they are. Accordingly, the eigenvalues were re-scaled by reducing the total variance to the proportion left unex-

**Table C.4**
Eigenvalues for Second-Order Analysis
(unrotated factors before iteration)

| Group | Second order factor | | | |
|---|---|---|---|---|
| | I | II | III | IV |
| | *Raw* | | | |
| Business | 2.00 | 1.95 | 1.65 | 1.62 |
| Farm | 2.12 | 1.92 | 1.75 | 1.59 |
| Intellectuals | 1.94 | 1.73 | 1.65 | 1.46 |
| Media | 1.89 | 1.85 | 1.73 | 1.57 |
| Republicans | 2.21 | 2.01 | 1.76 | 1.68 |
| Democrats | 2.23 | 1.86 | 1.84 | 1.65 |
| Blacks | 2.02 | 1.88 | 1.73 | 1.63 |
| Feminists | 1.86 | 1.74 | 1.68 | 1.63 |
| Youth | 1.85 | 1.76 | 1.59 | 1.47 |
| Labor | 1.93 | 1.83 | 1.65 | 1.60 |
| | *Corrected* | | | |
| Business | 1.20 | 1.17 | 0.99 | 0.97 |
| Farm | 1.09 | 0.99 | 0.91 | 0.82 |
| Intellectuals | 0.86 | 0.77 | 0.73 | 0.65 |
| Media | 0.93 | 0.91 | 0.86 | 0.77 |
| Republicans | 1.16 | 1.05 | 0.92 | 0.88 |
| Democrats | 1.00 | 0.84 | 0.83 | 0.74 |
| Blacks | 1.16 | 1.08 | 0.99 | 0.94 |
| Feminists | 0.81 | 0.76 | 0.73 | 0.71 |
| Youth | 0.77 | 0.73 | 0.66 | 0.61 |
| Labor | 0.91 | 0.86 | 0.78 | 0.76 |

plained by the original overall solution. As a result, one could legitimately add the variance explained within a group by the overall structure to the variance explained by any within-group structure.

Any concern with second-order within-group structures is largely academic. Even the uncorrected eigenvalues are hardly impressive. Had the initial analysis not been performed at all and were a researcher therefore looking at this eigenvalue structure by itself, the most likely conclusion would be that there was no structure at all. The highest eigenvalue observed in any of the groups is 2.23. Moreover, the scree test leaves no clear justification for taking any of the factors.

The corrected eigenvalues make the case even clearer. The corrected eigenvalues, expressed in terms of the variance in an original variable, are very low, and there is hardly any within-group factor that explains even as much as an original variable. The scree test leads to no different result here. Thus, the criteria of classical factor analysis do not support any real within-group structure. The six-factor solution for the groups taken together accounted for a substantial portion of the interrelationships among the variables but not for all the variance. Thus, one would expect to find some residual structure in each group, even if it were not truly group-specific but only had elements of the overall common structure beyond the six factors extracted. There is no evidence either that the common structure fails in any groups or that a substantively interpretable structure is particular to individual groups.

The analysis has thus established that there is no strong within-group structure on top of the overall solution. Moreover, it has shown, using a more conservative measure, that the overall structure accounts for a good deal of the within-group variation. The detailed search for a within-group structure has led to several conclusions. First, the overall structure fits the patterns within groups quite well. While there is evidence of "fine-tuning," so that factor scores representing the underlying dimensions do not relate precisely the same way to items across groups (nor would they be expected to), by any measure the overall factors seem to have real meaning within groups. In particular, the fit is close enough so as to validate the use of the results of the overall solution to discuss the nature of equality as an issue and to use the factor scores as a useful summary of the information in the original items. Finally, an investigation of the possibility of significant group-specific structure over and above the overall solution yielded the conclusion that no such structure existed for any of the groups.

# D. Scale Construction and Group Differences

The results of the factor analysis reduce the data to manageable proportions by providing a way of using the individual items as a means of estimating the "scores" individuals might have on the more general dimensions of equality. The factor scores may then be used in place of individual items in subsequent analysis.[1] Unlike the observed variables, some of which were originally measured on a 1-4 scale (the agree/disagree items) and others of which were originally measured on a 1-7 scale, the derived factor scores have no inherent metric. Since they are estimated from standardized data (correlations among items, where each is weighted to have an equal variance of 1.0 and a mean of 0.0), it is customary for factor scores to be extracted to have means of 0.0 and variances (as well as standard deviations) of 1.0. Vagaries of the estimation process lead to minor discrepancies from this goal, and typically the standard deviation of the factor scores is less than 1.0, but the key is that the amount of variance among cases on the factors is defined to be approximately equal, and the mean position approximately 0.0.

This makes comparison across the several scales for all leaders together impossible, but it allows a full range of comparisons of the relative positions of groups on any one scale as well as a comparison of those relative positions across scales. Specifically, comparison of group means on the factors shows the average positions of the groups. For example, is the typical business leader more or less liberal than the typical labor union leader on racial issues? It also shows whether a particular group is closer to one group or another on a given scale. For example, is the typical farm leader closer to Democratic or Republican leaders on the redistribution scale? Further, it shows the relative closeness of two pairs of groups on the *same* scale. For instance, are Republicans closer to business leaders on the racial scale than Democrats are to civil rights leaders on *that same* scale? And finally, it shows if the groups are arrayed in a similar order across the various dimensions.

For any variable, both the mean and standard deviations at least are necessary truly to describe the distribution on that variable. The mean indicates what the typical value is, since it is the value from which the average deviation is 0 and from which the average squared deviation is least. The standard deviation, on the contrary, tells how far, in squared deviation terms, the typical case is from the value typical of all cases. It is possible to compare these values for different groups on the same variables.

A table of means and standard deviations of factor scores thus tells how far apart, on average, members of different groups are and whether the within-group differences on a given factor are greater or lower than the within-group differences for a different group on that same factor. This is true even though in absolute terms it is impossible to say that a particular group is more or less united on one issue than it is on another, since a unit difference on the one issue may correspond to a greater or lesser actual difference on the other issue.

Finally, for a given factor, the within-group variation can be compared to the between-group variation. It is possible to partition the differences among respondents on a factor into those that exist between typical members of a particular group and typical members of another group and those that exist among the members of the same group.

This leads to the eta-square measure, which is the amount of difference among individuals in the amalgamated samples that can be ascribed to differences among the groups to which they belong compared to the total amount of difference. An eta-square of .33, for example, says that twice as much difference (two-thirds of the total) is accounted for by within-group differences as by systematic differences between groups (one-third of the total). At one extreme, an eta-square of 0.0 means that knowing what groups two individuals belong to tells nothing about how different they are likely to be. At the other extreme, an eta-square of 1.0 indicates that knowing what groups two individuals belong to tells exactly how different they are, since all members of a given group have identical positions. This measure is roughly comparable to the $R$-square of regression analysis and, indeed, would be mathematically equal to the $R$-square from a regression in which the variable was predicted solely by dummies representing group membership.

# E. Leadership Questionnaire

A slightly different version of the questionnaire was used for each of the leadership groups. The version here was used for the media.

# LEADERSHIP SURVEY

A Joint Project of The Washington Post and The Harvard University Center for International Affair~

● Here is a series of statements. For each, please indicate whether you agree strongly with it, agree somewhat, disagree somewhat, or disagree strongly.

Please use the following numbers and place them in the blanks below.

| Agree<br>Strongly:1 | Agree<br>Somewhat:2 | Disagree<br>Somewhat:3 | Disagree<br>Strongly:4 | No<br>Opinion:9 |
|---|---|---|---|---|

_____ If a company has to lay off part of its labor force, the first workers to be laid off should be women whose husbands have jobs.

_____ If blacks are not getting fair treatment in jobs, the government should see to it that they do.

_____ The country would be better off if business were less regulated.

_____ White people have a right to refuse to sell their homes to blacks.

_____ There should be a law limiting the amount of money any individual is allowed to earn in a year.

_____ It is the right of a woman to decide whether to have an abortion.

_____ The majority of American women do not agree with the leaders of the feminist movement.

_____ Racial integration of the public elementary schools should be achieved even if it requires busing.

_____ Businessmen have too much power for the good of the country.

_____ Lesbians and homosexuals should not be allowed to teach in the public schools.

_____ Women are usually less reliable workers than men.

_____ The news media are too critical of American institutions.

_____ The Equal Rights Amendment, which aims at eliminating distinctions in the treatment of men and women, should be ratified.

_____ All except the old and the handicapped should have to take care of themselves without social welfare benefits.

_____ The government should work to substantially reduce the income gap between rich and poor.

_____ Trade unions have too much power for the good of the country.

_____ The interests of employers and employees are, by their very nature, basically opposed.

_____ The news media pay too much attention to minority groups.

_____ Public financing is a fairer way to pay for political election campaigns than is private financing.

● Rank the national goals below in terms of importance to you. Place a "1" next to the most important goal; a "2" next to the second most; and a "3" next to the third most important. Place a "9" next to the least important goal; an "8" next to the second least; and a "7" next to the third least important goal.

_____ Achieving equality for women

_____ Maintaining a strong military defense

_____ Protecting freedom of speech

_____ Curbing inflation

_____ Developing energy sources

_____ Reducing the role of government

_____ Fighting crime

_____ Achieving equality for blacks

_____ Reducing unemployment

_____ Giving people more say in government decisions

● Some people say the two-party system is vital to our form government. Others express disenchantment with the two-pa system.

Generally, how satisfied are you with the present two-pa system?

☐ Very satisfied    ☐ Satisfied    ☐ Dissatisfied

☐ Very dissatisfied    ☐ No opinion

Do you think that the emergence of third or fourth politi parties would be beneficial to our political system?

☐ Yes    ☐ No    ☐ Don't know

Would you favor our two political parties becoming m politically homogenous, with liberals in one party and c servatives in the other?

☐ Yes    ☐ No    ☐ Don't know

● Would you approve or disapprove a government takeover of major existing oil firms in order to reduce the threat of ene crises?

☐ Approve takeover    ☐ Disapprove takeover    ☐ Don't Kn

● In light of increasing charges to consumers by public utiliti would you favor government takeover of the utilities?

☐ Favor takeover    ☐ Oppose takeover    ☐ Don't kno

● Do you own a handgun?    ☐ Yes    ☐ No

Would you approve a plan calling for:

☐ Registration of all firearms

☐ Registration of handguns only

Or are you:

☐ Opposed to registration but desirous of some other for of gun control legislation

☐ Opposed to gun control legislation.

● The following questions cover issues that are in the news th days. In each scale, "1" represents a position held by some peop "7" represents an opposing position, and the other numbers sta for positions between these two. Please circle the number th best represents your opinion on each issue.

| The government in Washington should see to it that everyone has a job. | | | In Between | It is not the role of government to see to it that everyone has a job. | | | N Opi |
|---|---|---|---|---|---|---|---|
| 1 | 2 | 3 | 4 | 5 | 6 | 7 | |

| If women tried harder, they could get jobs equal to their ability. | | | In Between | Discrimination makes it almost impossible for most women to get jobs equal to their ability. | | | N Opi |
|---|---|---|---|---|---|---|---|
| 1 | 2 | 3 | 4 | 5 | 6 | 7 | |

| The main cause of poverty is that the American system doesn't give all people an equal chance. | | | In Between | Those who are poor almost always have only themselves to blame. | | | N Opi |
|---|---|---|---|---|---|---|---|
| 1 | 2 | 3 | 4 | 5 | 6 | 7 | |

| Quotas in school admissions and job hiring should be used to insure black representation. | | | In Between | School admission and job hiring should be based strictly on merit. | | | N Opi |
|---|---|---|---|---|---|---|---|
| 1 | 2 | 3 | 4 | 5 | 6 | 7 | |

| Workers should have more say in important decisions than they do now. | | | In Between | The important decisions should be left to management. | | | N Opi |
|---|---|---|---|---|---|---|---|
| 1 | 2 | 3 | 4 | 5 | 6 | 7 | |

| If blacks would try harder, they could be just as well off as whites. | | | In Between | Social conditions make it almost impossible for most blacks to overcome poverty even if they try. | | | N opir |
|---|---|---|---|---|---|---|---|
| 1 | 2 | 3 | 4 | 5 | 6 | 7 | |

nder a fair economic system . . .

| people would earn about e same. | | In Between | People with more ability would earn higher salaries. | No Opinion |
|---|---|---|---|---|
| 1 | 2 | 3 | 4 | 5 | 6 | 7 | --- |

| notas in job hiring should be ed to increase the number women in good jobs. | | In Between | Job hiring should be based strictly on merit. | No Opinion |
|---|---|---|---|---|
| 1 | 2 | 3 | 4 | 5 | 6 | 7 | --- |

| he private enterprise sys- m is generally a fair sys- m for working people. | | In Between | Under private enterprise, working people do not get a fair share of what they prod- uce. | No Opinion |
|---|---|---|---|---|
| 1 | 2 | 3 | 4 | 5 | 6 | 7 | --- |

| dministration of justice in e U.S. mainly favors the ch. | | In Between | Administration of justice in the U.S. benefits most Ameri- cans equally. | No Opinion |
|---|---|---|---|---|
| 1 | 2 | 3 | 4 | 5 | 6 | 7 | --- |

| axing those with high in- omes to help the poor is nly fair. | | In Between | Taxing those with high in- comes to help the poor only punishes the people who have worked hardest. | No Opinion |
|---|---|---|---|---|
| 1 | 2 | 3 | 4 | 5 | 6 | 7 | --- |

| acial integration not going fast nough | Racial integration is going just about right | Racial integration is going too fast | | No Opinion |
|---|---|---|---|---|
| 1 | 2 | 3 | 4 | 5 | 6 | 7 | --- |

general, women will be better off if they . . .

| ay home and raise families. | | In Between | Have careers and jobs just as men do. | No Opinion |
|---|---|---|---|---|
| 1 | 2 | 3 | 4 | 5 | 6 | 7 | --- |

n general, government grows bigger as it provides more ervices. Do you favor:

| maller government | | In Between | More government services | No Opinion |
|---|---|---|---|---|
| 1 | 2 | 3 | 4 | 5 | 6 | 7 | --- |

ere are two ways to deal with inequality; which do you refer?

| quality of opportunity: giv- g each person an equal ance for a good education nd to develop his or her bility. | | In Between | Equality of results: giving each person a relatively equal income regardless of his or her education and ability. | No Opinion |
|---|---|---|---|---|
| 1 | 2 | 3 | 4 | 5 | 6 | 7 | --- |

ome occupations are listed below. In the first column, please dicate what you think the average annual earnings are for omeone in that occupation before taxes. In the second column, lease indicate what you think someone in that occupation should arn, again before taxes. (Most people do not have precise infor- aation on salaries in other occupations, but we would like your est estimate.)

| | Average Annual Salary Is | Fair Annual Salary Would Be |
|---|---|---|
| grade school teacher with five years' expe- ience in a midwest school. | $____ | $____ |
| resident of one of the top hundred corpora- ions. | $____ | $____ |
| semi-skilled worker in an auto assembly lant. | $____ | $____ |
| tar center, NBA basketball team. | $____ | $____ |
| bank teller. | $____ | $____ |
| J.S. Cabinet member (Secretary of Com- merce, Labor, HEW, etc.) | $____ | $____ |
| n elevator operator. | $____ | $____ |
| policeman in a midwest city with five ears' experience. | $____ | $____ |
| An aeronautical engineer. | $____ | $____ |
| college professor | $____ | $____ |
| A doctor in general practice in a large city. | $____ | $____ |
| omeone at your level in your own occupation | $____ | $____ |
| A plumber | $____ | $____ |

• Some people say that we must concentrate on fighting either in- flation or unemployment but that if we make an equal effort to fight both we probably will solve neither problem. If you had to choose where to place the emphasis, which would you consider the more important?

☐ Emphasize fight against unemployment.

☐ Emphasize fight against inflation.

☐ Emphasize both equally, even at risk of solving neither.

☐ No opinion.

• Please indicate how strongly you agree or disagree with each of the following statements concerning America's role in the world.

(Please use these numbers for your answers)

| Agree Strongly: 1 | Agree Somewhat: 2 | Disagree Somewhat: 3 | Disagree Strongly: 4 | No Opinion: 9 |
|---|---|---|---|---|

____ The United States has a moral obligation to prevent the destruction of Israel.

____ There is nothing wrong with using the CIA to help support governments friendly to the U.S. and to try to undermine hostile governments.

____ We shouldn't think so much in international terms but should concentrate more on our own domestic problems.

____ The U.S. should give economic aid to poorer countries even if that means higher prices at home.

____ It is not in our interest to have closer relations with the Soviet Union because we are getting less than we are giving to them.

____ To protect our supply of oil, the U.S. should be more pro- Arab in the Middle East conflict.

____ The main goal of those who make foreign policy is to pro- tect the interests of U.S. big business.

____ The U.S. should take all steps including the use of force to prevent the spread of communism.

____ Even though it could mean higher prices at home, it is worth selling grain to the Soviet Union since it may im- prove our relations with Russia.

• Please check the appropriate box to indicate how you feel about U.S. military power vis a vis Russian military power.

☐ The U.S. should try to maintain a large margin of superior- ity.

☐ The U.S. should reduce armaments even if we risk falling behind Russia.

☐ The U.S. should be militarily equal to Russia.

☐ Don't know.

• Under what circumstances should the U.S. supply arms to other countries? (Check one box only.)

☐ Never

☐ To democratic countries that are fighting communism.

☐ To any democratic country that wants arms.

☐ To any country fighting communism, even if it is not demo- cratic.

☐ To any non-Communist country that wants arms.

• As a last resort, how much financial assistance should the federal government provide to each of the following if they are in seri- ous financial trouble?

| | Substantial Support | Moderate Support | No Support |
|---|---|---|---|
| Corporations doing national defense work | ☐ | ☐ | ☐ |
| Corporations providing necessary services, such as railroads | ☐ | ☐ | ☐ |
| City or state governments | ☐ | ☐ | ☐ |
| Individuals who can't support themselves | ☐ | ☐ | ☐ |
| Foreign countries friendly to the U.S. | ☐ | ☐ | ☐ |

• Government spending for military defense should be:

☐ Increased    ☐ Reduced    ☐ Kept at present level

☐ Don't know

2

- How would you describe your interest in international, national and local affairs? (Please write the appropriate number in the spaces allotted.)

One of my major concerns — 1

2

3

Moderate concern — 4

5

6

I pay little attention — 7

International affairs  _ _ _ _ _ _
(answer here)

National affairs  _ _ _ _ _ _
(answer here)

Local affairs  _ _ _ _ _ _

---

- Over the past several years, how frequently have you engaged in these activities?

| | More than Once a Month | A few times A year | Once a year Or less | Never |
|---|---|---|---|---|
| Made a speech at some public meeting | ☐ | ☐ | ☐ | ☐ |
| Appeared on radio or television | ☐ | ☐ | ☐ | ☐ |
| Contributed articles to newspapers or magazines | ☐ | ☐ | ☐ | ☐ |
| Written to a member of the U.S. House or Senate | ☐ | ☐ | ☐ | ☐ |
| Talked to a member of the U.S. House or Senate | ☐ | ☐ | ☐ | ☐ |
| Talked to a state or local elected official | ☐ | ☐ | ☐ | ☐ |

---

- If you have contacted government officials in the past several years, how would you describe the results of those contacts in terms of obtaining what you wanted:

| | Generally Successful | Mixed | Generally Unsuccessful | Did Not Contact |
|---|---|---|---|---|
| Member of U.S. House or Senate | ☐ | ☐ | ☐ | ☐ |
| Local or state officials | ☐ | ☐ | ☐ | ☐ |

---

- We would like to know how much influence you think various groups **actually have** over American life, and how much influence you think they **should have**. Here is a scale in which "1" represents "very influential" and "7" represents "very little influence."
(Please place your answers below)

Very Influential — 1

2

3

In Between — 4

5

6

Very Little Influence — 7

No Opinion — 9

| | Actual Influence | Influence They Should Have |
|---|---|---|
| Labor Unions | _ _ _ _ | _ _ _ _ |
| Farm Organizations | _ _ _ _ | _ _ _ _ |
| Business Leaders | _ _ _ _ | _ _ _ _ |
| Media | _ _ _ _ | _ _ _ _ |
| Intellectuals | _ _ _ _ | _ _ _ _ |
| Banks | _ _ _ _ | _ _ _ _ |
| Consumer Groups | _ _ _ _ | _ _ _ _ |
| Feminist Groups | _ _ _ _ | _ _ _ _ |
| Black Leaders | _ _ _ _ | _ _ _ _ |
| The Political Parties | _ _ _ _ | _ _ _ _ |

---

- Which political party do you think better promotes the interests of people like you?

☐ Democrats by a lot          ☐ Democrats by a little

☐ Neither more than the other

☐ Republicans by a little          ☐ Republicans by a lot

- How do you regard yourself politically? (Please check the appropriate box.)

☐ A strong Republican          ☐ A Republican

☐ Independent, closer to Republicans          ☐ Totally Independent

☐ Independent, closer to Democrats          ☐ A Democrat

☐ A strong Democrat          ☐ Don't Know

3

---

- If there were some national issue on which you wanted to have your voice heard, are you personally acquainted with any of the following kinds of people whom you would feel free to contact?

☐ Senator

☐ Congressman

☐ Member of U.S. Cabinet

☐ Government official (bureau chief or higher)

☐ Member of national news medium

☐ Member of local news medium

- Which Democratic candidate for President in 1976 is the most acceptable to you? _ _ _ _ _ _ _ _ _ _ _ _ _ _ _ _ _ _

- Which Democratic candidate is the least acceptable? _ _ _ _

- Which Republican candidate for President in 1976 is the most acceptable to you? _ _ _ _ _ _ _ _ _ _ _ _ _ _ _ _ _ _

- Which Republican candidate is the least acceptable? _ _ _ _

- If the candidates you have listed as being most acceptable did get their parties' nominations, which of the two would you prefer as President? _ _ _ _ _ _ _ _ _ _ _ _ _ _ _ _ _

---

- Please indicate what effects you feel the following groups have on the ability of the **media** to accomplish their goals: which groups help a lot, which help and hinder equally, which hinder a lot, and which fall in between.

(Record answers below)

Helps a Lot — 1

2

3

Helps and Hinders Equally — 4

5

6

Hinders a Lot — 7

Irrelevant; No effect — 9

| | |
|---|---|
| _ _ _ _ | Labor Unions |
| _ _ _ _ | Big Business |
| _ _ _ _ | Federal Government |
| _ _ _ _ | State Government |
| _ _ _ _ | Local Government |
| _ _ _ _ | Consumer Groups |
| _ _ _ _ | Banks |
| _ _ _ _ | Civil Rights Groups |
| _ _ _ _ | Feminist Groups |

- When it comes to issues of public policy, how divided do you find the media to be?

☐ Greatly divided          ☐ Moderately divided

☐ Generally in agreement          ☐ Fully in agreement

☐ Don't Know

- Do you think the influence of the media has been increasing or decreasing?

☐ Increasing          ☐ Staying the same          ☐ Decreasing

---

- Please indicate how you feel about each of these statements.
(Use the following guide for your answers.)

Agree Strongly: 1          Agree Somewhat: 2          Disagree Somewhat

Disagree Strongly: 4          No Opinion: 9

_ _ _ _ The media make the world confusing rather than understandable.

_ _ _ _ The news media should give full coverage to disturbing events, such as presidential assassination attempts, even if coverage could breed other such events.

---

- Do you work more in the print media or in the electronic media?

☐ Print Media          ☐ Electronic Media

We would like to know about various aspects of people's lives. Please check the appropriate boxes to indicate where you would place yourself in relation to the following activities:

| | ● Do you feel you have adequate time for them? | | ● When you do engage in them, how satisfying do you find them? | | |
|---|---|---|---|---|---|
| | Adequate Time | Inadequate Time | Very Satisfying | Somewhat Satisfying | Very Unsatisfying |
| Family life | ☐ | ☐ | ☐ | ☐ | ☐ |
| Work | ☐ | ☐ | ☐ | ☐ | ☐ |
| Organizations and public activities | ☐ | ☐ | ☐ | ☐ | ☐ |
| Relations with friends | ☐ | ☐ | ☐ | ☐ | ☐ |
| Leisure activities | ☐ | ☐ | ☐ | ☐ | ☐ |

About how often do all the members of the immediate family living in your household eat dinner together?

☐ Most nights   ☐ Several times a week
☐ About once a week   ☐ Less than once a week

About how often do you see relatives not living in your household?

☐ Once a week or more   ☐ One to three times a month
☐ A few times a year   ☐ Once a year or less

There is talk about the changing responsibility of men within the household. In your household, how much change has there been in recent years?

☐ Male members take many more household responsibilities than they used to
☐ Male members take a few more responsibilities
☐ No change
☐ Does not apply

A few questions on your work: There are various things about a job that can be satisfying or unsatisfying. How do you rate your own work in the following respects:

| | Very Satisfying | Somewhat Satisfying | Mixed | Somewhat Unsatisfying | Very Unsatisfying |
|---|---|---|---|---|---|
| Chance to be creative | ☐ | ☐ | ☐ | ☐ | ☐ |
| Chance to get ahead | ☐ | ☐ | ☐ | ☐ | ☐ |
| Chance to use your talents | ☐ | ☐ | ☐ | ☐ | ☐ |
| Job security | ☐ | ☐ | ☐ | ☐ | ☐ |
| Chance to earn adequate income | ☐ | ☐ | ☐ | ☐ | ☐ |

HERE ARE SOME ITEMS FOR BACKGROUND INFORMATION.

How did you vote in recent presidential elections?

1964: ☐ Johnson ☐ Goldwater ☐ Other
☐ Did not vote ☐ Don't recall ☐ Ineligible to vote

1968: ☐ Humphrey ☐ Nixon ☐ Wallace ☐ Other
☐ Did not vote ☐ Don't recall ☐ Ineligible to vote

1972: ☐ McGovern ☐ Nixon ☐ Other
☐ Did not vote ☐ Don't recall ☐ Ineligible to vote

How would you describe your views in political matters?

☐ Far left   ☐ Very liberal   ☐ Somewhat liberal
☐ Moderate   ☐ Somewhat conservative
☐ Very conservative   ☐ Far right   ☐ Don't know

In what year were you born? _____

What is your sex?   ☐ Male   ☐ Female

Are you married and living with your spouse, or are you widowed, divorced, separated, or have you never been married?

☐ Single ☐ Married ☐ Divorced ☐ Separated ☐ Widowed
☐ Never married ☐ Other

● What was the highest level of schooling that:

| | You Completed | Your father Completed | Your mother Completed |
|---|---|---|---|
| Grade school or less | ☐ | ☐ | ☐ |
| Some high school | ☐ | ☐ | ☐ |
| High school graduate | ☐ | ☐ | ☐ |
| Some college | ☐ | ☐ | ☐ |
| College graduate | ☐ | ☐ | ☐ |
| Some graduate school | ☐ | ☐ | ☐ |
| Graduate degree (Specify highest) | ___ | ___ | ___ |

● If you attended college or university, what was the name of the last college or university you attended?

Undergraduate school _ _ _ _ _ _ _ _ _ _ _ _ _ _ _ _ _

Graduate School _ _ _ _ _ _ _ _ _ _ _ _ _ _ _ _ _

Was your high school (check one): ☐ public ☐ private ☐ parochial

● What is your occupation? Please describe it fully.

_ _ _ _ _ _ _ _ _ _ _ _ _ _ _ _ _ _ _ _ _ _ _ _ _

● What was your father's occupation when you were growing up?

_ _ _ _ _ _ _ _ _ _ _ _ _ _ _ _ _ _ _ _ _ _ _ _ _

● In general, who has been the chief wage earner in your family?

☐ You ☐ Your spouse ☐ Other(please specify)

● What is your race? ☐ White ☐ Black ☐ Other(please specify)

● In what religion were you raised? (Include denomination)

_ _ _ _ _ _ _ _ _ _ _ _ _ _ _ _ _ _ _ _ _ _ _ _ _

● What is your present religious preference? (Include denomination)

_ _ _ _ _ _ _ _ _ _ _ _ _ _ _ _ _ _ _ _ _ _ _ _ _

● How often do you attend religious services?

☐ Almost every week or more   ☐ Once or twice a month
☐ A few times a year   ☐ Almost Never   ☐ Never

In addition to being an American, from which nationality groups (Irish, Japanese, German, etc.) are you mainly descended?

_ _ _ _ _ _ _ _ _ _ _ _ _ _ _ _ _ _ _ _ _ _ _ _ _

● In what state(s) did you live most when you were growing up?

_ _ _ _ _ _ _ _ _ _ _ _ _ _ _ _ _ _ _ _ _ _ _ _ _

● In what state do you now live?

_ _ _ _ _ _ _ _ _ _ _ _ _ _ _ _ _ _ _

● Please check the box that indicates your approximate family income last year, before taxes.

| | | |
|---|---|---|
| ☐ None | ☐ Less than $1,000 | ☐ $1,000-$2,999 |
| ☐ $3,000-$4,999 | ☐ $5,000-$9,999 | ☐ $10,000-$14,999 |
| ☐ $15,000-$19,999 | ☐ $20,000-$24,999 | ☐ $25,000-$29,999 |
| ☐ $30,000-$49,999 | ☐ $50,000-$74,999 | ☐ $75,000-$149,999 |
| ☐ $150,000 and over | | |

Now please check the box that indicates your approximate personal income last year, before taxes.

| | | |
|---|---|---|
| ☐ None | ☐ Less than $1,000 | ☐ $1,000-$2,999 |
| ☐ $3,000-$4,999 | ☐ $5,000-$9,999 | ☐ $10,000-$14,999 |
| ☐ $15,000-$19,999 | ☐ $20,000-$24,999 | ☐ $25,000-$29,999 |
| ☐ $30,000-$49,999 | ☐ $50,000-$74,999 | ☐ $75,000-$149,999 |
| ☐ $150,000 and over | | |

Thank you very much for your cooperation. A return envelope is enclosed for mailing, addressed to:

LEADERSHIP SURVEY, 1150 15th St., N.W., Washington, D.C. 20071

4

# Notes

## 1. Egalitarian Dilemmas

1. Lester C. Thurow, *Dangerous Currents: The State of Economics* (New York: Random House, 1983), p. 217.

2. Michael Walzer, *Spheres of Justice: A Defense of Pluralism and Equality* (New York: Basic Books, 1983), pp. 82, 79, 66, 320.

3. Phillips Cutright, "Political Structure, Economic Development and National Social Security Programs," *American Sociological Review* 70 (1964): 537–550; Robert Jackman, *Politics and Social Equity* (New York: Wiley, 1975); Harold L. Wilensky, *The Welfare State and Equality* (Berkeley: University of California Press, 1975); Douglas A. Hibbs, Jr., "Political Parties and Macro Economic Policy," *American Political Science Review* 71.4 (Dec. 1977); David T. Cameron, "The Expansion of the Public Economy: A Comparative Analysis," *American Political Science Review* 72.4 (Dec. 1978); Alexander Hicks and Duane H. Swank, "Governmental Redistribution in Rich Capitalist Democracies," paper presented at meeting of American Political Science Association, Chicago, September 1983; Alexander Hicks and Duane H. Swank, "On the Political Economy of Welfare Expansion: A Comparative Analysis of Eighteen Advanced Capitalist Democracies, 1966–1971," *Comparative Political Studies* 17.1 (Apr. 1984); Edward Tufte, *Political Control of the Economy* (Princeton: Princeton University Press, 1978). Robert A. Dahl has put the point clearly: "In a private-enterprise, market oriented economy, the proper distribution of income is not primarily a technical question but a political and moral question." Dahl, *Dilemmas of Pluralist Democracy* (New Haven: Yale University Press, 1983), p. 135. There are

notable exceptions which emphasize the role of values. See, e.g., Seymour Martin Lipset, *The First New Nation: The United States in Historical and Comparative Perspective* (New York: Basic Books, 1963); Robert Lane, *Political Ideology: Why the American Common Man Believes What He Does* (New York: Free Press, 1962); Jennifer L. Hochschild, *What's Fair? American Beliefs about Distributive Justice* (Cambridge: Harvard University Press, 1981).

4. Equality is a recurrent theme in the writings of foreign visitors to the United States. See Alexis de Tocqueville, *Democracy in America* (New York: Random House, 1945, first published in 1835); James Bryce, *The American Commonwealth* (New York: Commonwealth Publishing, 1908); Gunnar Myrdal, *An American Dilemma* (New York: Harper & Bros., 1944). See also J. R. Pole, *The Pursuit of Equality in America* (Berkeley: University of California Press, 1978).

5. Douglas Rae, *Equalities* (Cambridge: Harvard University Press, 1981).

6. Pole, *The Pursuit of Equality in America*, p. 354. See also Sanford Lakoff, *Equality in Political Philosophy* (Cambridge: Harvard University Press, 1964).

7. Lipset, *The First New Nation*. See also John Schaar, "Equality of Opportunity and Beyond," in J. Roland Pennock and John W. Chapman, ed., *Equality* (New York: Atherton Press, 1967).

8. David Riesman, personal correspondence.

9. Lyndon B. Johnson spoke of the need for "not just equality as a right and a theory, but equality as a fact and a result." Commencement address, Howard University, June 4, 1965.

10. Daniel Bell, "On Meritocracy and Equality," *The Public Interest*, Fall 1972, p. 40. Like Bell and others, we have contrasted equality of opportunity and equality of result. It may be analytically more precise to think of this as a continuum stretching from equality of rights to equality of result, with equality of opportunity occupying a somewhat unstable position in between. Full equality of opportunity implies going beyond equal rights, but it probably cannot exist without some prior degree of equal result. Nonetheless, the formulation we have adopted distinguishes between equal opportunity and equal result, if only to remain consistent with common usage.

11. Walzer, *Spheres of Justice*, pp. 17–19, 107–110.

12. In this respect Walzer's argument is reminiscent of the Fabian socialists. See also R. H. Tawney, *Equality*, 4th ed. (London: Allen and Unwin, 1952).

13. Charles A. Beard, *The Economic Basis of Politics* (New York: Vintage Books, 1960), p. 69. Of course, the two principles are not contradictory if one has an overriding commitment to liberty.

14. In discussions of income distribution, it is common to refer to the income share of each quintile, or fifth, of the population. The Gini index

named after its originator, Corrado Gini, measures the ratio between the fraction of the area between two Lorenz curves (one representing perfect equality and one the actual income distribution) and the area under the line of perfect equality. Generally, the larger the fraction, the greater the inequality. See Alan Blinder, "The Level and Distribution of Economic Well-Being," in Martin Feldstein, ed., *The American Economy in Transition* (Chicago: University of Chicago Press, 1980), pp. 419–422.

15. The basic story of the history of income distribution in the United States is "simple enough to summarize in a few words but complex enough to require volumes for a complete account." The central fact is one of "constancy," but this "conceals a host of controversies and puzzles." Blinder, "The Level and Distribution of Economic Well-Being," pp. 415–479. Those controversies and puzzles involve a long list of methodological problems, including the need to correct for demographic shifts in population; the impact of adjustments for taxes, in-kind transfer payments, and nonmonetary fringe benefits; and the effect of changing the accounting period from annual to lifetime incomes. Yet even after demonstrating the sensitivity of the distribution of income to these and other calculating rules and lamenting the limitations of the census data, most economists conclude that the trend in the distribution has remained impressively stable during the postwar period.

16. Charles Lewis Taylor and Michael C. Hudson, *World Handbook of Political and Social Indicators,* 2nd ed. (New Haven: Yale University Press, 1972), p. 229; Christopher Jencks et al., *Inequality: A Reassessment of the Effect of Family and Schooling in America* (New York, Basic Books, 1972); Arnold Heidenheimer, describing the American response to late nineteenth-century demands for equality and security, writes: "The United States responded more to equality demands by enhancing mobility opportunities for individuals through the initiation of an unprecedented expansion of post-primary education opportunities, largely through state and local governments." "Education and Social Security Entitlements in Europe and America," in Peter Flora and Arnold Heidenheimer, *The Development of the Welfare State in Europe and America* (New Brunswick, N.J.: Transaction Books, 1981), p. 275.

17. Although the Senate was elected indirectly in the early years (for over one hundred years in some states), the electors were state legislators who had entered office by popular vote.

18. Sidney Verba and Norman H. Nie, *Participation in America* (New York: Harper and Row, 1972), ch. 20; Charles E. Lindblom, *Politics and Markets* (New York: Basic Books, 1977), ch. 13. Thomas Edsall argues that there has been a recent shift in the balance of power in favor of corporate and affluent interests in the U.S. See Edsall, *The New Politics of Inequality: How Political Power Shapes Economic Policy* (New York: Norton, 1984).

19. Jeane Kirkpatrick, *The New Presidential Elite: Men and Women*

*in National Politics* (New York: Russell Sage Foundation and the Twentieth Century Fund, 1976), chs. 3, 8.

20. Buckley v. Valeo 424 U.S. 1 (1976). Only Venezuela allows political advertising on television at a scale comparable to that in the United States. Canada permits the selling of time for political ads, but only to political parties for a strictly limited amount of time. "The Overselling of Candidates on Television," *Transatlantic Perspectives* 11 (Apr. 1984): 4.

21. Jencks et al., *Inequality*; Verba and Nie, *Participation in America*, ch. 8, pp. 273–275. See also Sidney Verba, Norman H. Nie, and Jae-on Kim, *Participation and Political Equality: A Seven-Nation Comparison* (New York: Cambridge University Press, 1978).

22. Herbert McClosky, "Consensus and Ideology in American Politics," *American Political Science Review* 58 (June 1964): 367. See also Samuel P. Huntington, *American Politics: The Promise of Disharmony* (Cambridge: Harvard University Press, 1981).

23. The opposition to such laws is not entirely antiegalitarian but often stems from a preference for other widely held values, like liberty. See Buckley v. Valeo, U.S. 1 (1976).

## 2. The Two Hundred Years' War

1. J. R. Pole, *The Pursuit of Equality in American History* (Berkeley: University of California Press, 1978), p. 3.

2. Pole, *The Pursuit of Equality*, p. 9.

3. Pole, *The Pursuit of Equality*, p. 15.

4. Bernard Bailyn, *The Ideological Origins of the American Revolution* (Cambridge: Harvard University Press, 1967), p. 98; Louis Hartz, *The Liberal Tradition in America* (New York: Harcourt, Brace, and World, 1955); Allan Nevins and Henry Steele Commager, *A Short History of the United States* (New York: Alfred A. Knopf, 1966), p. 77.

5. Samuel P. Huntington, *American Politics: The Promise of Disharmony* (Cambridge: Harvard University Press, 1981), p. 154. On the impact of denominational religion on American values, including its influence on egalitarianism, see Seymour Martin Lipset, *Revolution and Counterrevolution: Change and Persistence in Social Structures* (New York: Basic Books, 1968), p. 53; Lipset, "The Paradox of American Politics," *The Public Interest* 41 (Fall 1975); Lipset, *The First New Nation: The United States in Historical and Comparative Perspective* (New York: W. W. Norton, 1979), pp. xxxvi, 159–169.

6. James Q. Wilson, "Reagan and the Republican Revival," *Commentary* (Oct. 1980): 29; William G. McLaughlin, *Revivals, Awakenings, and Reforms* (Chicago: University of Chicago Press, 1978).

7. Wilson, "Reagan and the Republican Revival," p. 28; Pole, *The Pur-*

*suit of Equality*, p. 92; Edmund Burke, quoted in Huntington, *The Promise of Disharmony*, pp. 45–46.

8. Huntington, *The Promise of Disharmony*, p. 24.

9. Pole, *The Pursuit of Equality*, p. 48; Martin Diamond, "The Declaration and the Constitution: Liberty, Democracy, and the Founders," *The Public Interest* 41 (Fall 1975): 48.

10. Pole, *The Pursuit of Equality*, pp. 117, 57.

11. Pole, *The Pursuit of Equality*, pp. 125–128.

12. Jeffrey G. Williamson and Peter H. Lindert, *American Inequality: A Macroeconomic History* (New York: Academic Press, 1980), p. 16; Pole, *The Pursuit of Equality*, pp. 38–39, 28.

13. Pole, *The Pursuit of Equality*, pp. 32–33.

14. Marvin Meyers, *The Jacksonian Persuasion* (Palo Alto: Stanford University Press, 1957), pp. 18–19.

15. Richard Hofstadter, *The American Political Tradition* (New York: Vintage Press, 1948), p. 51.

16. Nevins and Commager, *A Short History of the United States*, p. 197.

17. Quoted in Huntington, *The Promise of Disharmony*, p. 97.

18. Pole, *The Pursuit of Equality*, pp. 34–35.

19. Mari Jo Buhle and Paul Buhle, ed., *The Concise History of Woman Suffrage* (Urbana: University of Illinois Press, 1978), pp. 86, 94.

20. Pole, *The Pursuit of Equality*, pp. 134, 136–137.

21. Pole, *The Pursuit of Equality*, p. 144.

22. Eric Foner, *Free Soil, Free Labor, Free Men: The Ideology of the Republican Party Before the Civil War* (New York: Oxford University Press, 1970), pp. 11–39.

23. Robert V. Remini, *The Revolutionary Age of Jackson* (New York: Harper and Row, 1976), passim.

24. Pole, *The Pursuit of Equality*, p. 175.

25. Huntington, *The Promise of Disharmony*, p. 110.

26. Kenneth M. Stampp, *The Era of Reconstruction, 1865–1877* (New York: Alfred A. Knopf, 1966), p. 102.

27. Morton Keller, *Affairs of State: Public Life in Late Nineteenth-Century America* (Cambridge: Harvard University Press, 1977), pp. 64–65.

28. Stampp, *The Era of Reconstruction*, p. 106.

29. Pole, *The Pursuit of Equality*, p. 202.

30. Keller, *Affairs of State*, p. 70.

31. Keller, *Affairs of State*, p. 143. See also Stampp, *The Era of Reconstruction*, pp. 96–97.

32. Keller, *Affairs of State*, p. 235.

33. Pole, *The Pursuit of Equality*, p. 163.

34. Pole, *The Pursuit of Equality*, p. 164.

35. Everett Carll Ladd, Jr., *American Political Parties: Social Change and Political Response* (New York: W. W. Norton, 1970), p. 115.

36. Pole, *The Pursuit of Equality*, p. 205.

37. Pole, *The Pursuit of Equality*, pp. 134, 216.

38. Richard Hofstadter, *The Age of Reform* (New York: Vintage Press, 1955), p. 136.

39. Quoted in Keller, *Affairs of State*, p. 573.

40. Pole, *The Pursuit of Equality*, p. 209.

41. Keller, *Affairs of State*, p. 573.

42. Hofstadter, *The Age of Reform*, p. 122.

43. Williamson, *American Inequality*, p. 105.

44. Pole, *The Pursuit of Equality*, p. 207; Keller, *Affairs of State*, p. 169.

45. Calculated from U.S. Bureau of the Census, *Historical Statistics of the United States, Colonial Times to 1970* (Washington, D.C.: U.S. Government Printing Office, 1975), pp. 127, 138, 139, 457.

46. Quoted in Hofstadter, *The Age of Reform*, p. 132.

47. Hofstadter, *The Age of Reform*, p. 267; Ronald Steel, *Walter Lippmann and the American Century* (Boston: Atlantic Monthly Press, 1980), p. 59.

48. Quoted in Pole, *The Pursuit of Equality*, pp. 218–219.

49. Hofstadter, *The Age of Reform*, pp. 266–267.

50. Susan B. Hansen, *The Politics of Taxation: Revenue Without Representation* (New York: Praeger, 1983), pp. 82–83. See also Sidney Ratner, *American Taxation: Its History as a Social Force in Democracy* (New York: W. W. Norton, 1942).

51. William E. Leuchtenburg, *Franklin D. Roosevelt and the New Deal* (New York: Harper & Row, 1963), p. 347.

52. Leuchtenburg, *Franklin D. Roosevelt*, p. 47.

53. Samuel H. Beer, "In Search of a New Public Philosophy," in Anthony King, ed., *The New American Political System* (Washington, D.C.: American Enterprise Institute, 1978).

54. See Beer, "In Search of a New Public Philosophy," p. 11. See also John Kenneth Galbraith, *American Capitalism: The Concept of Countervailing Power* (Boston: Houghton Mifflin, 1952).

55. Beer, "In Search of a New Public Philosophy," p. 12.

56. Leuchtenburg, *Franklin D. Roosevelt*, pp. 186, 235.

57. Leuchtenburg, *Franklin D. Roosevelt*, p. 187.

58. Susan Ware, *Beyond Suffrage: Women in the New Deal* (Cambridge: Harvard University Press, 1981), pp. 32–34.

59. Peter Steinfels, *The Neoconservatives: The Men Who Are Changing America's Politics* (New York: Simon and Schuster, 1979), pp. 214, 215.

60. Huntington, *The Promise of Disharmony*, pp. 101–102.

61. James L. Sundquist, *Politics and Policy: The Eisenhower, Kennedy, and Johnson Years* (Washington, D.C.: The Brookings Institution, 1968), pp. 278–279.

62. Pole, *The Pursuit of Equality*, p. 280.

63. Christopher Jencks, Review in *The New York Review of Books* 30.3 (Mar. 3, 1983): 35.

64. Pole, *The Pursuit of Equality*, p. 309.

65. U.S. Bureau of Census, *Statistical Abstract of the U.S., 1982–1983* (Washington, D.C.: U.S. Government Printing Office, 1983), p. 388.

66. Pole, *The Pursuit of Equality*, p. 316. See also Caroline Bird, *Born Female* (New York: McKay, 1968), pp. 1–7.

67. Speech by Lyndon Johnson, Howard University, June 4, 1965.

68. Pole, *The Pursuit of Equality*, pp. 293–294.

69. J. R. Pole, personal correspondence, Feb. 28, 1984.

70. Williamson and Lindert, *American Inequality*, pp. 3–31, 33–53.

71. Williamson and Lindert, *American Inequality*, pp. 49, 75–82, 289, 134; Simon Kuznets, *Shares of Upper Income Groups in Income and Savings* (New York: National Bureau of Economic Research, 1953).

72. Huntington, *The Promise of Disharmony*, p. 38.

73. Keller, *Affairs of State*, p. 171.

74. Huntington, *The Promise of Disharmony*, p. 107.

## 3. The Leaders

1. Jo Freeman, *The Politics of Women's Liberation* (New York: David McKay, 1975); Clare K. Fulenwider, *Feminism in American Politics* (New York: Praeger, 1980).

2. See, e.g., Robert Putnam, *The Comparative Study of Political Elites* (Englewood Cliffs, N.J.: Prentice-Hall, 1976), pp. 93–94.

3. *Fortune*, May 1976, p. 172. See also Thomas R. Dye, "Identifying Change in Elite Structures," paper delivered at meeting of American Political Science Association, Denver, Colorado, Sept. 1982.

4. Sidney Verba, Norman H. Nie, and Jae-on Kim, *Participation and Political Equality: A Seven Nation Comparison* (New York: Cambridge University Press, 1978), ch. 9.

5. This is especially clear if one considers the high percentage of black and feminist leaders who have done graduate work. The low level of college education among blacks in general, compared with black leaders, is confirmed by the fact that in 1980 only 8.4 percent of blacks over age twenty-five had four years of college, compared to the 70 percent found among black leaders in the study.

6. The youth sample was deliberately half male and half female. The study of chief executive officers by *Fortune* (May 1976) found no blacks and one woman.

7. C. Wright Mills, *The Power Elite* (New York: Oxford University Press, 1956).

8. University of Michigan, Center for Political Studies, 1978 American National Election Study.

## 4. Accord and Discord

1. Jennifer L. Hochschild, *What's Fair? American Beliefs about Distributive Justice* (Cambridge: Harvard University Press, 1981); Kay Lehman Schlozman and Sidney Verba, *Injury to Insult: Unemployment, Class, and Political Response* (Cambridge: Harvard University Press, 1979); Robert E. Lane, *Political Ideology: Why the American Common Man Believes What He Does* (New York: Free Press, 1962); Herbert McClosky and John Zaller, *The American Ethos* (Cambridge: Harvard University Press, 1985).

2. The preference of the leaders is paralleled by that of the public. In 1979 the public was asked whether it agreed with either or both of the following: "It is all right for the good things in life to be distributed unequally, as long as everyone has an equal opportunity to compete for them," and "The good things in life should be distributed equally, even if some people have made more of their opportunities than others." Many more people (73 percent) agreed with the first statement than with the second (33 percent). The strong preference for equal opportunity held across all occupational levels. Yankelovich, Skelly, and White, Survey for American Council on Life Insurance, May 1979.

3. J. R. Pole, *The Pursuit of Equality in America* (Berkeley: University of California Press, 1978).

## 5. A Common Language of Equality

1. There is also a methodological reason for not relying exclusively on people's attitudes on specific equality issues. Responses to any particular survey question contain some degree of "error." The specific wording or the particular response categories that are offered in a questionnaire may distort or imperfectly measure the real position of the respondent. Creating summary attitude measures, which combine people's responses to several related questions, is one antidote to this problem.

2. See Philip E. Converse, "Attitudes and Non-Attitudes: Continuation of a Dialogue," in Edward Tufte, ed., *The Quantitative Study of Politics* (New York: Addison-Wesley, 1971); Philip E. Converse, "The Nature of Belief Systems in Mass Publics," in David E. Apter, ed., *Ideology and Discontent* (New York: Free Press, 1964); Norman Nie and Kristi Andersen, "Mass Belief Systems Revisited: Political Change and Attitude Structure," *Journal of Politics* 36 (Aug. 1974): 540–587; John C. Pierce and Douglas D. Rose, "Non-Attitudes and American Public Opinion: The Examination of a Thesis," *American Political Science Review* 68 (June 1974): 626–649; Norman H. Nie, Sidney Verba, and John R. Petrocik, *The Changing American Voter* (Cambridge: Harvard University Press, 1980), ch. 8, Epilogue; George Bishop, Alfred J. Tuchfarber, and Robert W. Oldendick, "Change in the Structure of American Political Attitudes: The Nagging Question of Question Wording," *American Journal of Political Science* 22 (May 1978):

250–269; John L. Sullivan, James E. Piereson, and George E. Marcus, "Ideological Constraint in the Mass Public: A Methodological Critique and Some New Findings," *American Journal of Political Science* 22 (May 1978): 233–249; Norman Nie and James N. Rabjohn, "Revisiting Mass Belief Systems Revisited: Or, Why Doing Research Is Like Watching a Tennis Match," *American Journal of Political Science* 23 (Feb. 1979): 139–175; John Petrocik, "The Changeable American Voter: Some Revisions of the Revision," in John C. Pierce and John L. Sullivan, ed., *The Electorate Reconsidered* (Beverly Hills: Sage Publications, 1980).

3. See Norman R. Luttbeg, "The Structure of Beliefs among Leaders and the Public," *Public Opinion Quarterly* 32 (Fall 1968): 388–409; George F. Bishop, "The Effect of Education on Ideological Consistency," *Public Opinion Quarterly* 40 (Fall 1976): 337–348.

4. Our argument is supported by findings from other studies which relied on very different kinds of evidence. See Douglas Rae, *Equalities* (Cambridge: Harvard University Press, 1981); Jennifer Hochschild, *What's Fair? American Beliefs about Distributive Justice* (Cambridge: Harvard University Press, 1981).

5. See R. J. Rummel, "Understanding Factor Analysis," *Conflict Resolution* 11 (1967): 444–480; H. H. Harman, *Modern Factor Analysis* (Chicago: University of Chicago Press, 1976); Jae-on Kim and Charles W. Mueller, *Introduction to Factor Analysis: What It Is and How To Do It* (Beverly Hills: Sage Publications, 1978); Jae-on Kim and Charles W. Mueller, *Factor Analysis: Statistical Methods and Practical Issues* (Beverly Hills: Sage Publications, 1978).

6. If we consider "loadings" of .30 and above.

7. Kirk H. Porter and Donald B. Johnson, ed., *National Party Platforms: 1840–1972* (Urbana: University of Illinois, 1974); Edward Tufte, *Political Control of the Economy* (Princeton: Princeton University Press, 1978), pp. 72, 74.

8. Methodologically speaking, either the four- or six-factor solution is acceptable. The two most widely used criteria to determine the number of factors deemed sufficient to explain a set of variables are Kaiser's criterion and the scree test. The first holds that a factor with an eigenvalue less than 1.0 ought not in general to be retained, since a factor identical to a single variable would necessarily have an eigenvalue at least that large. The second criterion holds that the factor analyst ought to look for discontinuities in the amount of variance accounted for by factors. A case could be made on either criterion for either a four- or six-factor solution. It is in such situations that a substantively informed judgment based on the results comes into play. H. F. Kaiser and John Rice, "Little Jiffy, Mark IV," *Educational and Psychological Measurement* 34 (Spring 1974): 111–117; Rummel, "Understanding Factor Analysis."

9. This conclusion is similar to that reported in a study which found

more stereotypical thinking about women than about blacks. Both men and women are more likely to assign shared traits to women than they are to blacks. This suggests that gender categories are more important than racial ones. Mary R. Jackman and Mary Scheuer Senter, "Images of Social Groups: Categorical or Qualified?" *Public Opinion Quarterly* 44 (Fall 1980): 340–361.

10. These results are consistent with a study of attitudes toward inequality in the United States and Britain, which discovered that race and class perceptions are too highly correlated to be considered separate in the United States but are separate dimensions in Britain. The difference between Britain and the United States might be explained by the relative newness in Britain of the race issue, which, like the gender issue in the United States, has not yet been incorporated into other issues. Wendell Bell and Robert V. Robinson, "Cognitive Maps of Class and Racial Inequalities in England and the United States," *American Journal of Sociology* 86 (Sept. 1980): 320–349.

## 6. Group Positions

1. *Eta²* is analogous to *r²* as a measure of variance explained. For instance, as shown in Table 6.1, 41 percent of the variance in New Deal attitudes is explained by group membership. All the *Eta²* statistics are significant at the .001 level or better.

2. Farmers have the largest standard deviation on the New Deal scale, indicating that they are internally divided over such issues.

3. See Allen H. Barton, "Consensus and Conflict among American Leaders," *Public Opinion Quarterly* 38 (Winter 1974–75): 507–530; Stanley Rothman and Robert Lichter, "A Look at the Media," *Public Opinion*, Oct.–Nov. 1980, pp. 10–15; Lichter and Rothman, "Media and Business Elites," *Public Opinion*, Oct.–Nov. 1981, pp. 42–46. Although these studies find that the media hold more liberal views than other elites, the disparity between their conclusion and ours is not so great. Rothman and Lichter, for instance, show that the media elite are particularly liberal on social matters, while their views on economic matters, as we show here, couple support for the capitalist economy and income disparities with a welfare state orientation. Their media sample is somewhat more likely than ours to consider private enterprise "fair to workers" and to believe that the government should reduce the income gap between rich and poor. Thus, in one case their media sample is somewhat more conservative than ours, and in another somewhat more liberal. Some of these differences may result from differences in the wording of questions. A lot also depends on the groups compared. When Rothman and Lichter compare media leaders to business leaders, they too find that the former are far to the left of the latter. Rothman and Lichter, "Are Journalists a New Class?" *Business Forum*, Spring 1983, pp. 12–17.

4. A similar analysis appeared in Chapter 5, but for all the leaders taken together. Here we analyze each of the leadership groups separately.

5. One indication of this greater emphasis is that in 1983 a group of 40 national women's organizations prepared a report analyzing the impact of government policies on women's economic well-being. They distributed the report throughout Congress and used it to lobby for changes in the Congressional budget. The first chapter of the report documents the "feminization of poverty," the growing proportion of the poor who are women or children. Coalition on Women and the Budget, "Inequality of Sacrifice: The Impact of the Reagan Budget on Women," Washington, D.C., March 1983.

6. Race and sex cannot be put into the equations because almost all feminist and civil rights leaders are female or black respectively and almost no other leaders have those characteristics. In this sense, race and sex cannot be isolated from membership in a leadership group; the boundaries of two of the groups are coterminous with race or sex differences.

7. There is a tendency for certain groups to appear more liberal on the race and gender issues after controlling for the demographic characteristics of the leaders. The liberalism applies to labor leaders and farm leaders on race and to labor, black, Republican, and farm leaders on gender. This probably reflects the fact that the more highly educated leaders of these groups are more liberal on these issues. Nevertheless, the groups remain in their approximate positions even after the adjustment for demographics.

8. These findings are consistent with the concept of "status inversion," by which higher status people are more conservative economically but more liberal on social issues. See Everett Carll Ladd, Jr., with Charles D. Hadley, *Transformations of the American Party System,* 2nd ed. (New York: W. W. Norton, 1978).

9. National priorities naturally rise and fall over time, depending on events and social conditions. The rankings in Figure 6.3 tap the salience of issues at the time of the study, not today or always. Nonetheless, the pattern of relative priorities across the leadership groups is revealing.

## 7. Political Parties

1. See Seymour Martin Lipset, *Political Man* (Garden City, N.Y.: Doubleday, 1960), ch. 9; Seymour Martin Lipset, *The First New Nation: The United States in Historical and Comparative Perspective* (New York: Basic Books, 1963), esp. chs. 9–10; Everett Carll Ladd, Jr., *American Political Parties* (New York: Norton, 1971), esp. ch. 1.

2. Gerald M. Pomper, *Elections in America: Control and Influence in Democratic Politics* (New York: Dodd, Mead, 1970), pp. 179–203.

3. Edward R. Tufte, *Political Control of the Economy* (Princeton: Princeton University Press, 1978), pp. 71–75; Kay L. Schlozman and Sidney

Verba, *Injury to Insult: Unemployment, Class, and Political Response* (Cambridge: Harvard University Press, 1979), p. 295.

4. See Kirk H. Porter and Donald Bruce Johnson, *National Party Platforms, 1840–1972* (Urbana: University of Illinois Press, 1974); Republican Party Platforms of 1976 and 1980, Republican National Committee; Democratic Party Platforms of 1976 and 1980, Democratic National Committee.

5. Everett Carll Ladd, Jr., with Charles D. Hadley, *Transformations of the American Party System*, 2nd ed. (New York: W. W. Norton, 1978), pp. 31–87, 111–114; Robert S. Erikson, Norman R. Luttbeg, and Kent L. Tedin, *American Public Opinion* (New York: Wiley and Sons, 1980), p. 170; Robert Axelrod, "Where the Votes Come From: An Analysis of Electoral Coalitions, 1952–1968," *American Political Science Review* 66 (Mar. 1972): 11–20; Axelrod, "Communications," *American Political Science Review* 68 (June 1974): 717–720; Arthur H. Miller, "The Emerging Gender Gap in American Elections," *Election Politics* 1 (Winter 1983–1984): 7–12.

6. Everett Carll Ladd, Jr., and Charles D. Hadley, *Political Parties and Political Issues: Patterns of Differentiation since the New Deal* (Beverly Hills: Sage Publications, 1973), pp. 21–26; Ladd, *Transformations of the American Party System*, pp. 31–87; Erikson et al., *American Public Opinion*, pp. 153–157, 165–168; Gerald Pomper, "From Confusion to Clarity: Issues and American Voters, 1956–1968," *American Political Science Review* 66 (June 1972): 415–428.

7. Steven Kelman, "Party Strength and System Governability in the Face of New Political Demands: The Case of Feminism," unpublished manuscript, John F. Kennedy School of Government, Harvard University, January, 1984, esp. pp. 35–42.

8. Norman H. Nie, Sidney Verba, and John R. Petrocik, *The Changing American Voter* (Cambridge: Harvard University Press, 1976), pp. 200–205.

9. Regression equations estimating the effects of party affiliation, demographic characteristics, and group membership on the equality attitude scales show the magnitude of the party effects in a familiar order: the party coefficients (partial betas) are .41, .33, and .17 for the New Deal, race, and gender equality, respectively.

10. Herbert McClosky, Paul J. Hoffman, and Rosemary O'Hara, "Issue Conflict and Consensus among Party Leaders and Followers," *American Political Science Review* 56 (1960): 406–429.

11. Jeane Kirkpatrick, *The New Presidential Elite: Men and Women in National Politics* (New York: Russell Sage Foundation and The Twentieth Century Fund, 1976). The 1972 data are at variance with the experience of county chairpersons in that period, which shows that the Republican leaders were still further removed from their rank-and-file supporters than were the Democratic leaders. R. S. Montjoy, W. R. Shaffer, and R. E. Weber, "Policy Preferences of Party Elites and Masses: Conflict or Consensus," *American Politics Quarterly* 8 (July 1980): 319–344. To confuse things a

bit more, another study found that Republican leaders in 1980 were more homogeneously on the right than were Democratic leaders on the left. On some issues, Democratic county chairpersons were even more moderate than Democratic supporters in the public. J. S. Jackson, III, B. L. Brown, and D. D. Bositis, "Herbert McClosky and Friends Revisited: 1980 Democratic and Republican Party Elites Compared to the Mass Public," *American Politics Quarterly* 10 (Apr. 1982): 158–180. These various conclusions appear to depend on variations from election to election in the selection of convention delegates and on differences between county chairpersons and convention delegates.

12. Party leaders on the county level differ sharply from those on state committees. Jackson et al., "Herbert McClosky and Friends."

13. There are two different views on the degree of difference between the two parties. "Party cleavage" theories predict substantial differences, while "spatial model" or "public opinion" theories predict slight differences. A study of the policy views of the public and candidates during the Presidential campaigns of 1952 to 1976 concluded that although there was some tendency for the parties to offer up candidates with views near the midpoint of public opinion, there was substantial divergence between the two parties. Benjamin I. Page, *Choices and Echoes in Presidential Elections* (Chicago: University of Chicago Press, 1978).

14. Lipset, *Political Man,* pp. 311–312; Lipset, *The First New Nation,* p. 30.

15. Gary R. Orren, "Candidate Style and Voter Alignment in 1976," in Seymour Martin Lipset, ed., *Emerging Coalitions in American Politics* (San Francisco: Institute for Contemporary Studies, 1978), pp. 12–13; Warren E. Miller and Teresa E. Levitin, *Leadership and Change* (Cambridge: Winthrop Publishers, 1976).

16. There are signs that this has changed in recent years. The emergence of the gender gap in the 1980 and 1982 elections, wherein Democratic candidates fared better against their Republican opponents among women voters, has enhanced the role of women and their concerns in the party. At the 1982 mid-term Democratic convention, gender issues were prominent, as they were in 1984.

### 8. Equality of Income

1. Angus Campbell, Philip E. Converse, and Willard L. Rodgers, *The Quality of American Life: Perceptions, Evaluations and Satisfactions* (New York: Russell Sage Foundation, 1976), pp. 75–76, 382–384. See also Burkhard Strumpel, ed., *Subjective Elements of Well-Being* (Paris: Organization for Economic Cooperation and Development, 1974).

2. Campbell et al., *The Quality of American Life,* p. 381.

3. Lee Rainwater and Richard Coleman, *Social Standing in America:*

*New Dimensions of Class* (New York: Basic Books, 1978), p. 29.

4. See Malcolm Sawyer, *Income Distribution in OECD Countries: OECD Economic Outlook* (Paris: OECD, 1976), pp. 3–11; Alan Blinder, "The Level and Distribution of Economic Well-Being," in Martin Feldstein, ed., *The American Economy in Transition* (Chicago: University of Chicago Press, 1980), pp. 415–479.

5. Most economists argue that earnings are determined by market forces on the basis of contribution to marginal productivity or that earnings are paid to compensate for a worker's worry and responsibility. See Albert Rees, *Economics of Work and Pay* (New York: Harper and Row, 1973), chs. 4–5; Harold F. Lydell, *The Structure of Earnings* (Oxford: Clarendon Press, 1968), pp. 125–127. Some economists point out that although the efficient productivity of the market requires some differential in earnings—the kibbutz factories in Israel notwithstanding—this necessity by no means completely explains the existing income disparity. Wage differences also reflect the impact of nonmarket forces, including people's values. See e.g. Henry Phelps Brown, *The Inequality of Pay* (Berkeley: University of California Press, 1977); Jan Pen, *Income Distribution* (London: Allen Tate, The Penguin Press, 1971), esp. p. 40; Derek L. Phillips, *Equality, Justice, and Rectification* (London: Academic Press, 1979). For example, people's attitudes toward how much money different occupations deserve affect not only the decisions of those who set wages but also the willingness of people to work at a particular job for a given wage. The equilibrium price for labor depends on how many people are willing to work at a given price, which may depend on how much they think various jobs are worth.

6. Arthur Okun, *Equality Versus Efficiency: The Big Tradeoff* (Washington, D.C.: The Brookings Institution, 1975). Some sociologists have offered a "functionalist" variant of the work-incentive justification for income differentiation, seeing it as a means to motivate individuals to take positions of responsibility and invest in training. See Kingsley Davis and Wilbert E. Moore, "Some Principles of Stratification," *American Sociological Review* 10 (Apr. 1945): 246.

7. Peter Wiles, *Distribution of Income: East and West* (Amsterdam: North-Holland, 1974).

8. Lester Thurow, "The Pursuit of Equality," *Dissent* (Summer 1976): 253–258. Robert Kuttner argues that an expanding economy does not require current inequalities of income. Kuttner, *The Economic Illusion: False Choices Between Prosperity and Social Justice* (Boston: Houghton Mifflin, 1984). Peter Wiles shows that top wages could be cut a lot without reducing incentives. Wiles, *Distribution of Income*, pp. 72–76.

9. P. T. Bauer, *Equality, the Third World, and Economic Delusion* (Cambridge: Harvard University Press, 1981), ch. 1.

10. Kay L. Schlozman and Sidney Verba, *Injury to Insult: Unemployment, Class, and Political Response* (Cambridge: Harvard University Press,

1979), p. 221; Guillermina Jasso and Peter H. Rossi, "Distributive Justice and Earned Income," *American Sociological Review* 42 (1977): 639–651; Lee Rainwater, *What Money Buys* (New York: Basic Books, 1974).

11. Warren E. Miller, Arthur H. Miller, and Edward J. Schneider, *American National Election Studies Data Sourcebook, 1952–1978* (Cambridge: Harvard University Press, 1980), p. 172.

12. Robert J. Lampman, *The Share of the Top Wealth-Holders in National Wealth* (Princeton: Princeton University Press, 1962).

13. Pechman and Okner estimate various effective tax rates for those at different income levels in the United States based on different assumptions about the incidence of taxes. Under most sets of assumptions, the overall tax bite is about the same across all income categories. Only for the set of assumptions stipulating that taxes would have the most progressive incidence do effective rates differ substantially across incomes, and these differences tend to appear at the top and bottom of the income scale. This allows us to locate the worst distortion that our choice of pretax estimates could produce: a comparison between the top earning occupation and the bottom under the most progressive assumptions. The occupation that the leaders perceive as highest in earnings is the top executive; they place the elevator operator at the bottom. The top executive, is, on average, perceived to earn before taxes $206,000; the elevator operator, $7,200. The ratio of their incomes is 28.6 to 1. Under the most progressive assumption about taxes, the ratio becomes 21.5 to 1. Under the least progressive taxes, the after-tax ratio becomes 26.9 to 1, not appreciably different from the pretax ratio. Joseph A. Pechman and Benjamin A. Okner, *Who Bears the Tax Burden?* (Washington, D.C.: The Brookings Institution, 1974), pp. 48–50, esp. Table 4-3. Greater disparity between incomes before and after governmental intervention is found if one takes into account both taxes and governmental transfers. Okner and Rivlin found that taxes do not change income shares much in the United States, but a combination of taxes and transfers does. Before taxes and transfers, the lowest quintile of earners receives 1.7 percent of income; after taxes and transfers they receive 6.3 percent. The figures for the top quintile are 53.1 percent and 47.1 percent respectively. However, much of this change comes from transfers to the aged, who do not figure in our occupational analysis. For those under 65, the figures for the bottom quintile are 1.0 percent and 2.4 percent respectively, and for the top quintile 50.1 percent and 44.0 percent respectively. Benjamin Okner and Alice M. Rivlin, "Income Distribution Policy in the United States," in *Education, Equality, and Life Chances* (Paris: OECD, 1975), II, 191–193. If these comparisons were between a pair of occupations other than the top and bottom earnings, the pre- and post-tax income gaps would be more similar than in this worst case. Clearly, the choice of pretax earnings does not introduce enough distortion to undercut our analysis.

14. Pechman and Okner, *Who Bears the Tax Burdern?* p. 61.

15. The leaders' estimates are also close to those made by ordinary

citizens. A nationwide sample of the public in 1977 estimated the annual earnings of an auto assembly worker as $12,200, compared with the leaders' estimate of $12,600. The college-educated members of the nationwide sample approximated the leaders even more closely—$12,560. *Roper Reports,* May 1977.

16. The income data in this chapter are logged, for several reasons. First, a logged income measure eliminates extremes that can distort a simple arithmetic mean. The average income of the residents of a small town, for example, may be highly dependent on the town's only millionaire. Since the study asked about the incomes of occupations with very high salaries, such as top executives and sports stars, "outlying" income estimates could easily distort the results. Second, a logged measure is symmetric. If half the leaders want to double the executive's salary and the others want to cut it in half, the logged measure appropriately shows the average person favoring no change. Third, the measure applies consistently to simple income, desired change from present income levels to the ideal, the difference in earnings between high- and low-paying occupations, or the desired amount of change in the spread between particular occupations. Finally, the logged measure corresponds to the way that people actually think about income. People think in ratio, not absolute terms, as shown by studies of the relationship between income and prestige and of the perceived value of different amounts of money. Given a declining marginal value of income, ratio figures make more sense. An increase in income from $10,000 to $20,000 is closer in meaning to an increase of $100,000 to $200,000 than it is to an increase from $100,000 to $110,000. It makes no sense to say that a $10,000 difference is the same on a base of $100,000 as on a base of $10,000. This is corroborated by salary negotiators, who typically describe an across-the-board raise of 10 percent as fair, even though this means that those earning more are getting larger raises in absolute terms. To compute income estimates, we first log the income for each individual leader, compute the mean for the leaders within a particular group, and then take the antilog of the mean to convert back to the original scale in dollars. For ratio comparisons we first compute the ratios for individuals, log them, compute the group means, and take the antilog.

17. Most leaders would raise the earnings floor somewhat. Whether there should be an income floor for the poorer groups in society and, if so, how high a floor is not clear. An income floor deals with transfer payments, welfare benefits, and the like—policies that supplement earnings.

18. The party differences also appear in the public at large. When asked about over- and underpaid occupations, 76 percent of Democrats in 1976 said that executives were overpaid, in comparison with 66 percent of Republicans. When asked about a skilled factory worker, 10 percent of Democrats but 25 percent of Republicans considered them overpaid. *Roper Reports,* June 1976.

19. Technically, the fair/perceived or "ought/is" ratio is not a desired

ratio. The groups indicate what they think a "fair" income would be for the various occupations. A "desired" income is not necessarily equivalent to a fair income. For several reasons, people may diverge in the income levels or distribution that they regard as fair as opposed to desirable. The fair system might be seen as economically inefficient and therefore undesirable. Or the fair system might be a desirable vision of utopia but too radical a change and too destabilizing for people to desire it for America today. They may conclude that the transactional costs of restructuring the American economic system into a truly fair one would be prohibitive and therefore undesirable. Finally, at least for those near the top of the income ladder, the fair system might not be in their self-interest. There is no logical inconsistency in the position of uncommonly honest business executives who agree that a fair salary would be lower than what they currently receive but who still adamantly deny that they would desire that system. Nonetheless, words like *desire* and *want* are occasionally used here, albeit imprecisely, with reference to the income distribution that the leaders consider to be fair.

20. Judgments of fairness of earnings have been found to be based on the education and occupational prestige of the occupation. Clearly executives require higher education than do athletes. Executives' prestige, at least among leaders, is thus higher as well. See Jasso and Rossi, "Distributive Justice and Earned Income."

21. These evaluations of earnings are consistent with the public view of which occupations are over- and underpaid. In 1976 presidents of large corporations and doctors were considered to be overpaid by 70–75 percent of the public, and almost no one—one percent for executives and two percent for doctors—considered them underpaid. In 1977 public school teachers and policemen were seen as somewhat underpaid, while skilled factory workers were most frequently perceived as earning about the right amount. *Roper Reports,* June 1976; June, 1979.

22. Everett Carll Ladd, Jr., and Seymour Martin Lipset, *The Divided Academy: Professors and Politics* (New York: The Norton Library, 1976).

23. A full comparison of data for the United States and Sweden will appear in subsequent publications.

24. The national business leaders believe that top executives ought to earn somewhat more than "someone in their own occupation" ought to earn by a ratio of 1.6. Since they themselves are top executives, this seems anomalous. The reason is possibly that they are selected from the top executives of companies in the Fortune 500 list, while the question is about an even more rarefied group, top executives in one of the top 100 corporations. Local businessmen deviate from the other groups in considering a ratio of 4.6 between their own earnings and those of a top executive to be fair.

25. National business leaders believe that they actually earn 17.4 times

the earnings of an elevator operator and ought to earn 17.6 times as much.

26. Brown, *The Inequality of Pay.*

27. Wayne M. Alves and Peter H. Rossi, "Who Should Get What? Fairness Judgments of the Distribution of Income," *American Journal of Sociology* 84 (Nov. 1978): 54–65.

28. Coleman and Rainwater, *Social Standing in America,* pp. 58–59. The Coleman and Rainwater ratings are derived from a mass sample, while our estimates of perceived and fair income come from American leaders. Furthermore, not all of our occupations appear on their list of rated occupations. The comparisons, therefore, must be interpreted with caution. In Table 8.8 we report estimates of general standing for those occupations on both lists, indicating those cases where the occupational designations do not match exactly.

29. The coefficients for membership in each of the leadership groups are not reported. We already know that groups differ in their attitudes on these issues; here we are interested in the effect of other variables on income attitudes above and beyond the effects of group affiliation.

## 9. Equality of Influence

1. The terms *political influence* and *political power* are used in many ways, sometimes interchangeably, sometimes referring to very different relationships. We consider the terms interchangeable for our purposes, and we use the term *influence* here because that is what we asked our respondents about. We assume that they understood the term to refer to the ability of a group to have its preferences prevail in the struggle over public policy— by whatever means.

2. Peter Bachrach and Morton S. Baratz, *Poverty and Power* (New York: Oxford University Press, 1970), ch. 3; Frederick W. Frey, "Comment: On Issues and Non-Issues in the Study of Power," *American Political Science Review* 65 (Dec. 1971): 1081–1107; Roger W. Cobb and Charles D. Elder, *Participation in American Politics: The Dynamics of Agenda Building* (Boston: Allyn and Bacon, 1972); Charles O. Jones, *An Introduction to the Study of Public Policy,* 2nd ed. (North Scituate, Mass.: Duxbury Press, 1977), ch. 3.

3. For contrary views, see Nelson W. Polsby, *Community Power and Political Theory: A Further Look at Evidence and Inference,* 2nd ed. (New Haven: Yale University Press, 1980); Kenneth Newton, *Second City Politics* (Oxford: Clarendon Press, 1976).

4. Two strands in American political thought, however, call for differential political influence among the citizenry. One argues for limited citizen involvement and for rule by political elites, subject to the control of periodic elections. This argument is based on the presumed lower capacity of ordinary citizens to take the long view and to discern the public interest.

Joseph A. Schumpeter, *Capitalism, Socialism, and Democracy* (New York: Harper and Row, 1942), esp. ch. 22; Walter Lippmann, *Public Opinion* (New York: Free Press, 1965). The other strand prefers elite participation because the public is less committed to civil liberties than are organizational leaders, political activists, and the more educated segment of the public. Samuel Stouffer, *Communism, Conformity, and Civil Liberties* (New York: Wiley, 1966). Each of these strands of thought implies a desire for unequal political influence. The first wants greater influence among elected officials and wise bureaucrats. The second wants greater influence among the more educated members of society. But neither wants some interests to have more political influence than others, such as labor more than business and liberals more than conservatives. The interests of business and labor are adversarial, whereas the interests of the leader or educated citizen are common to all—if all are as enlightened as the leader or educated citizen. Another argument of limited participation stresses the dangers of ungovernability, or of too many extreme demands being placed on government. Samuel P. Huntington, "The Crisis of Democracy: The United States," in Michel J. Crozier, Samuel P. Huntington, and Joji Watanuki, *The Crisis of Democracy* (New York: New York University Press, 1975), p. 114; Richard Rose, "The Nature of the Challenge" in Richard Rose, ed., *Challenge to Governance: Studies in Overloaded Politics* (Beverly Hills: Sage Publications, 1980), pp. 3–28. Neither work argues for inequality in participation. Huntington, for example, does not want greater noninvolvement through the withdrawal of marginal poor and minority groups: "Less marginality on the part of some groups thus needs to be replaced by more self-restraint on the part of all groups."

5. The pervasive antipower ethic in America opposes the concentration of influence. Americans consider the exercise of authority by one person or group over another or by government over citizens as in some way illegitimate and to be avoided. Samuel P. Huntington, *American Politics: The Promise of Disharmony* (Cambridge: Harvard University Press, 1981), pp. 33–39.

6. The few studies of power and influence perceptions have usually dealt with either the real or the ideal, not both. Some studies tapped citizens' views on whether certain institutions or groups have too much or too little influence. See Richard Klorman, "The Public's Perception of Group Influence in the United States," *Social Forces* 56 (Mar. 1978): 770–794. Another study focused on the perceptions of groups. Arnold Rose, *The Power Structure* (New York: Oxford University Press, 1967). One study looked at both the "is" and "ought" of power. William H. Form and Joan Rytina, "Ideological Beliefs on the Distribution of Power in the United States," *American Sociological Review* 34 (Feb. 1969): 19–31.

7. Actually, the business leaders in the leadership study do include the heads of the two hundred largest banks in the country and the presidents of large local banks.

8. Huntington, *American Politics*, p. 75; Charles E. Lindblom, *Politics and Markets: The World's Political-Economic Systems* (New York: Basic Books, 1977), ch. 13. Our point is consistent with Lindblom's argument but not the same one he makes. He does not argue that individual business leaders have influence which they and others do not notice. Rather, he emphasizes the structural linkage between business and government: it is so essential that the economy perform well that the government accords business a privileged position.

9. Other studies of the perception of influence have similarly found big business and the rich to be the most influential, with labor unions second. Form and Rytina, "Ideological Beliefs." One study ranked big business highest in having too much influence, followed by politicians, labor unions, and newspaper editors. Klorman, "The Public's Perception." A 1981 *Washington Post*/ABC News poll found big corporations, the media, and labor unions to be rated as most influential in that order. Another study found that unions were most frequently mentioned by American leaders as one of the most powerful groups in America, followed by business. Business leaders were more likely (74 percent) to think labor powerful than labor leaders (63 percent), while labor was more likely (89 percent) to see business as powerful than were businessmen (43 percent). Rose, *The Power Structure.*

10. Gary R. Orren, "The Impact of the Press on Government," paper prepared for Study of How the Press Affects Federal Policy Making, Institute of Politics, John F. Kennedy School of Government, Harvard University, May 1983.

11. The denial of influence, especially on the part of business and labor, is paralleled by a sense of decreasing influence. The leaders were asked whether they thought their group's influence was rising or falling. The index of influence loss or gain for each group—that is, the percentage of a group's leaders who say their own influence is increasing minus the percentage saying it is decreasing—is: business, $-79$; farm, $+1$; labor, $-30$; media, $+38$; Democrats, $-68$; Republicans, $-70$; blacks, $+2$; and feminists, $+56$. Business as well as both parties perceive a decline in their influence, as does labor with less unanimity, while the media and feminists think their influence is increasing. See Rose, *The Power Structure*, pp. 304–309.

12. Their ratings are very similar, with the exception of the media's perception of intellectuals' influence compared with the intellectuals' self-perception. Like most other groups, the intellectuals see themselves as less powerful than they are seen by others.

13. Klorman, "The Public's Perception," p. 773. See also Seymour M. Lipset and William Schneider, *The Confidence Gap* (New York: Basic Books, 1983).

14. The criterion of equality of political influence is a collective one: business equal to labor equal to consumers. Such an equality is very unequal from an individual perspective. The fact that the norm of equality is usually

a norm referring to individuals, while political conflict is seen as taking place among corporate actors, creates yet another inconsistency which allows egalitarian norms to coexist with inegalitarian reality.

15. The exact wording of the question was, "Please indicate what effects you feel the following groups have on the ability of (the respondent's own group) to accomplish its goals: which groups help a lot, which help and hinder equally, which hinder a lot?" "Help a lot" and "hinder a lot" represent the two end-points of a seven-point scale. The target groups about which the respondents were asked varied a bit across the respondent groups, but most groups were asked about the same groups that form the leadership sample, plus banks and consumer groups, about which influence questions had also been asked. We present the data only for the most contesting groups: business, farmers, labor, blacks, and feminists. Other groups were not asked the helpfulness question in a way that is useful for this purpose.

16. The public too perceives both big business and labor unions as having too much power and influence in society today, standing ahead of almost all other institutions. Some surveys have found labor unions to lead the pack in this respect; others have found big business in this position. *Roper Reports,* Sept. 1973; Sept. 1974; Sept. 1977; Sept. 1979.


## 10. Economics and Politics

1. Irving Kristol, "Poverty, Taxes, and Equality," *The Public Interest* 37 (Fall 1974): 27.

2. Political power and influence are resources that can expand to the benefit of all society. Talcott Parsons, "The Distribution of Power in American Society," in Talcott Parsons, *Structure and Process in Modern Societies* (Glencoe, Ill.: The Free Press, 1960), pp. 199–225. Similarly, more influence is exerted in some industries than in others over the behavior of the participants, not necessarily by management but by all participants. Arnold Tannenbaum et al., *Hierarchy in Organizations* (San Francisco: Jossey-Bass, 1974), p. 220. The contrary position holds that influence is a fixed quantity. Ralf Dahrendorf, *Class and Class Conflict in Industrial Societies* (Stanford: Stanford University Press, 1968). Everything depends on the issue over which political influence is applied. For Northern Ireland Catholics, an increase in Protestant influence is seen as negative.

3. James Tobin, "On Limiting the Domain of Equality," *Journal of Law and Economics* 13 (Oct. 1970): 454.

4. Although people need not spend money on themselves and could spend it on friends, they generally do not since they are not obliged to do so. But since governments are often precluded from giving special benefits to individuals, allies sometimes have little choice but to use their influence to acquire decisions and favors for the general benefit of all those who share their interests. Furthermore, people usually only need their own money to

buy what they want, given the typical range of prices and incomes. They do not need to pool income with allies. However, few groups have so much influence that they need not worry about the support of their friends. One generally does not need an ally's money to get by, but one often needs its vote.

5. See Lester C. Thurow, *The Zero-Sum Society* (New York: Basic Books, 1980); Richard Easterlin, "Does Money Buy Happiness?" *The Public Interest* 30 (Winter 1973): 3; Lee Rainwater, *What Money Buys* (New York: Basic Books, 1974), ch. 3.

6. Samuel P. Huntington, *American Politics: The Promise of Disharmony* (Cambridge: Harvard University Press, 1981). John Rawls also has emphasized the greater normative commitment to equality in political matters than in economic. His "first principle" takes a radically egalitarian view of basic political liberties, while his "second principle" allows for inequality in economic position, subject to the "difference" principle that the inequality helps out the worst-off. He allows for inequalities in income where there is a positive-sum game and where the least well-off gains from the inequality. In relation to political equality, he demands complete equality of result. Rawls, *A Theory of Justice* (Cambridge: Harvard University Press, 1971).

7. For a similar differentiation in public attitudes between economic and political spheres, Jennifer Hochschild, *What's Fair? American Beliefs about Distributive Justice* (Cambridge: Harvard University Press, 1981). For public support for income differentiation, see Guillermina Jasso and Peter H. Rossi, "Distributive Justice and Earned Income," *American Sociological Review* 42 (Aug. 1977): 639–651; Rainwater, *What Money Buys*. When participants in another study were asked about influence, 41 percent spontaneously said that "all should be equal," compared to the 8 percent of participants in the leadership study who opt for equal pay. William H. Form and Joan Rytina, "Ideological Beliefs on the Distribution of Power in the United States," *American Sociological Review* 34 (1969): 19–31.

8. 411 U.S. 1 (1973).

9. The scales for measuring income and influence are not directly comparable, since the metrics are different. The income scales refer to individual incomes; the influence scales refer to the power of large societal actors. Consequently, income and influence are not compared directly here. Rather, the relationship of the real to the ideal in income, both measured on the same scale, is compared with the relationship of the real to the ideal in influence, both also measured on the same scale.

10. These findings are consistent with the study's other findings that leaders agree on the ranking of occupations in terms of a fair income distribution but disagree on the ranking of groups in terms of a fair influence distribution, because what is at stake here is the relative agreement over the real and ideal within each domain. Groups disagree about what influence

ought to be, but they disagree more about what it is. The opposite is true for income. Whether they disagree more about the ideal of income than about the ideal of influence is harder to determine since the metrics differ in the two domains.

11. Another indication of the consensus on perceived income that does not exist in relation to influence is the wide disparity between business's perception of its own influence and others' perception of business influence, compared to their similar estimates of business' income. Business executives see business as much weaker politically than do other observers. However, there is much more consensus across groups in their perception of business executives' incomes:

| Group | Perceived income of business executives |
|---|---|
| National business executives | 199,295 |
| Labor leaders | 173,907 |
| Intellectuals | 189,151 |
| Media | 179,410 |

Unlike the situation in relation to influence, national business leaders' estimates of their own income are close to the estimates that others make.

12. The views of business leaders are not reported since the comparison with top corporate executives would be redundant.

13. The situation in relation to the influence of allies is less clear. A gain in influence by allies of a group will redound to its benefit if that influence is used to further positions with which it agrees. If the influence of an ally is increased, the overall influence of the group's side grows. However, the group's influence within the coalition diminishes. This ambivalence to allies is manifested in the attitudes of Democratic party leaders to the influence of labor unions. Though unions are a crucial part of the Democratic coalition, Democratic leaders would cut their influence. Despite this, all groups probably want their friends to be relatively more influential than their enemies.

14. The comparison is probably more precise in terms of business, since the power of business is held by business executives and the study inquires about executive income, than in terms of labor, where the power is held by union leaders but the study asks about the income of unionized workers.

15. It is not that groups are so generous when it comes to the influence of their friends. They do not want to raise the influence of their allies nearly as much as they would increase their own influence. In general, they favor more of a cut in the influence of opponents than an increase in the influence of friends. This pattern—improve your own position; reduce your opponents'; improve your friends', but not so much as to challenge your own position—is exactly what one would expect for some valued commodity

such as influence, which has a constant-sum quality. In this case a coalition with others is a mixed blessing, providing a group with a stronger position vis-à-vis the other side but also requiring the sharing of a scarce commodity with others.

16. For the greater conflict associated with a change of rankings in a hierarchy compared with a change in distribution of rewards that maintain positions, see Dan Usher, *The Economic Prerequisite to Democracy* (New York: Columbia University Press, 1981), pp. 28–31.

17. For evidence on how the economic and political views of American leaders compare with the views of leaders in Japan and Sweden, see Sidney Verba and Gary R. Orren, "Political and Economic Equality: A Theoretical and Empirical Comparison," in Samuel P. Huntington and Joseph S. Nye, Jr., ed., *Global Dilemmas* (Cambridge: Center for International Affairs and University Press of America, 1985).

## 11. Equality in Perspective

1. Samuel P. Huntington, *American Politics: The Promise of Disharmony* (Cambridge: Harvard University Press, 1981), ch. 5.

2. *The New York Times*, May 10, 1983, p. A19.

3. Michael J. Boskin, "Reaganomics and Income Distribution: A Longer-Term Perspective," *Journal of Contemporary Studies* 5 (Summer 1982): 31–44.

4. See John L. Palmer and Isabel V. Sawhill, ed., *The Reagan Record* (Cambridge: Ballinger, 1984); Frank Levy and Richard C. Michel, *The Way We'll Be in 1984: Recent Changes in the Level and Distribution of Disposable Income* (Washington, D.C.: The Urban Institute, Nov. 1983); Bob Kuttner, "The Declining Middle," *The Atlantic Monthly*, July 1983, pp. 60–72; Bruce Steinberg, "The Mass Market Is Splitting Apart," *Fortune*, Nov. 28, 1983, pp. 76–82; Robert J. Samuelson, "Middle-Class Media Myth," *The National Journal*, Dec. 31, 1983, pp. 2674–2678; Sheldon Danziger, "Poverty and Equality under Reaganomics," *Journal of Contemporary Studies* 5 (Summer 1982): 17–30. Although the data are somewhat sketchy, it appears that the middle class has been declining in size and more families are either in the upper or lower ends of the income hierarchy. Most of the above authors agree that the policies of the Reagan administration in cutting expenditures on such programs as welfare and food stamps and in changing the tax structure increased income inequality. Government transfers had been the main source of the modest reduction in inequality in the fifteen years before the Reagan administration; the Reagan cuts in these programs reversed the trend.

5. Michael Walzer, *Spheres of Justice* (New York: Basic Books, 1983), pp. 10–20.

6. The Swedish study was conducted by us in collaboration with Pro-

fessor Leif Lewin of the University of Uppsala and Professor Steven Kelman of the John F. Kennedy School of Government, Harvard University.

7. Tamar Lewin, "A New Push to Raise Women's Pay," *The New York Times*, Jan. 1, 1984, sec. 4. Aside from the argument that it is difficult if not impossible to define and measure "comparable worth," the opponents also phrase their opposition in opportunity terms. As a Justice Department lawyer who opposed the proposal put it, "If the women with low-paying jobs had an equal opportunity to work at the jobs with higher salaries but never took advantage of that opportunity, if they never sought the higher paying jobs, where's the discrimination?" *The New York Times*, Jan. 22, 1984, p. 10.

8. Walzer, *Spheres of Justice;* Harper v. Virginia State Board of Elections 383 U.S. 663, 666 (1966).

9. Buckley v. Valeo, 424 U.S. 1 (1976).

10. Robert Dahl, *Dilemmas of Pluralist Democracy* (New Haven: Yale University Press, 1982), p. 174.

11. Theodore H. White, "New Powers, New Politics," *The New York Times Magazine*, Feb. 5, 1984, p. 22.

12. White, "New Powers, New Politics," p. 51.

13. Comments by Ronald Reagan, *New York Times*, July 14, 1984, p. 1, and Patrick Buchanan, ABC-TV "Nightline," July 12, 1984.

14. *New York Times*, July 13, 1984, p. A8.

15. Labor, civil rights groups, and feminist groups form a liberal coalition on issues of manpower policy and employment, but each group has a more central set of priorities that limit its commitment on that issue. Kay L. Schlozman and Sidney Verba, *Injury to Insult: Unemployment, Class, and Political Response* (Cambridge: Harvard University Press, 1979).

16. "Sexism vs. Racism," *The Boston Globe*, January 18, 1984.

## Appendix A

1. F. L. Filion, "Estimating Bias Due to Non-Response in Mail Surveys," *Public Opinion Quarterly* 39 (1975): 482–492; Don A. Dillman, *Mail and Telephone Surveys: The Total Design Method* (New York: Wiley-Interscience, 1978), pp. 12–27, 160–198.

## Appendix B

1. See e.g. R. J. Rummel, "Understanding Factor Analysis," *Conflict Resolution* 11 (1967): 444–480; H. H. Harman, *Modern Factor Analysis* (Chicago: University of Chicago Press, 1976); Jae-on Kim and Charles W. Mueller, *Introduction to Factor Analysis: What It Is and How To Do It* (Beverly Hills: Sage Publications, 1978); Jae-on Kim and Charles W. Mueller, *Factor Analysis: Statistical Methods and Practical Issues* (Beverly Hills: Sage Publications, 1978).

**Appendix D**

1. See Jae-on Kim and Charles W. Mueller, *Introduction to Factor Analysis* (Beverly Hills: Sage Publications, 1978); Kim and Mueller, *Factor Analysis: Statistical Methods and Practical Issues* (Beverly Hills: Sage Publications, 1978).

# Index